The Spanish Political System

Other Titles in This Series

Communism and Political Systems in Western Europe,
David E. Albright

Ideology and Politics: The Socialist Party of France,
George A. Codding, Jr., and William Safran

Westview Special Studies in West European Politics and Society

The Spanish Political System:
Franco's Legacy
E. Ramón Arango

In few places, contends Professor Arango, do illusions obscure reality as they do in Spain. The Spaniard as well as the foreigner has believed and sustained the myths; the scholar as well as the poet. For the Spaniard, myth became the substitute for action in a world in which Spain was increasingly a nonparticipant. It replaced the reality of Spain's inability to move, either politically or economically, into the modern world during the nineteenth century. For the foreigner, Spanish myths were used to fashion an existence more romantic than the one endured at home. At the turn of the twentieth century the notion of Spanish "differentness" found fertile ground among the critics of modernity in Europe and the United States.

Scholars have judged Spanish historical events through the prism of these myths and illusions. This volume is an attempt to counter the resulting distortion. Within the historical context of Spanish politics from the time of the country's emergence as a nation-state, Professor Arango analyzes the political system created by Franco. His study continues into the present period of transition between an authoritarian past and a democratic future. The myths put to rest, Spain is viewed as a contemporary modernizing nation and is examined as such.

E. Ramón Arango, associate professor of government at Louisiana State University, Baton Rouge, received his Ph.D. from the University of Florida. He previously taught at Kenyon College, Texas A&M University, and the Institute for Mediterranean Studies in Rome. Professor Arango is author of *Leopold III and the Belgian Royal Question.*

Españolito que vienes al mundo
te guarde Dios;
una de las dos Españas
ha de helarte el corazón.

Little Spaniard, coming into the world,
May God watch over you.
One of the two Spains
Will benumb your heart.

—Antonio Machado

The Spanish Political System:
Franco's Legacy

E. Ramón Arango

Westview Press / Boulder, Colorado

Westview Special Studies in
West European Politics and Society

Copyright © 1978 by Westview Press, Inc.

Published in 1978 in the United States of America by
  Westview Press, Inc.
  5500 Central Avenue
  Boulder, Colorado 80301
  Frederick A. Praeger, Publisher

Library of Congress Cataloging in Publication Data
Arango, Ergasto Ramón.
    The Spanish political system.
    (Westview special studies in West European politics and society)
    Includes bibliographical references.
    1. Spain—Politics and government—20th century.
I. Title.
DP233.A73   320.9′46′08   78-8979
ISBN 0-89158-177-4

Printed and bound in the United States of America

CAROLINE AND ERGASTO ARANGO

To their memory

I would like to say thank you to Jimmy Rooks, who took most of the burdens in order that this book could be finished.

E. Ramón Arango
Baton Rouge, Louisiana

Contents

PART 4. AFTER FRANCO

APPENDIXES

Introduction

An astute Spaniard once said that unwittingly Georges Bizet caused terrible harm to Spain. He could have said the same thing about Ernest Hemingway, V. S. Pritchett, Claude Debussy, André Malraux, Washington Irving, George Orwell, Maurice Ravel, James Michener, and, in some of their writings, Gerald Brenan, Havelock Ellis, Franz Borkenau—among many others less luminous. These men—most of them nonscientists and therefore forgivable, to a degree—number among those beguiled by the myths of Spain. It must be added, however, that it has been not only the foreigner but also the Spaniard who has believed and sustained the myths, and not only the poet but the scholar as well. In few places do illusions obscure reality as they do in Spain. To write, to speak, even to think about Spain must be a wary exercise in self-discipline. From time to time, the most distinguished and careful authors are caught by the myths. To artists, this enticement can be rewarding; to those who aspire to academic detachment—among others, historians and political scientists—the entrapment can be hazardous.

Why have I singled out Spanish myths? No country is without them. All myths must serve a purpose; otherwise they would not exist universally. As Robert MacIver says: "Myth is the all-pervading atmosphere of society, the air it breathes."[1] Are Spanish myths different from others? Are they more potentially harmful? Perhaps they are because for many—foreigner and Spaniard alike—Spanish myths have not ratified values and sanctioned reality; they have replaced reality. For the Spaniard, myths became the substitutes for action in a world in which Spain was increasingly nonparticipant. For the foreigner, Spanish myths were used to fashion an existence more tolerable than the one he endured at home. (It is difficult to decide upon the correct tense to be used in these sentences. The myths are still active even though less so than they once were, and their influence is still powerful even on those who question their authority.)

1

All Spanish myths are variations on a single theme: Spain is different. Sophisticated Spaniards laugh out loud at the statement, but the lucrative tourist industry—the new El Dorado—is built on the solid foundation of its reality, over 30 million foreigners come yearly to discover this differentness, many millions leave convinced that they did, and Spaniards believe (and disbelieve) it with the same conviction that Frenchmen believe (and disbelieve) the superiority of French culture, Britishers believe (and disbelieve) the superiority of British character, and Americans believe (and disbelieve) the superiority of American morals.

The basis of the myths is the Spanish rejection of modern civilization—the industrialized, urbanized, mechanized, competitive, rational, scientific world culture. For the Spaniard, the reality that the myths replaced was Spain's inability during the nineteenth century to move, either politically or economically, into the modern world. The world "inability" carries no pejorative connotations. Whether the inability was a weakness that could have been overcome by disciplined effort, whether the inability sprang from conditions that could not have been remedied, such as the absence of raw materials essential for industrial growth, or whether the inability was a carefully weighed, purposeful rejection are evaluations I will not now make. It is enough to say that Spain did not move toward what is called modernity when her European neighbors did. The myths came into being in order to explain the failure to move in terms of Spanish superiority, expressed more congenially by calling superiority "differentness." (No people ever calls itself different and means inferior.)

Undeniably, Spain is different. She was ruled for over 700 years by Islamic invaders from the East who transformed most of the peninsula with a dazzling culture far more developed than that found in Europe.[2] Christians expelled the Muslims along with the Jews after a centuries-long religious crusade that burned into the Spaniard a deep and abiding Catholicism. The Reformation, the Renaissance, and then the Enlightenment were prevented from rooting in Spain, and the Industrial Revolution is taking place only now, in the latter part of the twentieth century. This does not mean that Spain had not partially industrialized earlier, beginning in the latter part of the nineteenth century, nor that Spain had not experienced recurring, bloody conflicts between the possessing and the dispossessed classes, first in the late nineteenth century and again in the twentieth century, culminating in the Civil War in 1936. Notwithstanding, the profound cultural changes implied in the words "Industrial Revolution" did not begin to have a major impact on Spanish society until recent years. Spain *is* different.

Whether she is superior is moot, but the myths of differentness have reassured the Spaniard—particularly since the nineteenth century, which early on saw Spain lose nearly all her colonies and which, at the end, saw the nation retracted almost totally into her peninsula for the first time since 1492. (The only exceptions were the unimportant African possessions that made Spain's claim to colonial status seem sadly ludicrous; the dogged, prideful maintenance of those possessions sparked a series of events that led eventually to disaster.)

The myths manifested themselves in the exaltation of characteristics that have become synonymous with Spain: pride, honor, stoicism, asceticism, tenacity, dignity. Many of these qualities could have described the Spaniard long before the 1800s. In earlier generations these traits were genuine because they were the psychological manifestations of the evolution of a unique people. The attributes did not then have an existence divorced from reality. It was only during the nineteenth century that these characteristics were mythologized and used almost genetically as a defense against what was called the worldly materialism of modernizing Europe. Poverty, which was the base of this defense, was given a Christian blessing, while progress was cursed as being corruptive and beneath contempt. Spanish dignity, simplicity, and lack of affectation, Spanish nobility and forbearance were lifted to the realms of nearly biologic certainty, and Spaniards came to believe that what was unjustly called national inferiority as judged by foreign standards was in reality personal, moral superiority within Spain— apotheosized in Spanish individualism. Spain was different, and, moreover, Spaniards were different.

It was not important to the foreigner how the Spaniard became different, nor was it important to him how the Spaniard rationalized that differentness. At the turn of the twentieth century, the myths of Spanish differentness found fertile ground among the creative and sensitive critics of modernity in Europe and in the United States. As these observers recoiled from the brutality and inhumanity of contemporary culture, Spain became a place of refuge suspended in time. By going to Spain one seemed to reenter premodern history; one could live again in a era before pride, honor, stoicism, asceticism, tenacity, and dignity became revered only in fiction. This could have been done as well by traveling to China or India or Japan or Egypt, but these were non-Western cultures. Spain was Western (albeit with a deep-dyed Eastern heritage), and even though much that was Spanish was remote from Western European and American experience, Spain was a part of the West, had been one of the great creative forces shaping the Western world, and could be identified with it. Spain became the anodyne of modernization and industrialization, and its differentness and its myths were embraced with desperate tenacity by those who wanted to believe that existence did not have to be as repellant as it was. The mere fact that "eternal" Spain existed contemporaneously with societies suffering profound transformation made those disillusioned by modernity believe an alternative way of life was possible without having to embrace a completely alien and far-off culture.

Thus, the myths that Spaniards held about themselves for their own national reasons assumed a double life and became sustaining myths for many non-Spaniards, particularly those among the influential intelligentsia. In the disillusionment with himself and with his own society, the foreigner thought he saw in Spain what he believed he could not see at home and idealized a society that seemed different and worthy of emulation. The Spaniards' myths of their own differentness conjoined the non-Spaniards' myths about Spanish culture, which appeared by comparison to what was being rejected by the foreigner as in some way superior.

Before discussing the significance of these observations, it is necessary to mention another myth—not one that the Spaniard and the foreigner share but one that is sole property of the non-Spaniard, particularly the Anglo-Saxon Protestant. This is the myth of Spanish religious fanaticism—*la Leyenda Negra* (the Black Legend), as it is called. It is just as romantic as the antimodernity myth, but portrays the Spaniard as worse than he is rather than better. It characterizes him as cruel, bloodthirsty, irrational, and intolerant—a death-fixated guerrilla fighter for a Catholic Christ wielding fire and sword for religious orthodoxy. The myth comes to awesome life in the single word *Inquisition*. Catholicism and its role in Spanish society will be analyzed in subsequent chapters. It suffices here to mention that in Protestant countries the antique but still lively Black Legend is one more obscurant to the reality of modern Spain.

The analysis of myth is significant because the foreigner has seen Spain through the prism of these illusions in much the same way as the Spaniard has seen himself. Moreover, the foreigner has judged Spanish historical events through this refraction. The distortion has particularly affected scholarship on the Second Republic (1931-36), the Civil War (1936-39), and the Franco era (1936-1975). Many valuable studies become warped when their authors attempt to evaluate these events. It is my opinion that the lack of dispassion originates to a great extent in the myths discussed earlier. Let us take two examples. The myths say otherwise, but the Second Republic was not an interlude of greening freedom between autocratic regimes. The Republic was a period of chaos unsalvageable by a few well-intentioned men among an obstinate majority totally unwilling to make the concessions necessary for a viable democracy. The republican idea throughout the nineteenth century was called *la niña bonita,* the pretty girl. The Second Republic may have been a "pretty girl," but she was ravished by men of every political family from Right to Left and was dead long before she was buried in April, 1939.

The myths have romanticized the Spanish Civil War. The war was bestial, but no more so than the American Civil War or the French Revolution (which, of course, was a civil war) or the English Civil War. It was no more cruel and vicious than the recent civil war in India that separated Pakistan, the even more recent one in Pakistan that separated Bangladesh, or the civil wars in the Congo or Nigeria. As in all such wars there were thousands of atrocities on both sides committed with that exquisite, obscene savagery best performed among intimates.[3] To die in Madrid was no more (or less) glorious than to die in the Midlands, or Paris, Karachi, Léopoldville, or Vicksburg. These civil wars were different, however. The wars on the Indian subcontinent and in Africa took place in "strange" lands beyond the experience of the West, between "strange" peoples whom the West looks on bloodlessly, intellectually with emotional detachment. The civil wars in America, France, and England took place in a past distant enough so that they can be considered almost not to have taken place at all—like a dead loved one who, once a certain number of years has passed, seems never to have lived, much less to have died. The British have almost completely blocked their war out of their memory. The French and the Americans cannot do so as easily as the British because all the wounds opened by these wars have not yet healed. But the ravages are old, and their origins have lost importance even if their consequences have not. The civil war in Spain happened in our time between people like ourselves.

The fact that war could erupt in a legendary land between brothers whom the West thought it knew and understood and could be fought with a butchery that one imagines to occur only in foreign, far-off places, or only back in times considered less humane, frightened and horrified the West. Reality confronted the myths. Spain was supposed to be different, a land of noble people with virtuous instincts (if you forget the Black Legend), a land where civility was more important than money, where honor was more durable than contract, a land where poverty was not ignominy, where wealth could not buy dignity—a place where the perversions of modern civilization had not invaded and corrupted a simple and honest society.

The Second Republic and the Civil War shattered these illusions about Spain, but the illusions could not be allowed to disappear. If the myths perished in Spain, then they died everywhere in the Western world. Explanations had to be found; scapegoats had to be created. A great part of the response in Europe and in the United States to the Spanish Civil War and to the Spain that emerged from it has been an emotional reaction to hopes shattered and faith ill placed. Those who believed in the illusions of Spain can be forgiven for not allowing them to die, for hallowing the ground where they last seemed to flourish. For the present generations—those born since the end of the Second World War, the Armageddon of all conceits of decency—Spain of the myths no longer exists. Spain is simply a modernizing nation much like many others to be found in Africa, Latin America, the Near East, the Far East, and parts of Europe, and I will evaluate her as such.

I am a part of the last generation to believe in the myths of Spain. It is my hope that I have been able to put them to rest.

Notes

1. Robert M. MacIver, *The Web of Government* (New York: Macmillan, 1948), p. 39.

2. Among the best accounts of Muslim rule in Spain are these studies: Claudio Sánchez Albornóz, *España: Un enigma histórico*, 2 vols. (Buenos Aires: Editorial Sudamericana, 1956) and *La España Musulmana*, 2 vols. (Buenos Aires: Libreria "El Ateneo" Editorial, 1960); Américo Castro, *The Structure of Spanish History*, trans. Edmund L. King (Princeton, N.J.: Princeton University Press, 1954).

3. See Hugh Thomas, *The Spanish Civil War* (New York: Harper & Row, Colophon Books, 1963), chaps. 19, 20, 21, and 22.

PART 1
BEFORE FRANCO

Lo que nos pasa a los españoles es que no sabemos lo que nos pasa, y ésto es lo que nos pasa.

The thing that is the matter with us Spaniards is that we do not know what is the matter with us, and that is what is the matter with us.

—*José Ortega y Gasset*

1
The Foundations of Spanish Politics

The Reconquest and the Creation of the Modern Nation-State

From the point of view of the political scientist, modern Spanish history is an account of unsuccessful attempts to sustain a viable nation-state. It begins in 1492 with the final battle of the Reconquest—the fall of Granada to Ferdinand and Isabel, *los Reyes Católicos* (the Catholic Kings).[1]

Spain was forged as a state by dynastic marriages among the heirs to the Christian realms that divided the peninsula. Except for the Moorish kingdom of Granada, unity was finally achieved in 1479, ten years after the wedding of Isabel of Castile to Ferdinand of Aragon. Married as prince and princess of the two controlling Christian royal houses on the peninsula, each monarch kept intact his and her sovereignty in the kingdoms that each inherited during the early years of their marriage. This unique political alliance, which created Spain, was expressed in their heraldic motto: *"Tanto Monta, Monta Tanto Isabel como Fernando."* Fully if stiffly translated it means: "Isabel mounts the throne with sovereignty equal to that of Ferdinand, who mounts the throne with sovereignty equal to that of Isabel."

Spain was forged as a nation by the reconquest of the peninsula from the Moors, who had arrived victoriously in 711. In 718 the Muslim expansion was stopped in Asturias in northern Spain at the battle of Covadonga, which marked the beginning of the Reconquest. In 1492 the last Moorish sovereign surrendered at the battle of Granada. During these seven centuries, a nation evolved whose legitimacy was purchased with the Christian blood—or more precisely with the Catholic blood—of those who gradually but relentlessly pushed out the invader in the name of Christ's apostle who was to become Spain's patron saint—Santiago (James).[2] The battle cry of the liberating Christians—*"¡Santiago y Cierre España!"*—reflected a way of thinking that has characterized Spain up to the present time, yet the slogan may be interpreted in two ways. It can mean, "Fight in the name of Santiago and close ranks for Spain!" Or it can mean, "Fight in the name of Santiago and close Spain [against all invaders, all foreigners, all alien things and ideas]!" Spain the state and Spain the nation germinated simultaneously during the crusade to liberate the peninsula from foreign, non-Christian domination. The year 1492 is the most significant date in Spanish history not because America was discovered but because Spain was born, a Spain that would become the modern world's first nation-state.

During the seven centuries of reconquest, Catholicism was burned into the Spaniard. It was as a Catholic that the provincial came to identify himself as Spanish—not as Castilian, Aragonese, Andalusian, Catalan, Gallegan, but Spanish. Even today the Spaniard identifies emotionally first with his *patria chica* (little country), the province in which he was born and raised and whose language or dialect he speaks before he learns Spanish. Before the unification, a man thought of himself almost exclusively as the native of the region in which he lived. Spain, the nation-state, took form as the peninsula was freed from Islamic dominion. Thus to be Spanish was to be Catholic. This statement must be understood fully because it explains not only the motivation behind the central event of Spanish history—the Reconquest —but also clarifies a great part of all subsequent Spanish history. In this perspective, the expulsion of the Jews and Muslims after 1492 can be seen as an early form of denaturalization. The fact that, after centuries of living on the Iberian peninsula, the Jews and the Muslims were as Spanish as the Catholics in birthright and in cultural heritage makes their expulsion a moral abomination. The additional fact that they were the most gifted and creative people of their time caused their banishment to deliver a blow to the arts and sciences of Spain from which the nation has yet to recover fully. Be that as it may, in the strategy of the Catholic Kings and their heirs, the Jews and the Muslims were not *politically* Spanish and therefore were expendable in the name of nationalism.[3] The Inquisition was employed by the Catholic sovereigns to root out the false believer—the false Spaniard, the infidel-traitor—and was a weapon used against the Muslims and the Jews long before it was used against the Protestants. This explanation does not make the Holy Office (the formal name for the Inquisition) any less repugnant (particularly when seen in retrospect from the present where more subtle, supportive methods of maintaining loyalty abound), but it does make clear the intimate, symbiotic relationship between religion and politics that exists in Spain. To use sociological terms, Catholicism became and remained the prime agency of political socialization.[4]

The religious means of achieving national unity eventually proved to be inadequate, however, and Spain imperceptibly but ineluctably began to pull apart. The disintegration was slowed because of the agglutinative strength of Catholicism, but, as will be seen in later pages, the faith grew weak as the Church became corrupt. The first nation to be born was also the first not actually to die but to sicken and languish. Only the distance of time allows us to see that the Golden Age of the 1500s was the end of an old era and not the beginning of a new one. The glorious sixteenth century was the exuberant extension of the dynamism of the Reconquest given incalculable impetus by the discovery of the Americas. The zeal to defend and propagate the faith throughout Europe and pagan America, plus the passion to accumulate gold that quickly followed the discovery of riches in the New World, provided the impulsion for the century that saw Spain become the most powerful and influential nation on earth. The momentum was broken by England when her navy destroyed the Armada in 1588, but more significantly it was broken within Spain herself.

Historians continue to debate the causes of this collapse of commitment and loyalty. Moreover, the reasons lie buried too deeply in time to allow political scientists to do anything more than muse unscientifically. But some attempt must be made to grapple with a reality that while unprovable is undeniable. The speculations of José Ortega y Gasset are acceptable not only because his ideas aid in understanding the remote past but also because they assist in understanding the recent past and the present as well. Paraphrased, Ortega states in his most celebrated and provocative work, *Invertebrate Spain*, that a nation is great not because of what she has done in the past, she is great because of what she does in the present and even more because of what she plans to do in the future.[5] Expanding this insight, it could be argued that, since the Reconquest and the age of discovery and colonization, Spain has had a sense of national purpose insufficiently strong to prompt the masses to continue to legitimize the state and its pursuits. Moreover, for those who became the elites, the Reconquest and the century of discovery had calamitous consequences. The Reconquest turned peasants into soldiers and soldiers into gentlemen. Gentlemen fight, conquer, plunder, and govern, but they do not work and without work no polity can prosper for long. It can survive, just as Spain has survived, but its existence becomes mean, and its people—particularly its elites—grow resentful and envious, taking refuge from failure behind vainglorious claims to moral superiority. Elena de la Souchère has fascinating statistics giving the number of *hidalgos* who swelled the aristocratic ranks in post-Reconquest Spain.[6] Etymologically *hidalgo* means *hijo de algo* (literally, son of something), a *somebody*, and the caste of the *hidalgos* forbade its members manual labor or even commercial enterprise. Even had discovery and colonization provided the vital sense of national mission, the era of international dominance came to an end with the defeat of the Armada. Thus, as the nation deteriorated for lack of purpose, so in turn did the state, and the history of modern Spain can be read as the attempt once again to form what was cast and lost between 1492 and 1588—a viable nation-state.

The writings of Hermann Weilenmann can help clarify the plight of Spain. Weilenmann says that the people who make up any polity must possess and maintain three wills if they are to live successfully politically: the will that creates a people, the will that creates a state, and a political will.

> The aim of the will that creates a people is to maintain the common good so that it may be uninterruptedly utilized and enjoyed. Not every people with this desire has the will that creates a state as well—the will to create an organization that has the power to protect the common good against attacks from within and without. Political will, in its narrow sense, is achieved completely only by those members of the state who can determine for themselves, from one case to the next, what is to be done and what is left undone, so that the purpose of the union will be fulfilled.[7]

The will to create a people and the will to create a state were powerful during the seven centuries of the Reconquest and the century of discovery and colonization. Inexplicably, beginning in the seventeenth century these wills wasted away. The Spanish polity held together, but it resembled the victim of a chronic, debilitating ailment. Only during the war against Napoleon in the early 1800s were these two wills reanimated, but even then only sufficiently to rid Spain of the invader, not sufficiently to reestablish an effective political system. As for the political will, it can be safely said that Spaniards have never possessed it.

The Hapsburgs

Salvador de Madariaga suggests that perhaps Charles V (Charles I in Spain) was the only Spanish monarch since the Reconquest to have had the vision necessary to have galvanized the new nation and to have turned the Spanish people into supportive citizens.[8] Yet Charles was not a true Spaniard. He was born and reared in Flanders, spoke no Spanish, and came to Spain for the first time as an adult. His contemporaries considered him to be a German. He inherited the Spanish throne in 1516 and by craft obtained the Holy Roman throne in 1519. He was simultaneously king and emperor and by temperament and conviction an internationalist at the beginning of the age of nationalism. He dreamed of and worked toward creating a Europe politically unified through the Hapsburgs and spiritually unified through Catholicism. To this European nucleus he would add the Spanish colonial possessions in the Americas, Africa, and the Far East and establish a Hispano-Christian hegemony over the known world. By the end of his reign, Charles had come to consider himself Spanish, and therefore he saw Spain as the heart and brains of his worldwide empire. This would have been a magnificent destiny for Spain and the heirs of Charles—a future with a sense of purpose fit for a people who had spent seven centuries proving its militant faith and who considered itself to be the first child of the Church. Unfortunately for Spain, Charles' grand scheme was thwarted by the spirit of nationalism growing in France and England that rejected the concept of political internationalism and by the spirit of Protestantism that challenged Catholic spiritual universality. Exhausted and unsuccessful in his endeavors, Charles abdicated and retired to a monastery in a remote part of Spain. Before doing so, however, he divided his world, giving the German kingdom to his brother Ferdinand and Spain to his son Philip, who came to the throne as Philip II.[9]

Philip II was the first authentic king of Spain and the first authentic Spaniard to rule Spain. His great-grandparents, the Catholic Kings, created Spain, but they were born and culturally remained Castilian and Aragonese and governed in a manner unique to themselves. His grandmother, the daughter of Ferdinand and Isabel, never really ruled; she had been declared mad and spent most of her adult life locked away in a convent. His father was Flemish and ruled an empire of which Spain was only a part, albeit eventually the most important. Philip, by contrast, was born, reared, and formed in Spain. Moreover, he was the first sovereign to be confronted with the political problems with which every subsequent Spanish ruler has had to grapple, down to and including Franco, whose successor, King Juan Carlos, faces the same task. Philip sought to make absolute the sovereignty of the state and to maintain the loyalty of the Spaniards. He was not successful in either task, nor were any of his successors, whether monarch, president, or caudillo. The reasons for their failure lay partly in the problems all governments face and partly in problems peculiar to the polity of Spain.

Every political system must balance the centripetal, sovereign, decision-making powers of the state against the centrifugal, resistant forces of the nation that seek to limit and define that power.[10] For effective government the balance must tilt slightly in favor of the authoritative power of the governors against the vigilant but acquiescent forces of the governed. This slightly askew equilibrium can survive unsustained by oppression only if the people have trust in a government that has earned their confidence by not abusing the slight edge of power it must possess in order to maintain the stability of the system. These maxims apply to all governments; what distinguishes democratic from nondemocratic government is the role the governed play in choosing the governors. Moreover, as governments evolve from autocratic to democratic, the powers of the governors come to be delimited and the rights of the people come to be guaranteed either in written constitutions or in customs and traditions grown sacred over time.

In Spain the resistant forces of the people have their origins in the ancient *fueros*.[11] The *fueros* predate the Romans and are thought to be of Celtiberian origin. They were an early form of common law found in the Cantabrian and Pyrenean mountain villages, and they evolved in order to institutionalize the rights of self-government. De la Souchère writes that "even the poorest free man sat as an equal with the *ricos hombres* (rich men) in the local assemblies which named magistrates invested with executive and judiciary power."[12] Thus direct democracy among the politically qualified was a heritage of many of the peoples who began the Reconquest.

In the territories reconquered from the Moors, the *fueros* took on additional significance. Still today, outside the cities and away from the coast, Spain is an empty and desolate land—particularly in the central mountains and plateaus. Scattered throughout this region are castles, many even now isolated and difficult to reach. They are a part of the romance of Spain, but more importantly for this study, they are a part of her politics. As the rulers of the Christian kingdoms pursued the Moors, volunteers were called upon to man the remote outposts at the frontiers between Arab and Christian land. Many of these settlements were self-governing under *fueros* established as a part of the agreements between the sovereign and the volunteers. These *fueros* differed from the ones that had grown organically in the northern mountain villages; the *fueros* of the frontier were guarantees of noninterference by the ruler in the local politics of the new settlements. They were not gifts from the sovereign, however; the rights had not been granted. These *fueros* were part of a contract and came to life simultaneously with the settlements themselves in places where before there had been no Christian law. Theoretically the *fueros* did not contain powers a future king could recoup since the authority never belonged to the state in the first place.

Thus the *fueros* expressed not only rights that had grown organically through custom among the people, they also set forth the contractual guarantees of self-government. As the Reconquest pushed farther and farther south between 718 and 1492, so did the *fueros* until finally they became part of the political tradition of most of the peninsula. Only in Andalusia was the tradition of the *fueros* weak. There the kings gave vast tracts of land not to pioneers but to the Church, to the nobility, and to the military orders (religious organizations of fighter-monks who had taken a vital part in the Reconquest).

After the Reconquest was complete, the *fueros* took on still further significance. They became the weapons of the local notables against the centralizing pressure of the monarchs. During the reign of the Catholic Kings, there was less concern for *political* centrality. Ferdinand and Isabel were the rulers of Spain, but they were also sovereigns of their respective kingdoms. Moreover, the pursuit of spiritual unity was an endeavor shared by all the Christians of the peninsula. The Catholic Kings sought little use of state power that ran counter to the will of the people. Politics was absorbed in religion, and religion was the universal force of the day. There was little conflict between the people and the sovereign, between the state and the nation.

Beginning in the 1500s, however, the Hapsburg kings acted to cement the loose political unity achieved by their predecessors and to consolidate the power of the state in the hands of the monarch. They were not successful. Charles V was forced to learn an early lesson when he attempted to impose alien political institutions on his new Spanish subjects. The revolt of the *comuneros* in 1520 was an uprising of Castilian town-dwellers who used the *fueros* to protect themselves against royal absolutism. Reluctantly Charles honored the *fueros*. In fact they were kept intact throughout the entire reign of the Hapsburgs (1516-1700), who learned to live with what de Madariaga describes as "the multitude of councils and boards, *fueros* and local liberty."[13]

As a consequence, the Hapsburgs changed their tactics, but they did not change their goals. If Spain could not be consolidated politically, she would be consolidated spiritually. Philip II and his Hapsburg heirs used religion as the surrogate for politics and turned to their political use the faith that had created Spain and that had become the symbol of citizenry by which Spaniards called each other brother. Beginning with Philip II, religion also became the symbol of political authority by which Spaniards called their sovereigns master. Spiritual unity was made the substitute for political unity. Whereas Catholicism during the Reconquest had been the vital spiritual force of positive commitment to the unified nation, Catholicism under Philip II and all the successive

Hapsburg kings became the repressive weapon of religious orthodoxy wielded by the Inquisition in the name of the unified state. Heresy became treason and treason became heresy, and the Spaniards who eluded the political power of the state by taking refuge in the *fueros* were trapped by the spiritual power of the Church. The repression notwithstanding, the people remained compliant believers because the Spaniards were yet unable to identify themselves as anything but Catholic. Their faith remained strong until the 1800s when the Church betrayed the people and the de-Christianization of the masses began. Only in retrospect can it be seen that the de-Christianization (or de-Catholicization to be more exact) was seeded by the Hapsburgs when they forced religion to perform a task unsuited to its nature.

The Bourbons

In 1700 the last Spanish Hapsburg, Charles II, died. He had no children and chose as his heir Philip of Anjou, the grandson of his sister Maria Teresa, the wife of Louis XIV of France. This inheritance was challenged by the Archduke Charles of Austria, but Philip's claim was upheld at the end of the War of Spanish Succession. Elena de la Souchère perceptively calls this war the first Carlist War because it was fought in Spain over the clash between central and local authority.[14]

During the seventeenth century, municipal unity, theretofore so essential for resistance to royal prerogatives, had begun to collapse because of class conflict and internal corruption within the cities. By this time, however, the *fueros* had lost much of their identification with municipal self-government and had taken on new significance as symbols of regional or provincial home rule. So intense had this resistance become that, during the War of Spanish Succession, Catalonia and Aragon fought, in the name of local liberties, on the side of the Hapsburg pretender against the Bourbon heir. Although the Hapsburgs had spent 150 years trying to consolidate unchallenged political authority, they learned to live with the complexity of local rights and honored them at least in theory. The new Bourbon king had different sentiments and intentions, and, following the solar pattern of his grandfather, Louis XIV, he began the relentless destruction of regional freedoms that continued to be the hallmark of that royal house until the abdication of Alfonso XIII in 1931. The Bourbons brought with them a concept of authority alien to Spain. De Madariaga writes: "The century dominated by French thought shifts the stress from the religious to the political, and the Spanish crown ceases to worry about religious unity but seeks to reduce Catalonia to the laws of Castile.

Gradually the Inquisition relaxes its hold over the people."[15] The Bourbons, unlike the Hapsburgs, would tolerate no challenge to the sovereignty of the state. They rejected the concepts that rights belonged to the people from time immemorial (the ancient mountain *fueros*) or that rights belonged to municipalities or regions springing from agreements made between ruler and people (the frontier *fueros* of the Reconquest). The power of the monarch was supreme, and any alleviation from his authority was ordained and repealed at his will, or *"notre bon plaisir,"* as the French phrased it. Unalloyed absolutism was the Bourbon dowry to Spain. The early Bourbons were not totally successful in destroying all *fueros*, however. Those in Catalonia and Aragon were eventually suppressed as retribution for supporting the Hapsburg pretender, but those in Navarre and in the Basque country survived until 1839.

Irrespective of the absolutism of the Bourbons, of the corruption and depravity of many of their kings and queens, and of their contemptuous and cruel disregard for the Spanish political heritage, the monarchist ideal remained strong among the people—kept alive by the Church. So tenacious was it, in fact, that when Spain was invaded by Napoleon, the masses rose up in arms against him in the name of their Bourbon king Ferdinand VII, one of the most execrable rulers in all Spanish history. The soldiers of Napoleon and the French revolutionary ideas that came with them were resisted with a conviction and ferocity that had not been seen among the Spanish people since the Reconquest. The defense of a state that had lost most of its legitimacy became the ironic motive for guerrilla warfare against a hated invader. Echoes of *"¡Santiago y Cierre España!"*

It is the opinion of many careful observers of Spanish history and politics that perhaps only a crusade against foreign invasion—whether of ideas or troops—gives the Spanish people a sense of mission sufficiently strong to unify them. It is not difficult to accept this observation when applied to the invasion of troops bent upon destruction. It is difficult to accept, however, when applied by a people to the rejection of ideas, foreign or otherwise, whose implementation would set it free from despotic rule. The revolutionary political theories that came in with the Bonapartes were based on concepts of liberty, fraternity, and equality (whether respected or not by Napoleon and his brother Joseph, whom he made king of Spain). These ideas were repudiated by the Spanish masses, and their rejection is a paradox that must be understood if the politics of the nineteenth and twentieth centuries is to make any sense at all to the non-Spaniard. The paradox is that an oppressed people fought a guerrilla war in the name of reactionary beliefs against an invader bringing with him revolutionary theories that could have freed the invaded people from the oppression of their historic masters.[16] The paradox is compounded by the fact that the historic Bourbon masters were also of French origin and had almost totally destroyed the vestiges of indigenous Spanish democracy they had found when they took power.

The key to the paradox lies in Catholicism. As already discussed, the Reconquest took place in order to establish Catholicism throughout the peninsula and to create a Catholic nation-state. The Spaniard came to identify himself as Spanish by being Catholic. The Inquisition was used primarily to guarantee this continued identification. Political socialization was achieved in large part through the maintenance of doctrinal purity among the people, producing thereby a nation of believers. The systemic political disruptiveness of the Renaissance, the Enlightenment, and Protestantism had been prevented by the Inquisition from taking root in Spain. In like manner, the revolutionary ideas coming from France during the eighteenth century were ruthlessly suppressed among the masses. As a consequence of these phenomena, the Napoleonic invaders bringing with them the anathematized theories of liberalism were attacked by the well-indoctrinated Spanish rank and file both as foreigners and as heretics. The Church had done a thorough job.[17]

The conquest of Spain by Napoleon and the reign of his puppet-king Joseph broke the continuity of Spanish history. Never since the Moors had the nation been invaded and never before had the forces that had shaped Spain been challenged so profoundly as they were from 1808 to 1814. Unfortunately for the future of Spain, after the ouster of Napoleon the Spaniards were unable to muster the will to take the political and economic direction necessary to enter the mainstream of European societies. In 1814, as a result of the successful National War of Independence (as the Spaniards call their war against France), Spain was more a nation than she had been since 1588, and her more progressive elements had hammered out an honorable constitution that could have been the vehicle for meaningful systemic change. But that was not to be the case.

The Nineteenth Century to the Second Bourbon Restoration

De Madariaga writes that "the nineteenth century in Spain can only appear as a turbulent and chaotic period without any meaning whatever unless it be realized that, in the history of Spain, it stands as an era of reconstruction from the ground upward."[18] The 1800s can be interpreted politically as the struggle to reestablish the political system destroyed by the Peninsular Wars. From 1814 to 1876 the antagonists in this conflict were the traditionalists and the liberals. The antagonism began in Cádiz, where a constituent assembly (the Cortes) met beginning in 1810 to erect the framework for the new state that would follow the expulsion of Napoleon. The results of the assembly's labor was the constitution of 1812. The liberals, who dominated the Cortes, represented the new bourgeoisie, a tiny minority in Spain, and had come to Cádiz to modernize Spain—to abolish the ancient prerogatives of the Church and of the aristocracy and to clear away the confusion of medieval property rights that often separated ownership from usage. These antique privileges made it difficult if not impossible to enter freely into contracts, a right essential to a liberal economy. Politically they sought to limit the authority of the king who, like William and Mary in England, would be invited to reign. Raymond Carr writes, quoting an earlier source: "The spirit and ideas of the liberals were republican although in order not to affront openly the opinions of the masses they pretended no other aim than a limited monarchy basing their projects on laws and events in the history of Spain adapted to their purposes."[19] Regarding the power of the state, the anticlerical liberals were uncompromisingly centralists. They accepted two principles unqualifiedly: "that the Cortes, as 'sole representative of the sovereign nation,' must enforce a uniform and centralized system and that within this system the municipalities were 'subaltern corporations.'"[20] Control over the central power of the state would be in the hands of a legislature chosen by limited suffrage. In short, a representative, constitutional monarchy would govern Spain. The traditionalists opposed the liberals on most all issues, defending their position by claiming that the liberals represented alien political ideas at variance with Spain's ancient customs and that they preferred artificial representative government over the organic, direct democracy embodied in the *fueros*.[21]

The paradoxes of Spanish politics in the nineteenth and twentieth centuries—which make dispassionate analysis so difficult—originate with these antagonists. The liberals supported concepts of national sovereignty that had been the property of the Bourbon autocrats, whose royal prerogatives the liberals sought to limit constitutionally. The traditionalists, who supported an autocratic monarchy, were advocates of the decentralization of power, a proposal anathema to the Bourbons. The liberals' impetuous disregard for traditional political institutions of self-government (sanctified by memory if not by usage) met the traditionalists' cynical defense of these same institutions in the name of liberty long since subverted by the provincial oligarchy and its liegemen, the caciques.[22] It should come as no surprise that the constitution and its legislative consequences remained ineffective. The restored monarch Ferdinand VII—the Desired One as he was called—flouted the constitution with undisguised contempt and established the precedent for royal interference in constitutional politics that was faithfully maintained by each of his descendents down to and including Alfonso XIII, who left Spain ignominiously in 1931.

Between the first Bourbon restoration in 1814 and the second Bourbon restoration in 1875, Spanish political history is a chronicle of the conflict between the liberals and the traditionalists. The antagonists appeared with different names from time to time—moderates, progressives, democrats, conservatives, among others—but the basic issues remained constant. During those sixty years Spain had six constitutions; one Royal Charter; thirty-five pronunciamientos (eleven considered successful);[23] one temporarily deposed king, Ferdinand VII, who was placed back on his throne with the aid of French soldiers sent into Spain by Louis XVIII (1823); the forced abdication of a queen regent, the first Maria Cristina, mother of Isabel II (1840); a military regency that ruled Spain until Isabel II reached her majority (1840-43); one revolution that ousted a monarch, the same Isabel II (1868); another military regency during which Spain searched for a sovereign (1868-70); one Italian prince, Amadeo of Savoy, the brother of King Victor Emmanuel II, who in 1870 was asked to become, agreed to become, and became king of Spain; one abdication (the same Amadeo in 1873); one republic (which lasted less than one year and had four presidents, 1873-74); and two civil wars (the First Carlist War, 1833-40, and the Second Carlist War, 1870-75).

The two civil wars are of special importance to this study. They were in reality two phases of a single war separated by several decades. In fact, it could be said that they were earlier parts of a multiphased campaign whose later battles were fought in the Civil War between 1936 and 1939. Its most recent manifestation is the urban guerrilla warfare being waged today by the Basque nationalists.[24] These wars were fought essentially to oppose the establishment of a centralized sovereign state with ultimate decision-making power. In addition they were fought to determine who would control the state that would emerge from the conflict. The First Carlist War broke out at the death of Ferdinand VII, who designated as his heir his infant daughter Isabel. By the time of his death, Ferdinand, who had despised and corrupted the constitution of 1812, had won the support of the liberals, who looked to his widow to continue through her regency the centralist political policy of Ferdinand so essential to liberal survival. In the name of regional self-determination, the traditionalists opposed the designation of Isabel and supported Ferdinand's brother Charles, whose claim was in reality more legitimate. The Salic law, which governed the Bourbon successional custom, precluded females from inheriting the crown. Consequently, Isabel had no right to the throne under Bourbon tradition. In the First Carlist war the forces of Isabel were victorious. Over thirty years later, during the chaotic years following the ouster of the same queen (whose scandalous personal life would read like pornography), the Carlist forces once again tried to seat their pretender on the throne and once again they were defeated. The Carlist strongholds in both wars were in the countryside of the north—the Basque provinces (Vizcaya, Álava, Guipúzcoa), Navarre,[25] and parts of Catalonia, Aragon, and Old Castile. These were the regions of the ancient mountain *fueros*, populated in the 1800s by devoutly, almost fanatically, Catholic, economically comfortable small farmers who damned all liberal concepts—economic, religious, and social. The Carlists were prosperous, liberty-loving regionalists fighting for the right to be reactionary. This paradox would endure for over sixty years and carry meaning that would color international reaction to the Civil War in 1936. Self-determination is a cause honored by most democratic systems. When self-determination is proclaimed in the name of undemocratic ideology, democratic critics are presented with a painful dilemma.

During this period of continuing conflict, two ancient institutions, the Church and the army, changed their natures and assumed their modern roles. It is essential that the student of contemporary Spanish politics understand this epochal transformation. Prior to the nineteenth century, the army had not been an independent participant in the political process. The army became a political force in Spanish history as a result of the Peninsular War and its consequent domestic and colonial upheavals. De Madariaga is correct, however, when he dissociates the army from militarism, and his observations in regard to the nineteenth century apply with equal validity to the twentieth, including part of the Franco era.

Militarism is hardly a correct word in the case of Spain. It is used here only to conform with the now traditional misuse of it. The position in Spain bears no resemblance to that of countries—such as prewar Russia—in which a military caste controlled the national policy, particularly in matters of defense and foreign affairs, with a warlike spirit and intention. In Spain there is no such thing, and the evil would be better described as *praetorianism*. For a body of officers, by no means a caste, controls the political life of the nation, giving but little thought to foreign affairs and intent on the preservation of power and on the administration and enjoyment of a disproportionate amount of the budget.[26]

When the Spanish colonies in Latin America revolted against the rule of the French puppet-king Joseph Bonaparte—thereby setting themselves free from Spain—the Spanish colonial armies came home, and their officers flooded an already swollen corps of personnel grown large during the campaigns against Napoleon. Many younger officers who had seen action in Spain resented the senior officers who returned from America to assume commands the young turks thought better deserved by those who had fought the French. These younger men became a strong force in the army and supported the liberals, who like themselves were seeking partially to reshape traditional institutions. The army would probably have returned to strictly professional affairs had the history of Spain in the nineteenth century been one of political stability, but the continued threat to the establishment of effective central government posed by the reactionary Carlists made inevitable the direct involvement of the army in Spanish politics until the second restoration of the Bourbons in 1874.[27] Moreover, it legitimized to the present day the tradition of military intervention in politics when such intrusion was deemed necessary to preserve national unity or to preserve the integrity of the armed forces.

The reader should not be misled by the "liberalism" of the army, however. By no means was the army a progressive institution. The military's liberalism sprang from its intention to maintain order and stability throughout the peninsula and from its refusal to allow any incursions against the sovereign authority of the state irrespective of the origins of those inroads—whether ancient *fueros*, seignorial and aristocratic prerogatives, or privileges of the Church. The army was liberal only because it was against certain things dear to the hearts and minds of the conservatives. Once army officers occupied political positions, they were indistinguishable from conservatives in the way they used and viewed power. The astute de Madariaga writes:

> Whether liberal or reactionary in his ideas, the military politician is a reactionary by temperament. He wants to have his way, not to pool his ideas or wishes. . . . Moreover, military education has disastrous effects on Spanish psychology. The Spanish character has an innate tendency to become overbearing. The military law of obedience from below and orders from above encourages such a tendency.[28]

The most powerful institution resisting the centralizing power of the state after the first Bourbon restoration was the Catholic Church. Gerald Brenan believes that the antagonism between the institutions had begun already in the latter part of the 1700s. By that time the Bourbon kings felt they no longer needed the political socializational functions of the Church, and so they sought to bring it under state control.[29] In spite of this power struggle, however, when Napoleon invaded Spain, the Spanish Church rushed to the defense of the Spanish monarchy—not because it loved the Spanish state but because it loathed Napoleon and his French revolutionary ideas. After the ouster of Napoleon in 1814, the Church returned to its stance of opposition to the state. Given the political theories of the liberals, the Church's opposition intensified especially during those times when more doctrinaire liberals were in control of the Spanish government. During the First Carlist War, in which the Church supported the Carlist cause, the liberal prime minister Juan Álvarez Mendizábal confiscated the lands of the Church.

Mendizábal's action was a stroke of political genius from a short range point of view. From a long range point of view, it began a trauma whose effects are still strong today after 150 years. The loss of the Church's lands and therefore of most of her wealth fundamentally changed the relationship between the Church and the state, between the Church and the army, and between the Church and the people. Prior to the confiscation, the Church had been an independent institution. Her intimate relationship with the Spanish state dated to the Reconquest, and the identification of Catholicism with citizenship gave the Church a secure place in politics that was vital to the existence of Spain. But the Church had been an equal partner; her vast riches insured her economic security and thus her independence from the state. That independence had often allowed the Church (in preachment if not always in practice) to protect the people from the arrogance of the upper classes and from the whims of the monarchs, and, as a consequence, the relationship between the Church and the masses had grown close over time. This intimacy was shattered when her lands were confiscated and the Church was left destitute and pregnable.

The liberal state did not give the lands of the Church to the poor. Liberalism in Spain was much like liberalism throughout the rest of Europe—a bourgeois phenomenon supported by a class that hated and feared the poor and the dispossessed as much as did the traditionalists. The liberals sought to eliminate not the conservatives as a class but only their antique, precapitalist political and economic privileges. Consequently the lands were sold to those who could afford to pay for them, not only the new liberal bourgeoisie but also the old conservative aristocracy. Greed to acquire more land lured the traditional elites (who were devout Catholics) to swallow their repugnance for the liberals, who had so generously provided their windfall, and to embrace the hated liberal state. This conservative conversion was the result of Mendizábal's acumen.

For the first time in the history of the Spanish nation-state, the Church found herself isolated from the centers of power and vulnerable to the will of others. Her strategy to correct this anomalous situation lost for her the support of the Spanish masses but gained for her the protection of the Spanish state and army and the affection of the Spanish elite. By custom the conservative elite had always been Catholic; out of discretion the liberal elite (excluding the liberal intellectuals) became so. The Church lost the Spanish masses when she abandoned them in order to court the new rich and the old rich grown richer. The Church still operated the keys to heaven, and the elites bought duplicates with legacies that became the nucleus of the Church's reestablished wealth. With priestly sanction the rich became richer and paid more and more for the warrants of salvation. The Church defended the political and economic philosophies of the rich against the increasingly desperate cries of the poor. The abandonment of the masses by the Church began the traumatic de-Christianization (or de-Catholicization) referred to earlier.[30]

In retaliation against the confiscation of her property, the Spanish Church brought the power of the Vatican to bear against the liberal Spanish state. In 1851, well over a decade after the confiscation, the Vatican and Spain signed a concordat that remained in force until the Second Republic in the 1930s. Under its terms the Church accepted the reality of the confiscation and renounced all claims for compensation. The state agreed to subsidize the Church, paying for the maintenance of temples and for the salary of the secular clergy.[31] Moreover, the treaty reestablished the *Real Patronato,* the ancient right of the Spanish monarchs to participate with the Pope in making episcopal appointments in Spain. As a result of the concordat, Catholicism became the official state religion, and the liberal state—the intrepid enemy of Catholicism—became the guarantor, protector, and subventioner of the Catholic Church—the imprecator of all liberal doctrine.

Notes

1. For an explanation of the terms "state building" and "nation building," see Gabriel A. Almond and G. Bingham Powell, Jr., *Comparative Politics, A Developmental Approach* (Boston: Little, Brown and Co., 1966), pp. 35-36.

2. For a fascinating account of the influence of St. James in Spain and Western Christendom, see Américo Castro, *The Structure of Spanish History,*

trans. Edmund L. King (Princeton, N.J.: Princeton University Press, 1954), pp. 130-58.

3. Before the reader judges Spain too harshly, it should be remembered that from that time to this, every new nation-state with no exceptions (including the present-day Arab nations and Israel) has claimed victims in the name of that exigent ideology which was nurtured in Spain.

4. For a provocative account of the Inquisition, see Henry Kamew, *The Spanish Inquisition* (New York: New American Library, 1968).

5. *España Invertebrada* (Madrid: Revista de Occidente, 1957), chap. 2.

6. *An Explanation of Spain*, trans. Eleanor Ross Levieux (New York: Vintage Books, 1964), pp. 68-70.

7. Hermann Weilenmann, "The Interlocking of Nation and Personality Structure," trans. Anna Johanna Lode-von Aesch, in *Nation-Building*, ed. Karl W. Deutsch and William T. Foltz (New York: Atherton Press, 1963), p. 43.

8. Charles was the son of Juana (*la Loca*, the Mad), daughter of Ferdinand and Isabel of Spain and of Felipe (*el Hermoso*, the Handsome), grandson and heir of Maximilian I, the Hapsburg emperor of the Holy Roman Empire.

9. Philip's inheritance included Portugal, all the colonies in the Americas, the Philippine Islands, the Canary Islands, the Low Countries, and parts of France, Italy, and North Africa.

10. For an explanation of these concepts see L. S. Amery, *Thoughts on the Constitution* (New York: Oxford University Press), chap. 1.

11. For a short but excellent account of the *fueros*, see Elena de la Souchère, *An Explanation of Spain*, chap. 2.

12. Ibid., p. 35.

13. Salvador de Madariaga, *Spain, A Modern History* (New York: Praeger Publishers, 1958), p. 47.

14. De la Souchère, *An Explanation of Spain*, p. 47. When the war spread to the New World, it was called King Philip's War.

15. De Madariaga, *Spain*, pp. 47-48.

16. Jaime Vicens Vives, the eminent Spanish historian, believes that the demand for social and political reform was also an important part of the popular uprising, but it is my opinion that Vicens Vives makes a weak case for the extensiveness of articulated, popular dissatisfaction. He writes in a well-known study: "The people were organized with varying degrees of efficiency by a few commanders of dubious military ability. Constantly engaged in guerrilla warfare, or in giving up their lives to defend strategic strongholds, they fought for certain concrete ideals: for their home, their God, and their king—in short, for their country. It would be a gross error, however, to ignore the ferment of social renovation, including a current anti-aristocratic feeling that motivated the bull goaders of Bailén in Andalusia (*los garrochistas*) the armed vigilantes of Bruch in Catalonia (*los somatenes*), and the guerrilla fighters of Saragosa." Joan Connelly Ullman, trans. and ed., *Approaches to the History of Spain* (Berkeley: University of California Press, 1967), pp. 122-23.

Surely ferment among the lowest element of the people cannot be considered symptomatic of widespread, national disaffection. Unless more evidence could be presented, I remain unconvinced of widespread popular demand for fundamental reform.

17. Vicens Vives explains: "Liberalism in Spain has both a political and a religious content. As elsewhere in Europe (where the term 'liberal' was adopted) its adherents defended a limitation on the absolute power of the monarch through a written constitution that safeguards the right of the Cortes to legislate as the representative of the people and the rights of the individual to defend his private interests against state intervention by guaranteeing freedom of speech, press and assembly. But the *Dictionary of the Royal Academy of Spain* (16th ed., 1956) does not mention these tenets and instead defines Liberalism as a 'political-religious system which proclaims the absolute independence of the state, i.e., its organization and actions, from all positive religions.' The Liberals' religious policy was one factor, but not the only one nor the most important one, in the Carlist Wars . . . and in the subsequent struggle to establish constitutional government in Spain." Ullman, *Approaches to the History of Spain*, p. 124.

18. De Madariaga, *Spain*, p. 56.

19. *Spain, 1808-1939* (Oxford: Clarendon Press, 1966), p. 97.

20. Ibid., p. 98.

21. This conservative argument is so disarmingly effective that even observers as unquestionably antiestablishmentarian as Elena de la Souchère can write the following sentence about representative democracy. True enough, she was writing about much earlier history, but her sentiments are revealing regarding the appropriateness of representative institutions for Spaniards. "This enlargement [the growth of cities beyond the effective control of direct democracy] was expressed through the disappearance of the old general assemblies composed of all free men; they were replaced by elected councils—*a cruel evolution for an activist race.*" [Italics mine.] *An Explanation of Spain*, p. 43.

22. Caciques are local, primarily rural, political bosses. The caciques functioned primarily in the mid- and later nineteenth century.

23. Vicens Vives defines *pronunciamiento* as follows: "A *pronunciamiento* (a term incorporated into the English language) is defined in the Dictionary of the Royal Academy of Spain as a military rebellion. Usually it consisted merely of subverting all or part of the army and sometimes the police force, thereby depriving a government of the means to defend itself. Many writers have pointed out the complexity of this phenomenon: the use of the armed forced of a nation to defend one party or one politician or one viewpoint; the paradoxical combination of justifying the right to act in defense of the 'national will' (against an arbitrary monarchy or corrupt politicians) and the use of force (but with a minimum of bloodshed or even of fighting)." Ullman, *Approaches to the History of Spain*, p. 125.

24. One of the most recent victims, and undoubtedly the most important, in this infinite war was Vice-Admiral Luis Carrero Blanco, the prime minister who was blown to bits in Madrid in December, 1973. See note 33, p. 239 in this study.

25. Navarre is often included among the Basque provinces, but, for reasons

which will be clarified when we speak of the Civil War, in this study it will be considered to be separate.

26. *Spain*, p. 170.

27. See Gerald Brenan, *The Spanish Labyrinth* (New York: MacMillan, 1944), chap. 9.

28. *Spain*, pp. 64-65.

29. Brenan, *The Spanish Labyrinth*, p. 42.

30. De-Christianization and de-Catholicization are inadequate terms, but they seem to be the only ones available to express a complex Spanish phenomenon. The Spaniard is always a Catholic even after he no longer goes to Mass. The identification between Catholicism and Spanishness seems indestructible. The Spaniard does not embrace other faiths. He simply leaves the Church, or rather he feels the Church leaves him. He renounces not so much Catholicism as its handmaidens, the priests. The Spaniard becomes more anticlerical than antireligious, and his anticlericalism is as obsessive as was his devotion to the faith.

31. The religious orders had to support themselves, but the concordat provided that only three be reestablished, two immediately and the third to be determined after future negotiation. Eventually, however, all the orders returned.

2
The Politics of the Second Bourbon Restoration

The constitution of 1876, which institutionalized the second return of the Bourbons, was not designed carefully enough for a polity whose people and leaders were as unpracticed in democratic politics as were the Spanish. For the constitution to have functioned properly, a number of fortuitous conditions would have had to converge and persist, conditions too unusual within Spain to be considered likely except for short-lived, almost accidental, occurrence. Under the constitution the monarch was given too much power, or was given power too ambiguously set forth for a political system that lacked the customs and conventions that would have operated to restrict the potentially capricious behavior of the sovereign. Title VI of the constitution proclaimed the person of the king to be sacred and inviolable and his ministers to be responsible for his actions. The king could initiate law. He sanctioned, promulgated, and executed all laws; commanded the armed forces; bestowed ranks, promotions, and military rewards; issued decrees; administered justice; pardoned criminals; declared war; made peace; conducted diplomacy; coined money; conferred civil employment; granted honors and distinctions of every class; convened, suspended, and closed the sessions of the Cortes (legislature); and freely appointed and dismissed his ministers. *But no order of the king could be executed unless countersigned by a minister who by that action became responsible.*[1] Unfortunately, no provisions existed for breaking a deadlock between a determined legislature and a stubborn king, nor did tradition exist to declare that the monarch was the servant of the government and was obliged to do its bidding. The potential for conflict was inherent in the document, and Spanish political conditions made contention inevitable, sooner or later.

It is regrettable for Restoration Spain that her political leaders and her sovereigns could not have learned from history and current events. The modern British monarch in theory possesses power little different from that held by rulers in predemocratic times, but in practice the power has not been used since the reign of Queen Anne (1702-14), the last sovereign to veto a parliamentary enactment. No modern British monarch forgets that his ancestors after Charles II were invited to reign, and the security of the Crown rests upon the good sense of the sovereign who knows that he rules because he is allowed to do so. The deference of the government to the Crown is exchanged for the deference of the Crown to the government. It is a fiction, a highly civilized charade perfected over generations, that is beneficial to the entire polity. The nonrational sources of legitimacy are fed by the dignified but powerless functions of the monarch, the head of state, while the prime minister, the head of government, carries on the business of the day unburdened by symbolic duties.[2] The British may challenge their government while remaining loyal to the Crown, thereby avoiding the terrible dilemma of the Americans, for example, who cannot distinguish between the president as head of state and the president as head of government and who thereby weaken both functions when they attack either.[3]

In Belgium King Albert, a contemporary of Alfonso XIII, reigned under a constitution whose provisions could have been interpreted to the advantage of the sovereign much as Spain's was. On paper the monarch had considerable power, and the first two Belgian kings, Leopold I (1831-65) and Leopold II (1865-1909), used it, but by the time of Albert's reign (1909-34) conditions in Belgium had changed, and the people were no longer tolerant of monarchical interference in politics. Albert, either out of conviction or discretion, was content to become a figurehead, the powerless symbol of unity, the only function possible for a modern, constitutional monarch irrespective of the wordings of a document.[4] What a pity for Spain that Alfonso XIII did not know how the crown was worn in Britain and Belgium and did not learn how to behave like his more temperate European cousins.

The Regency

In the early years of the Restoration, however, conditions seemed favorable for constitutional government, and Spain enjoyed relative political stability. The young king, Alfonso XII, appeared amenable to the constitutional process. Unfortunately, he died in 1855 at the age of twenty-eight, but fortunately his widow, Maria Cristina, was also comparatively tractable politically. The queen gave birth to their son after her husband's death, and she ruled Spain as regent until Alfonso XIII reached his majority in 1902. During her reign Maria Cristina had two celebrated prime ministers—Antonio Cánovas del Castillo, the leader of the Conservative party, and Práxedes Sagasta, the leader of the Liberal party. It was these men who were responsible for the stability that Spain enjoyed during the Regency, but it was they, too, who unwittingly corrupted the constitution and set in motion the collapse of the system that would take place long after their deaths.

The warring factions that had kept Spain torn for most of the first seventy-five years of the nineteenth century were brought into relative political harmony by the tacit pact between the two major contending political forces whose leaders, Cánovas and Sagasta, agreed to disagree and to govern in rotation. (The military counterpart to the political covenant had already been accomplished when Carlist officers were allowed to and consented to enter the national army following the end of the Second Carlist War.) Internal peace and stability existed at last, but they were achieved fraudulently. National elections were rigged by the Ministry of the Interior (ironically called the Ministerio de Gobernación, literally, the Ministry of Governing) primarily through caciques in the countryside, producing first a majority for the Liberal party, next for the Conservatives. Most adult males had the vote during the Restoration, so predetermined electoral results had to be achieved largely through intimidation and bribery.

There are reputable observers who, aware of the chaos and bloodshed that had convulsed Spain during the first three-quarters of the century, do not condemn the strategy of Sagasta and Cánovas. Violence of some sort seemed endemic in Spanish politics; order and peace did not. Between the choice of stability produced by veiled corruption, accompanied by latent violence, and protected behind a facade of constitutionalism and the choice of no stability, with recurring, open violence, and blatant political corruption, the former was an improvement over the latter and thus deserving of support if not of praise. For those who rush to denounce this cynical disregard for constitutional probity, in America during this period the city bosses were using much the same strategy as the Spanish leaders to manipulate the ignorant but enfranchised masses. In the years following the American Civil War, the United States was flooded with immigrants who were free to vote but were totally inexperienced in the ways of democracy. The city machines brought order out of the combustible chaos of races, colors, and religions by using intimidation, bribery, and coercion to achieve their goals. What saved America from the internal political rot that eventually infected Spain was the chance that men had in the United States after their apprenticeship in socialization to escape from the control of the bosses through prosperity that made dependence upon the machine and vulnerability to it no longer necessary.

For a few years at the end of the nineteenth century, Sagasta and Cánovas accomplished in Spain what the leaders of the Third Republic accomplished in France from 1876 until the late 1920s; they froze the Spanish state in attitudes favorable to the elites, the liberal and conservative "consensus groups" that supported the alternating governments. They achieved a "stalemate society" that produced little politically other than those things approved by the dominant classes represented by the two major political parties.[5] As in France, the values frozen were largely preindustrial, beneficial primarily to those socioeconomic elements seeking to delay industrialization. In Spain these elements included the landowners, the ranchers, the citrus and olive growers, and the mine owners and operators. In a situation peculiar to Spain, however, many elements of the new liberal bourgeoisie that arose in the nineteenth century shared preindustrial economic values with the classic conservative elites. Except for the entrepreneurial class in parts of Catalonia, Asturias, and the Basque country, much of the wealth of the emerging middle class in Spain came not from industry and commerce as it did in most of Europe but from land that had been confiscated from the Church by the state and then sold both to the old aristocracy and to the new bourgeoisie.[6] Another source of nonindustrial, bourgeois wealth—besides the liberal professions—was the bureaucracy, a bloated, featherbedded, nepotic institution with a vested interest in the continuity and growth of the regime. The larger the state, identified with Madrid, the more bureaucrats there were and the more money there was for the pockets of civil servants.

The price for this stability was paid by the peasants and by the lower urban classes, who found nothing within the two major parties supportive of their viewpoints and needs. Unlike the situation in France, however, the consensus groups controlling politics in Spain would not allow the underclasses to take a meaningful part in the electoral process. The masses of parochial-subject Spaniards never became participants in the affairs of government. In rural Spain the votes of the isolated and vulnerable peasants were produced by caciques on command of the landed elites. Only in those crowded industrial regions where the workers were too concentrated to be alone and vulnerable in their fear and where growing unionism gave them a sense of solidarity was there some electoral performance, but, for the Spanish masses in general, meaningful political participation was either too little or came too late to earn the system's legitimacy. In France the techniques that maintained the stalemate favorable to the controlling classes were much more subtle and less corruptive of the political system. No interference in the electoral process took place. The sentiments of the people were allowed full political expression in a wide spectrum of parties. When the representatives of the mutually antagonistic political parties reached parliament, their inability to produce an effective majority able to sustain a cabinet rendered positive governmental action almost impossible. The dominant socioeconomic groups, in little need of governmental action other than economic protection, were only too content with an incapacitated legislature unable to disturb the status quo. Yet the ruling elites of France could present themselves with clean hands because the electoral process was never tampered with; the very freedom of the process itself produced the excessive representation that paralyzed the legislature. In Spain, however, the unwillingness of the Liberal and Conservative party leaders to allow the normal electoral process to take place subverted not only the process but also whatever faith or hope the masses may have had in parliamentary democracy. The lower classes, forced out of democratic politics and deprived of effective electoral expression, turned to direct action—strikes, violence, and assassinations—and to new sources of political inspiration, socialism and anarchism.

The Accession of Alfonso XIII

The convergence of events that had given to Spain a generation of relative stability came to an end at the turn of the twentieth century. In 1897 Cánovas died. In 1898 Spain fought a war with the United States and lost to the victor her remaining American and Asian colonies. The reality of the fall from greatness that had been taking place for over three centuries could no longer be evaded. Spanish intellectuals responded to the collapse with a national soul-searching that questioned every facet of Spanish civilization, and their anguish reverberated throughout the entire society.[7] In 1902 Alfonso XIII reached his maturity and became king. In 1903 Sagasta was assassinated. In parts of Catalonia, Asturias, and the Basque country industrialization was making headway, and the urban masses were growing restive, particularly in Barcelona. The impact of the convergence of these events proved calamitous to the future of Spanish politics.

With Cánovas and Sagasta dead, the scramble for leadership fractionalized both the Liberal and Conservative parties. Moreover, dissatisfied elements within each defected, and new parties entered the arena. The dissension between the two old parties and the proliferation of new ones made durable governmental majorities almost impossible to achieve. Cabinet instability played into the hands of the new king. No longer was the sovereign confronted with alternating governments with established leadership as it had been during the Regency. Alfonso became an integral part of the political process and played off to his advantage the contending elements within each party and each party against the others. More and more the ministers became puppets of the king, their tenure assured not so much by support of the legislature as by favor of the monarch. Cabinets rose and fell with regularity, and between the accession of Alfonso in 1902 and the coup d'etat of Primo de Rivera in 1923, there were thirty-three governments (compared with eleven between 1885 and 1902 during the Regency). Perhaps had they lived, the authority and experience of Cánovas and Sagasta could have been used to control the impetuosity of the young king. Alfonso was not a stupid man. But he was politically unintelligent, and his education by reactionary clerics had done little to dissuade his conviction that, like his Bourbon ancestors, he had the right to rule. Moreover, the constitution could be interpreted to legitimize his claim. It is here that Alfonso's lack of exposure to the realities of political life in European constitutional monarchies worked to the great harm of Spain and eventually brought about the abdication of the king who became enmeshed in his own chicanery. A reading of British and Belgian history could possibly have aided Alfonso, but either he did not read them or, if he did, he did not comprehend.

Behind the throne stood the military. After the Spanish-American War, the overseas armies came home forever. Not since 1492 had Spain been locked within her peninsula. Only bits of Africa remained from her once extraordinary empire. The glory of Spain had come finally and irretrievably to an end. No longer could there be even a pretense of grandeur. Spain was finished as a world power, and the death throes had incalculable impact on the national psyche. The agonies particularly tormented the army (and the intellectuals as mentioned earlier). The army was not solely to blame for the imperial fall. An army is seldom stronger than the nation it defends, yet the Spanish army had done no defending against external enemies since 1814, and even then the colonial army could make no claim to the victory over Napoleon. But the military was sensitive and proud, and it reacted with that particular arrogance that usually accompanies the exposure of pretensions in those who have been accustomed to power exercised but not deserved. The army found the political process repugnant and reacted fiercely when it considered its honor besmirched. In 1905 a cartoon in a Barcelona newspaper made vicious sport of the swaggering military. Its enraged officers pressured the fractionalized Cortes to pass a law mocking the democratic pretenses of the government. The infamous Ley de Jurisdiciones (Law of Jurisdictions) declared that any verbal or written attack on military officers or institutions was to be henceforth judged before military tribunals.

In 1909 the army called reservists from Catalonia to fight in Morocco, an area of no importance to the Spanish masses but of economic interest to the elites and of deep symbolic significance to the military. Strikes of protest broke out in Barcelona and led to bloody confrontation between the army and the rank and file of Catalans. The *semana trágica* (tragic week), as the uprising was called, informed all of Spain that, having brutally crushed the workers, the army would brook no interference in its tactics to maintain order. In 1917 the army once again struck out against the masses during Spain's first general nationwide strike called to demonstrate the increasingly desperate plight of the proletariat. The cruelty of its repression in Asturias deepened the hatred of the lower classes for the army. The ultimate affront to civilian control over the military began sometime in 1916 when groups of disgruntled army officers secretly organized themselves into *juntas de defensa* (defense committees), which resembled nothing so much as trade unions, claiming not the military's subservience to but its equality with civilian authority. In 1917 the juntas became public with this pronouncement: "We do not want power for ourselves but we believe we have the right to insist that power should be in good hands." The episodes of 1916 and 1917 made it incontrovertibly clear that the army had once again become the arbiter of Spanish politics, as it had been throughout most of the nineteeth century. Six years later in 1923, the army, with the support and connivance of Alfonso, overthrew parliament and established a military dictatorship under Primo de Rivera.

The Deepening Crisis

Catalonia

During the second half of the Restoration—between the accession of Alfonso XIII and the coup of Primo de Rivera—the interrelated problems of Catalonia and labor deepened the convolution of Spanish politics. The plight of labor affected all of Spain, but it was most acute in Catalonia, the country's preeminent industrial region. Economics lay at the base of both phenomena, but the subcultural factors of history, race, and language made the matter of Catalonia considerably more complex.[8] Catalonia has always been different from the rest of Spain. Her location in the northeastern corner of the peninsula, facing the Mediterranean Sea and lying beneath the passes of the Pyrenees, has given her an access to Europe and to the East that the rest of Spain has never fully enjoyed. Until the discovery of America, when the nation's attention moved westward across the Atlantic and Seville was given the monopoly on trade with the American colonies, Catalonia's capital, Barcelona, had been the most prosperous, cultivated, and progressive city in non-Muslim Spain. During the Reconquest, Catalonia, far from the centers of Islamic domination, led a life relatively isolated from the rest of Spain and was oriented strongly toward the province of Languedoc in southern France and to the language of that region, Langue d'Oc.

When in the thirteenth century Languedoc was subjugated by the centralizing French kings and Langue d'Oc began to disappear, Catalonia lost her cultural and linguistic sources in France and turned back toward Spain. As a result of dynastic marriages, Catalonia eventually was absorbed into the more powerful Aragon and became as much a part of Spain as all the other separate entities finally joined together by Ferdinand and Isabel. She maintained her *fueros*, however, until the coming of the Bourbons in 1700, and it was not until the relentless centralization of the Liberal party after 1814 during the first Bourbon restoration that Catalonia lost her separate penal code (1822), her right to use Catalan in schools (1825), her commercial code (1829), her special tribunals (1834), her coinage (1837), and finally her regional administration (1845).[9]

Even after the disappearance of all the symbols of autonomy, Catalonia never lost her memories of former distinction, and gradually in the mid-1800s a rebirth of Catalanism began. Its first appearance was purely cultural, based on the poetic beauty of the Catalan language spoken then only by the lower classes. The revival dates to 1859 when the municipal council of Barcelona called back to life a medieval festival called *jochs florals* (floral games), a kind of tournament of poets. The history of the renaissance of Catalonia from these "games" is not pertinent to this study. It is sufficient to say, however, that no such phenomenon would have survived had it been sustained by culture alone. It is at the juncture where culture meets economics and politics that Catalanism becomes significant after the second restoration of the Bourbons in 1874.[10]

The stalemated society achieved by Sagasta and Cánovas proved too confining for Catalonia. The economics of the stalemate was based upon land and upon agricultural and mineralogical exploitation. The products of this economy moved as raw materials and foodstuffs into the industrial centers of Western Europe. It was to the advantage of the Spaniards who owned the land and to the Spaniards and foreigners who owned and worked the mines that goods move as cheaply as possible into and out of Spain. Any interference in trade in the form of tariffs was considered a threat both to the domestic producers of raw materials and to the foreign manufacturers and suppliers of finished goods who purchased the raw materials. The manufacturing interests in Catalonia found this policy discriminatory against Catalan infant industries and sought concession from the central government in Madrid in the form of protective tariffs. On this issue the laboring masses and the entrepreneurs were of somewhat similar opinion since both suffered monetarily from what they considered anti-Catalan bias among the predominantly Castilian political elite in Madrid. Moreover, Catalonia claimed she deserved special treatment from Madrid because the province occupied only one-sixteenth of the territory of Spain and her population made up only one-eighth of the national total, yet she paid almost one-quarter of the nation's taxes. Thus Catalan opposition to the political centralization of the state and to the economic policy of the stalemated society combined with the renaissance of culture and language to make up the combustible issue of Catalan separatism.

The major political voice of Catalan opposition to Madrid was heard through the party created by the Catalan oligarchy—the Lliga Regionalista (Regionalist League)—which became one of the fractions of opinion that proliferated after the Liberal and Conservative parties lost their monopoly on national politics at the turn of the century. For a time, the Lliga was able to win the support not only of the Catalan upper classes but of the lower classes as well. A large percentage of the proletariat living in Catalonia was not Catalan by birth and background. The workers had emigrated from poverty-stricken Andalusia and Murcia seeking a better life and had no interest whatsoever in Catalan cultural pretensions. That which briefly allied the two extremes of class was the opposition of each to the dictates of Madrid that were keeping Catalonia economically and politically subservient to the nonindustrial interests of Spain dominating national politics at the time.

This unnatural alliance did not survive for long. The needs of the urban proletariat were too desperate to be reconciled with the strategy of the possessing class; moreover, the Catalan oligarchy had no intention of acceding to the economic demands of the workers. On this issue the Catalan elite was no different from the preindustrial elite in the rest of Spain. Consequently, the lower classes in Catalonia found their earliest political spokesman not in the Lliga but in a new left-wing republican party—the Radicals—led by Alejandro Lerroux, a sample of whose rhetoric will give some idea of the emotional climate in Barcelona in the early years of the 1900s.

Young barbarians of today, enter and sack the decadent civilization of this unhappy country; destroy its temples, finish off its gods, tear the veil from its novices and raise them up to be mothers to civilize the species. Break into the records of property and make bonfires of its papers that fire may purify the infamous social organization. Enter its humble hearths and raise the legions of proletarians that the world may tremble before their awakened judges. Do not be stopped by altars nor by tombs. . . . Fight, kill, die.[11]

In 1909, during the *semana trágica*, the Catalan entrepreneurs reacted with typical class solidarity when the masses took to the streets and wrecked havoc in Barcelona. The army had called up reservists in Catalonia to fight in Morocco, but the reservists came only from the poor. The comfortable strata could always afford to purchase substitutes to perform their sons' military duties. What began as a protest against army service, however, became, during the course of five violent days, an uprising of the masses against all forces of oppression—military, political, and economic.

The result was five days of mob rule in which the union leaders lost all control of their men and twenty-two churches and thirty-four convents were burned. Monks were killed, tombstones were desecrated and strange and macabre scenes took place as when workers danced in the street with the disinterred mummies of nuns.[12]

As a consequence of this frightening manifestation of proletarian fury, the national political scene witnessed another of those paradoxical changes of allegiance that defy any clear and clean explanation of Spanish political life and that make ideological judgment about it almost impossible. The Catalan oligarchy came to realize that only the army could keep order in the event of mass insurrection in the future. Nevertheless, the Catalans hated the military as the instrument and symbol of central governmental authority. The army returned the sentiment because its officers considered the Catalan elite to be the strongest advocates of separatism in the nation and thus in the eyes of the military the most insidious enemy of the state. But the army, the Catalan economic oligarchy, and the political elites governing Spain from Madrid feared the masses more than they despised one another, and warily they began to reconcile their differences.

The move toward reconciliation slowed during the First World War when both labor and capital enjoyed windfall prosperity from supplying the Allies with war materiel. Following the armistice, the more moderate business elements in Barcelona and reformist groups within the army moved to renovate Spain and alter its political structure in order that the nation might more closely resemble her democratic neighbors, but labor, inspired by the events in Russia, sought more than renovation and manifested the depth of its alienation during the general strike in August, 1917. Fear once again unified the ruling elites, and the tentative steps toward change were abandoned in favor of completing the pact of reconciliation that had been agreed to but not fully implemented before the war. In exchange for the Catalan elite's seeking no further regional autonomy beyond that provided in the *Mancomunidad* granted by Madrid in 1912, the central government guaranteed protection by the army against proletarian violence and raised tariffs to shelter Catalan industry from foreign competition. To the advantage of the ruling classes throughout the peninsula, all of whom would suffer if the status quo were disturbed, Madrid (Castile) became the economic tributary of Barcelona (Catalonia), while Catalonia remained the political tributary of Castile.[13]

Labor

The oligarchy thereby achieved a solidarity never obtained by the working class. Whatever faith the lower classes may have had in the political system at the beginning of the Restoration in 1874 withered as a result of the machinations of Cánovas and Sagasta and of the deepening animosity emanating from the ruling elites. Paradoxically, the Restoration governments passed law after law to improve the plight of the working masses, but nothing was done to correct the extreme economic imbalance within the society.[14] As a result, the masses gradually turned away from the constitutional political process but dissipated the force of their numbers in ideological conflict. The short-lived solidarity that had drawn the Spanish working classes together in the First International crumbled following the split between the communist forces of Marx and the anarchist forces of Bakunin. Unlike their brothers in most of Western Europe who pledged their allegiance to Marx, the majority of the proletariat in Spain maintained its faith in Bakunin. Anarchism remained the dominant force in Spanish labor until the collapse of the Second Republic in 1939, but socialism attracted a dedicated minority.

The reasons for the ascendency of the anarchists will never be fully clarified. Many of the explanations put forth verge on the romantic. The ever insightful de Madariaga suggests that socialism and anarchism represented the two magnetic poles of the Spanish mentality with socialism expressive of sobriety and asceticism and anarchism expressive of passion and indiscipline.[15] Yet if both are the equally balanced

obverse and reverse of the Spanish soul, why, then, did anarchism claim
the more enthusiastic supporters? De Madariaga does not say. Brenan
sees the appeal of anarchism in its nostalgic millennialism, an
anachronism that is clear if one appreciates the hold of the past on the
Spanish mentality.[16] Anarchism was the means for destroying modern
life (which paradoxically was less advanced in Spain than in almost any
other Western European society) and for recapturing a mythologized
past where men had once been free—Spain of the ancient *fueros*.
Anarchism replaced religion among the masses and gave meaning to a
secular crusade: *"¡Bakunin y Cierre España!"*

Stanley Payne offers reasons less imaginative but more acceptable to
the political scientist. He feels that liberal democracy came prematurely
to Spain and that its failure destroyed the faith of the unprepared masses
not only in democratic government but in any government at all.
Additionally, Payne feels capitalism had not sufficiently developed to
keep pace with the political system.

> Anarchosyndicalism eventually gained a strong foothold in parts of a
> society living under the theory of liberal democracy and individual civic
> freedom but never achieving the substance of it. The Spanish economy
> had adjusted to a system of capitalist individualism. Yet, despite a slow,
> steady increase in living standards for most, it had not developed the
> industry and technology to realize the full benefits which the system was
> supposed to bring. In a more completely backward society anarchosyndi-
> calism might have been less appealing, but Spanish society was far
> enough evolved to have developed the ideal of personal freedom and
> plenty without reaching the degree of complexity that might have
> discouraged simplistic revolutionary notions of how to achieve it.[17]

For reasons inherent in anarchism, its proponents took decades to
decide upon the strategy to achieve their goals. Strategy requires
organization, but as David Apter writes, "As a moral phenomenon no
matter how much it waxes and wanes it [anarchism] has constant roots
in the fundamentally offending character of organization qua
organization."[18] The anarchists never formed a political party because
the doctrinal purists rejected all electoral activity. To have taken part in
the political process would have legitimized the existing political
structure through the automatic systemic exchange that takes place
when an individual votes. It took years for anarchism to overcome its
antipathy to organization and to stabilize its links with syndicalism. It
took even longer to determine what kind of syndicalist activity would
most effectively bring about the utopian destruction of government and
of the existing social and economic order. Not until 1910 did the

anarchosyndicalists create an effective organization, the Confederación Nacional del Trabajo—the C.N.T. (National Confederation of Labor) —which endured until the end of the Civil War. All efforts to organize before then, particularly the Federation of Workers of the Spanish Region and Workers' Solidarity, had proved futile. It was the brutality displayed by the army and the possessing classes during the *semana trágica* that finally galvanized the anarchists. The confederation was first designed along craft union lines, but this structure was abandoned after 1918 for the *sindicato único,* the single union, that marshalled all labor within a particular factory. By the early 1920s the C.N.T. had over 800,000 affiliates, and the unskilled industrial workers, the lumpen proletariat, who flooded the factory unions, made the confederation increasingly more radical. The strike was the primary armament of the C.N.T. and the general strike its ultimate weapon, but individual violence (primarily terrorism and assassination) was always a part of its arsenal. The strikes were not designed to bring about concessions from management on bread and butter issues; work stoppages were meant to disrupt and expected to destroy the political system.

By contrast, the socialists were able to organize with greater ease, yet their success was far less spectacular than that of the anarchists. The Socialist party was created in 1888, but it did not gain a seat in the Cortes until 1910 and then only because the socialists had entered into an electoral alliance with the republicans in Madrid. The socialist trade union, the Unión General del Trabajo (the U.G.T., General Union of Labor), was organized in the same year as the party, but thirty years later, after the First World War, the U.G.T.—structured along craft lines— numbered approximately 100,000 members compared to the approximately 800,000 associates of the C.N.T. The following words of Pablo Iglesias, the founder of Spanish socialism, express the spirit of the early socialist movement, and perhaps they give some account for the failure of socialism to attract the masses of Spanish workers.

> Shrill, insulting, reckless propaganda is used only by feeble political and economic movements that are here today and gone tomorrow, and invokes scant respect and less fear among those who tyrannize the working class.
> In propaganda one must reject the tactic of shrill oratory, of threats and of insults. . . . Nothing is gained by curses, threats and personal attacks against the exploiters or their supporters, and the discontent of the workers is not satisfied by arousing or sharpening hatred against management and its defenders.[19]

This statement notwithstanding, however, the socialists did take part in labor's antigovernmental and antientrepreneurial demonstrations in the teens of the 1900s (the general strike in 1917 was primarily of socialist instigation), but compared to the activity of the anarchists, that of the socialists was far less intense and less successful.

Domestic turbulence between 1910 and 1923 was dominated by the C.N.T. and the anarchists. The anarchists were active in the countryside of Andalusia, and from time to time they made spectacular attacks against the property of the landed aristocracy that controlled most of southern Spain. But the anarchists' effectiveness was diminished by rural isolation and by the absence of concentrated numbers of workers in confined urban areas. The center stage for the confrontations between the workers and the oligarchy was primarily Catalonia and in particular Barcelona. There was unrest in other large cities as well—Oviedo, Bilbao, and especially Madrid, the center of socialist strength—but it was in Barcelona where relentless violence reached major proportion. There the battles grew increasingly bloody while each side escalated its reaction to incitement from the other. Moreover, as radical anarchists came to dominate the C.N.T. after 1918, the number of political crimes grew larger. Tables 1, 2, 3, and 4 reflect the numbers and kind of political crimes committed in different Spanish cities from 1917 to 1921.

In 1913 factory owners in Barcelona retaliated and created a private employers' police force to battle the C.N.T. Fighting union fire with fire, the industrialists encouraged the formation of Catholic unions of Carlist persuasion, Sindicatos Libres (Free Syndicates), some of whose economic ideas the oligarchy could not stomach but whose Catholic hatred for the "godless and immoral" anarchists could be manipulated to the factory owners' advantage. The absurdities of Spanish politics continued to abound. Members of religiously conservative labor unions with many economically progressive ideas fought and killed their proletarian fellows belonging to anarchist and socialist unions in the name of a god who appeared to be primarily on the side of the rich and powerful who encouraged the imbroglio. Eventually all the antagonists—the socialist, anarchist, and Catholic unions and the oligarchy— came to use hired gunmen (*pistoleros*) from the Barcelona underworld who murdered for anyone who paid their price.

The intrigues surrounding Francisco Bravo Portillo—the head of the political section of the Barcelona police from 1917 to 1918—are symbolic of the putrefaction of Spanish politics during the last years of the Restoration. Bravo Portillo was in the secret pay of German espionage agents who operated within Spain seeking to disrupt the production of war materials being sold to the members of the Entente. With German money Bravo paid corruptible members of the C.N.T. to kill industrial

TABLE 1

The Incidence of Political Violence in Major Spanish Cities, 1917-21

	1917	1918	1919	1920	1921	Total
	Number of political crimes per year					
Barcelona	49	93	109	304	254	809
Bilbao	9	1	14	84	44	152
Valencia	5	6	41	77	22	151
Zaragoza	4	12	8	69	36	129
Madrid	5	6	66	37	13	127
Seville	0	7	22	63	12	104

SOURCE: Stanley G. Payne, The Spanish Revolution (New York: W. W. Norton and Company, 1970), p. 60.

TABLE 2

Objects of Political Crimes, 1917–22

| | Barcelona | | | | | | | |
	1910–17	1917–22	Total	Bilbao	Zaragoza	Madrid	Valencia	Seville
Against employers	25	126	151	7	10	7	16	3
Against foremen, etc.	8	58	66	8	4	3	5	5
Against workers	164	279	443	83	21	47	17	40
Group fights	0	4	4	6	0	0	2	0
Against CNT	0	49	49	5	0	0	5	0
Against Free Synd.	0	14	14	3	0	0	9	0
Against public officials	0	7	7	3	3	1	4	2
Against police, etc.	5	73	78	8	10	10	31	2
Against factories, etc.	52	119	171	22	21	26	39	22
Against the public	7	104	111	11	14	1	18	8

SOURCE: Stanley G. Payne, The Spanish Revolution (New York: W. W. Norton and Company, 1970), p. 60.

TABLE 3

Means Employed in Political Crimes, 1917-22

	Barcelona			Bilbao	Zaragoza	Madrid	Valencia	Seville
	1910-17	1917-22	Total					
Armed robbery	1	11	12	1	1	2	0	0
Firearms	90	344	434	50	23	29	61	15
Knife	13	32	45	5	1	7	1	7
Explosives exploded	9	150	159	8	24	3	55	31
detected	0	190	190	43	17	0	11	8
Beating	30	47	77	15	5	11	3	8
Stoning	46	10	56	3	9	6	7	3
Acid	2	1	3	0	1	0	0	3
Major sabotage	84	56	140	2	17	39	11	0
Major coercion	1	13	14	4	21	16	8	15
Looting	0	6	6	0	0	7	12	8
Kidnapping	0	0	0	0	0	1	0	0
Ley de fugas*	0	10	10	0	0	0	8	0

* Men released from jail and shot by Free Syndicate gunmen with police compliance.

SOURCE: Stanley G. Payne, The Spanish Revolution (New York: W. W. Norton and Company, 1970), p. 60.

TABLE 4

Results of Political Violence, 1917-22

	Barcelona			Bilbao	Zaragoza	Madrid	Valencia	Seville
	1910-17	1917-22	Total					
Against employers Killed	1	25	26	0	2	2	6	1
Injured	8	40	48	1	4	1	4	0
Against foremen Killed	1	23	24	2	3	1	3	1
Injured	7	27	34	3	3	1	2	3
Against non-union Killed	11	95	106	7	8	5	27	9
workers Injured	119	328	447	87	26	45	60	36
Against bystanders Killed	1	21	22	9	0	0	5	1
Injured	16	121	137	23	13	18	29	3
Against CNT or Killed	0	57	57	2	7	0	7	0
Free Synd. Injured	0	45	45	9	0	0	8	0
Against police Killed	0	20	20	1	3	0	9	0
Injured	7	15	22	13	5	7	17	0

Barcelona: 255 Dead, 733 Injured   Bilbao: 24 Dead, 145 Injured   Zaragoza: 23 Dead, 51 Injured
Valencia: 57 Dead, 120 Injured   Madrid: 8 Dead, 62 Injured   Seville: 12 Dead, 42 Injured

SOURCE: Stanley G. Payne, The Spanish Revolution (New York: W. W. Norton and Company, 1970), p. 61.

leaders in Barcelona. He then sold to the oligarchy the services of his own private gang of thugs to carry out reprisals against the C.N.T., and he terrorized those businessmen unwilling to purchase his protection.

Morocco

By the 1920s Spain was imperiled. The oligarchy had become increasingly rigid toward the proletariat, which in turn had become increasingly resolute. Both had become more violent and brutal. The elites and the masses faced each other across barriers of fear and hatred while among the working classes themselves conflict was growing deeper. The socialists and the anarchists loathed and mistrusted one another as only brothers can, and to this enduring animosity were added the Communists after 1917. Until after the Civil War began in 1936, the Communists did not become a major force among the Spanish proletariat, the greatest number of whom remained faithful to anarchism or to Marxist socialism. Moreover, Spanish workers were repelled by the elitist communism practiced in the Soviet Union. The Communist party was considered of such little importance during the first years of its existence in Spain that during the dictatorship of Primo de Rivera the party was never suppressed (as were anarchist organizations), and its press continued to appear.[20] Nevertheless, the Communists did add one more voice and one more fist to the violence that wracked Spain from the end of the First World War to the coup that put an end to parliamentary government in 1923.

The coup that brought down the constitutional monarchy had as its immediate cause the military disaster at Anual, Morocco, in 1921, where thousands of young Spaniards lost their lives. But Spain's involvement in Morocco dates to the 1400s when Melilla, a city on the North African coast, was made a garrison town and thereafter became a part of Spain as integral as if it had been located on the Castilian plateau. Ceuta, across the Straits of Gibraltar, was seized in the sixteenth century and joined Melilla as an extension of Spain in Africa. The loss of Gibraltar to the British in 1713 stopped more grandiose Spanish plans for the colonization of Morocco, but her possession of the garrison towns made whatever happened in North Africa a serious concern to Spain. During the nineteenth century, all of Africa became a colonial hunting ground for the major powers in Europe. France and England began to carve up the continent to their mutual advantage. Only Germany complicated their surgery, for Spain was too weak to be a major impedance. Yet Spain's historic claims to the coastal towns of Morocco and Britain's unwillingness to have French possessions just south of Gibraltar worked to the advantage of Spain, which was granted, in the

Franco-Spanish Treaty of 1912, a narrow zone of influence along the Mediterranean coast carved out of the French Moroccan protectorate.

Sadly, Morocco brought no glory to Spain. The zone was, from the beginning, a "death trap," as Brian Crozier calls it.[21] Not only was the climate murderous, but the territory became the stage for guerrilla warfare waged against the Spanish by Berber tribesmen who claimed the land for themselves. To the African clans their enemy was not only foreign but also infidel, and the Muslims followed their leaders into battle with a fanatical zeal like that of the Catholics in Spain centuries earlier. The garrison towns were never secure from raids, and the countryside outside the town limits became savage, open territory. In 1909 Spanish soldiers moving to protect a privately owned mining concession just outside of Melilla were ambushed by the mountain rebels and were almost totally annihilated. (It was the decision to replace these troops by calling up reserves in Catalonia that sparked the *semana trágica*, the catalyst for the organization of the C.N.T.)

The Spanish masses despised the Moroccan adventure because it brought them nothing while it bled their sons, but Morocco was valuable to the elite, who had economic investments there, and sacrosanct to the army, which declared after its defeat in the Spanish-American War that it would never again retreat and that Morocco would be forever Spanish. Alfonso encouraged the army intransigents and supported their stand on Morocco against the opinion and advice of his more moderate ministers. In 1921 Alfonso, eager to end the guerrilla warfare in Morocco and redeem Spanish honor, encouraged, against the advice of the war office, General Manuel Silvestre to march his troops from Melilla to Alhucemas Bay (about forty miles) across territory infested with rebels and to secure this newly established Spanish position. Silvestre's column was ambushed by a much smaller band of mountain tribesmen, and the Spaniards were butchered.

> Ten thousand were killed, four thousand were taken prisoner, all the rifles, artillery, machine guns and aeroplanes were captured. Scarcely anyone escaped. Silvestre himself committed suicide. A week or two later the fortified position of Monte Arruit was compelled to surrender. The men, some seven thousand, were massacred; the officers were carried off in chains and held to ransom. Melilla itself was only saved with difficulty.[22]

The reaction in Spain was volcanic. The country demanded an explanation from Alfonso, who sought to conceal his involvement. The army, defending the king, was under devastating attack because it had proved to be incapable of defending itself or the nation. The Cortes set up a commission of inquiry, but its report to the nation was never made. A week before it was to be delivered, General Miguel Primo de Rivera, with the support and collusion of Alfonso, who remained head of state and kept his throne, proclaimed himself dictator and brought an end to the Restoration.

The immediate course of the collapse of the constitutional monarchy followed Spain's disastrous involvement in Morocco, but the fundamental cause was the ambiguity of the constitution, the corruption of politics begun by Cánovas and Sagasta and continued by their successors, the irresponsibility of Alfonso XIII, the arrogance of the military, the selfishness of the oligarchy, and the violence of the working masses. Or less dispassionately and more accurately stated: the ultimate cause was an upper class hermetically sealed in ignorance; a brutalized lower class maintained in a festering thraldom; a corrupt and unctuous clergy within a Church bereft of decency or legitimacy; an army commanded by men not merely ignorant but stupid.

The Dictatorship of Primo de Rivera

Seen in retrospect, the dictatorship of Primo de Rivera was a nostalgic interlude between the attempt to create a new political system (the Second Republic) and the attempt to salvage an old one. It was nostalgic in the outdated, pre-Restoration, nineteenth-century tradition in which military coups and pronunciamientos took place in order to "save" Spain from herself. It was equally nostalgic in the person of the dictator himself who would have been more at home between 1814 and 1875 than he was in the 1920s. In many ways he was a quintessential Andalusian who toward the end of his brief regime became more a caricature than a portrait and lost even the support of those who had hailed him at the beginning. He was a man of "passion"[23]—a carouser, a voracious eater, a womanizer. He was voluble to garrulous among a people who worship speech, and he was courageous, earthy, and simple (but relatively well-born, a minor aristocrat) among a people who despise affectation and precious refinement but who admire style. He had the Spanish contempt for the intellect and its trust in the senses and in intuition. He was accused by some of being a fascist, but he was not; he was an old-fashioned caudillo with few fascist characteristics. He was neither racist, imperialistic, nor totalitarian, and his distrust of reason was viscerally Catholic rather than cerebrally philosophical. Moreover, the Unión Popular (Popular Union), which the general stoutly refused to call a political party (words he abhorred), was not a disciplined structure. The Popular Union was a loosely gathered agglomeration of those Primo de

Rivera hoped would rally to the regeneration of Spain—a kind of Spanish Rassemblement du Peuple Français (Rally of the French People, de Gaulle's "nonparty" of the 1940s). Nevertheless, he accepted none of the concepts of liberal constitutionalism and had what Samuel Beer might describe as an Old Tory concept of society's having an existence different from and superior to the individuals who comprise it.[24] To Primo de Rivera, "doctrines of individual rights were not merely moral suicide for a nation but artificial inventions—'the arabesques of unemployed intellectuals.' "[25]

Primo de Rivera's personality and his sensual approach to life and its dilemmas may have been appropriate in earlier generations, but they were anachronistic in the difficult 1920s and were too dependent for success upon luck, which eventually ran out. His responses to the political and economic problems that beset postwar Spain were impetuous and dramatic, and he saw his ideas as self-fulfilling wishes. The spectacular and costly exposition in Seville held to regenerate a destitute Andalusia and a similar exposition in Barcelona are classic examples of his mentality. Other projects—many of them of unquestionable worth—gained him the early, tenuous support of a people whom history has taught to be incredulous (but who have always been mesmerized by the flash of a man on horseback), but they were not thoroughly enough conceived to have endured and more importantly to have been maintained. The general came as a repairer but developed the dreams of a master builder with neither the will nor the way fundamentally to reconstruct his country. He was not a reformer, nor was he the "iron surgeon," as he has been called,[26] because he performed no radical operations on Spain. On the contrary, for those strata of society that sought profound, systemic change (primarily the proletariat and the peasantry), the general did far too little. As Stanley Payne has observed: "The Primo de Rivera regime was not a new order, but the old order on its last legs."[27]

Only the pacification of Morocco was an unqualified success, but in that achievement lay a paradox that contributed to Primo de Rivera's undoing. He came into power with the intrigue of Alfonso (and with the blessing of the oligarchy, which looked to him to end the civil strife in Spain). Primo and the king sought to prevent the publication of the report commissioned by the Cortes that would have implicated the monarch in the disaster at Anual and would have exposed the decay in the army. Once in power, Primo de Rivera would tolerate no public discussion of either the army or the king (a restriction tantamount to no public discussion of politics), and he clamped on the entire nation a rigid censorship that gained for him the relentless enmity of the intellectuals, whose authority as opinion-makers had grown immensely during the years of national flagellation following the Spanish-American War. His behavior revealed a failure (typical of the military) to understand his countrymen. Speech was one of the few things left that had value in Spain, and irrespective of the corruption and venality of the Restoration, speech had been free. Being deprived by the dictatorship of what had long since become a worthless ballot was no serious loss to the average Spaniard; being deprived of the right to speak his mind—particularly for the typical Spaniard who has traditionally spent a good part of his lifetime in a café, *talking*—was a kind of emasculation. This silencing eroded the legitimacy of a leader whose claim to it had never been strong, yet Primo de Rivera initially won the approval of the masses by doing (as did Eisenhower in Korea and de Gaulle in Algeria) what perhaps no civilian could ever have accomplished: he ended the decades of guerrilla warfare in Morocco that had bled the sons of the poor. By *retreating* to more modest positions that could be held and defended (seldom an honorable military alternative and one available only to a supreme commander answerable to himself alone) and by brilliantly executing an extraordinarily risky military operation in conjunction with the French, he destroyed the Berber tribesmen and finally pacified Morocco.

Unfortunately for Spain, however, Primo de Rivera met with only limited success in those endeavors in which a soldier's good sense seldom offers advantage—politics and economics. His grandiose plans for modernizing Spain were largely destroyed by the developing world economic crisis, but they had been unrealistic from the beginning. The initial success of his schemes was the result not so much of slow, carefully coordinated planning in Spain as it was of the fortuitous international economic conditions of the early and mid-1920s. The dictator overextended Spain's meager resources building highways, improving the railroads, constructing dams, irrigating the land, electrifying the countryside. To his distinction, all of these improvements were well done, and the country was proud of them, but they had to be paid for, and Spain lacked the economy to support what was basically infrastructural investment. During the postwar boom, Spanish goods and products sold well on the international market, and foreign investment was healthy. But the resulting prosperity proved to be artificial, and it vanished after the economy began to collapse in the late 1920s. Moreover, Primo de Rivera was obsessed with Spanish self-sufficiency, and he forced the state, often contrary to good economics, to intervene in, as Carr says, "everything from hydroelectric power to the rabbit-skin industry."[28]

The general's attempts to restructure the economic system through the creation of corporations did not succeed.[29] The corporations were only grudgingly accepted by the oligarchy, which had wanted suppression of the working classes, not enforced cooperation with them. The elites continued to support the dictatorship, however, because Primo de Rivera commanded the army, and it was the army that maintained order in the country. Labor was deeply divided over the dictatorship and its programs. Irrespective of what Primo de Rivera had to offer, no working man could forget for long that the dictator was an aristocrat (however minor), a landowner, and a soldier—traditional enemies of the laboring masses. The socialists fell out among themselves over Primo de Rivera. The majority, led by Francisco Largo Caballero, collaborated with the general and won his acceptance and tolerance, but a minority faction led by Indalecio Prieto rejected both Largo Caballero and Primo de Rivera. By accepting the socialists (whose discipline and organization he admired) and by making them a part of his economic experiments, the general hoped to draw strength away from the anarchists, whom he outlawed. By cooperating with the dictator, Largo Caballero and his followers hoped to gain adherents to the socialist cause, to the party and to the trade unions, at the expense of the anarchists—the Left betraying the Left, a classic Spanish scenario that would be repeated again and again during the Republic and during the Civil War.[30] The anarchists, however, still spoke for the majority of the Spanish proletariat and peasantry, and their tenacious evangelists went underground to create one of the most feared societies in modern Spanish history—the Federación Anarquista Ibérica (Iberian Anarchist Federation). The peasants believed that projects such as irrigation and rural electrification—so dear to the heart of the dictator—benefited primarily the landowners, and they rejected Primo de Rivera for failing to bring about the land reform that would have fundamentally altered the power structure in rural Spain. The general dared not antagonize the landowning class, which was a major pillar of his support and of which he, too, was a member—even though the most aristocratic of them found him vulgar.

The general's hold grew tenuous at every level of society. He courted the Church, which was given almost a free hand in education even in the state schools, but this relationship alienated the anticlericalists—not only the grumbling, de-Christianized working masses but also the vocal and articulate intelligentsia, primarily the university teachers and university students. Primo de Rivera vastly overestimated his authority when he attempted to permit a private Jesuit and a private Augustinian college the right to grant official university degrees—a privilege enjoyed exclusively by the state universities. The uproar forced him to retract his offer. In addition, he enraged Catalonia by revoking what were little more than token yet highly symbolic rights of self-determination in the *Mancomunidad* that had been won from Madrid a decade earlier. As an officer in the army, an institution that had historically condemned all forms of regional autonomy, Primo de Rivera's action should have come as no surprise, but, nevertheless, it weakened the general in an area of the country where proletarian violence had pushed many of the elites to favor the dictatorship initially. Gerald Brenan believes that this action on the part of the general did more than anything else to alienate the Catalan oligarchy and to lead it to vote for the Republic in the elections of 1931.[31]

Ironically it was the army that ultimately brought about the general's downfall. To his credit, Primo de Rivera sought to thin the gargantuan ranks of officers whose ratio to soldiers of approximately one to ten was the highest in Europe. He planned the modernization of the military, but in doing so he touched the most sensitive nerve in the most prestigious branch of the army—the seniority system of the artillery— and this powerful corps reacted by taking its complaint directly to the king, extracting from him a promise to countermand the general's orders. Alfonso had long wanted to rid himself of Primo de Rivera, who had come in as the king's protector but who had turned into his master. Alfonso had conspired with the general in the coup in 1923 because the king had hoped to rule Spain without legislative interference and had looked to Primo de Rivera to make possible the opportunity. But the dictator, with the backing of the army, proved to be stronger than the king, and Alfonso, by his very presence on the throne, was forced into the humiliating role of the legitimizer of Primo de Rivera. Moreover, the powerful aristocracy held Alfonso responsible for disgracing the Crown and for weakening the monarchy as an institution, thereby undermining the nobility as a political force. Alfonso was eager, therefore, to cleanse himself of the contamination of Primo de Rivera, and in the conflict between the army and the general, the king took the side of the majority of the officers against their commander. Faced with the rejection of his two main sources of strength—the king as his legitimizer and the army as his weapon—Primo de Rivera had no alternative but to resign. He left Spain in January, 1930, and died a few months later in Paris, where he spent the last days of his life alternately whoring and confessing.

The resignation of Primo de Rivera came too late to save either the monarch or the monarchy. During the last years of his regime, opposition to the Crown had spread from its traditional source on the Left to individuals and groups with impeccably conservative breeding.

The widening base of antimonarchical sentiment calmed the anxiety even of members of the aristocracy who disliked Alfonso but feared a republic because republican institutions had been historically associated with the most extreme Left and economic and social revolution.

Alfonso replaced Primo de Rivera with another general, Dámaso Berenguer, who became prime minister within a civilian cabinet. But as yet no elections had taken place. If the constitution of 1876 were considered to be still in force, then elections were mandatory under its provisions. If the dictatorship had broken constitutional continuity, then Spain was no longer a monarchy, and Alfonso had no right to the throne. Elections presented a painful dilemma to the king. If free elections were to be allowed, campaigning would be accompanied by the full and public airing of the dictatorship and would once again risk the exposure of the king. Yet if elections did not take place and the Cortes did not reconvene, then the prime ministership of Berenguer would be no different from the dictatorship of Primo de Rivera with the exception that the dictator would now be Alfonso himself because Berenguer was old and sick. The prime minister finally agreed to elections but with the provision that press censorship be lifted only twenty days before the polling date. All of the political parties refused these terms, and Berenguer resigned in February, 1931.

The reluctance of Berenguer to call elections had not delayed the formation of clandestine republican committees all over the country whose members included some of the most distinguished men in Spain. In August, 1930, progressive political leaders of variegated coloration (including many hues traditionally tending toward white rather than red) met secretly at San Sebastian. There they signed a pact declaring their support for a republic and for an autonomous Catalonia within the new republic and set up a revolutionary committee headed by a recently defected monarchist, Niceto Alcalá Zamora, a solid, devoutly Catholic, bourgeois lawyer, whose very presence comforted the unhappy but apprehensive conservative elements within Spain. A premature rebellion of republican army officers at Jaca in December, 1930, exposed the identity of the membership of the committee, and its leaders were jailed.

At this point Spanish politics came to resemble an operetta by Gilbert and Sullivan. After the resignation of Berenguer, Alfonso in effect went to jail to ask the imprisoned members to form a cabinet! They refused, and Alfonso appointed as his next (and last) prime minister an admiral, Agustín Aznar, whom Carr describes as a "nonpolitical figure famed for his novel-reading in moments of acute crisis."[32] Out of this new cabinet came the strategy for the long-delayed elections. There would be three successive elections: first, municipal, next, provincial, then lastly, parliamentary. The king hoped by this plan to cool antimonarchical sentiments so that when parliamentary elections were finally held the antirepublican forces would have regained their composure. The stratagem backfired. In the municipal elections held on April 12, 1931, every provincial capital city except Cádiz voted for men committed to a republic. Between April 13 and 14, the city councils of Oviedo, Seville, and Valencia, among others, proclaimed the Republic of Spain, and, in a premature moment of exultation, a group of delirious Catalan nationalists announced the Republic of Catalonia! When General José Sanjurjo, the commander of the Guardia Civil (Civil Guard), the national police force, declared for the Republic, Alfonso had nowhere to turn for protection since he had already lost the support of the army.[33] It was obvious that the results of the provincial and parliamentary elections would be even more overwhelmingly republican. Alfonso XIII realized that the monarchy was dead, and on the evening of April 14, 1931, he left Madrid. The following morning he sailed into exile from Cartagena. Ten years later he died in Rome, where his body still lies buried.

Notes

1. Emphasis added. Walter Fairleigh Dodd, *Modern Constitutions*, vol. 2 (Chicago: The University of Chicago Press, 1909), pp. 197-216.

2. For a development of these ideas describing the British monarchy, see Walter Bagehot, *The English Constitution* (Ithaca, N.Y.: Cornell University Press, 1966), chaps. 1 and 2.

3. At the time the Spanish constitution of 1876 was written, this analysis of the role of the British monarch had long been a reality.

4. Albert's son, Leopold III, did not learn from his father's experience. Like Alfonso, he allowed himself to become involved in politics and was eventually forced from the throne. See E. Ramón Arango, *Leopold III and the Belgian Royal Question* (Baltimore, Md.: Johns Hopkins University Press, 1964).

5. For a brilliant analytical study of France from which this author borrows the phrases "consensus groups" and "stalemate society," see Stanley Hoffmann and others, *In Search of France* (New York: Harper and Row, 1963).

6. See this study, p. 23.

7. These intellectuals made up what came to be called "the Generation of Ninety-eight," named after the year of the ignominious defeat. An analysis of their trauma is not pertinent to this study, but the quality of their works gave evidence that Spanish genius had been only dormant not dead. Not since the Golden Age had Spain witnessed such a stunning outpouring of artistic and intellectual creativity. The names Joaquín Costa, Angel Gavinet, Miguel de Unamuno, José Ortega y Gasset, Azorín, Valle-Inclán, among others, are now in

the pantheon of European men of letters.

8. For an analysis of political subcultures particularly applicable to Spain (to Catalonia, the Basque country, and to Galicia), see Gabriel A. Almond and Sidney Verba, *The Civic Culture* (Boston: Little, Brown and Co., 1965), pp. 26-29.

9. De Madariaga, *Spain*, pp. 214-15.

10. For a brief history of the Catalan question, see Raymond Carr, *Spain, 1808-1939*, chap. 13.

11. Brenan, *The Spanish Labyrinth*, p. 30.

12. Ibid., p. 34.

13. Ibid., pp. 65-66. There are those who claim that Madrid was so intent upon subduing Catalan regionalism that the central government in Madrid encouraged and supported proletarian violence in Barcelona in order to force the terrified oligarchy into the protective arms of Madrid.

14. Social welfare laws regulated child and female labor, guaranteed the eight-hour day and the forty-eight hour week, decreed Sunday a day of rest, and protected the worker against injury while on the job. Industrial Tribunals were established in 1918, and in 1920 the Ministry of Labor was created. Later, during the dictatorship of Primo de Rivera, accident insurance at the employers' expense became mandatory by law and compulsory arbitration boards were set up.

15. *Spain*, pp. 144-46.

16. *The Spanish Labyrinth*, chap. 7.

17. Stanley A. Payne, *The Spanish Revolution* (New York: W. W. Norton & Co., 1970), pp. 23-24.

18. David Apter, "The Old Anarchism and the New—Some Comments," in David E. Apter and James Joll, eds., *Anarchism Today* (New York: Doubleday & Co., 1971), p. 2.

19. Payne, *The Spanish Revolution*, p. 64.

20. Brenan, *The Spanish Labyrinth*, p. 223.

21. Brian Crozier, *Franco—A Biographical History* (London: Eyre and Spottiswoode, 1967), p. 40.

22. Brenan, *The Spanish Labyrinth*, p. 223.

23. The term "passion" is borrowed from Salvador de Madariaga's *Englishmen, Frenchmen and Spaniards*, 2d ed. (New York: Hill & Wang, 1969), a book whose methodology would give chills and fever to a tightly scientific student of politics but whose insights are rich and profound. It is an old-fashioned study written from the intellect and the imagination with no documentation, but for those interested in learning about Spaniards, the book is highly recommended. In many ways it resembles Luigi Barzini's *The Italians* (New York: Atheneum, 1964) or François Nourissier's *The French* (New York: Alfred A. Knopf, 1968) or Jean-François Revel's *The French* (New York: George Braziller, 1966).

24. Samuel Beer, "The Representation of Interests in British Government: Historical Background," *American Political Science Review* 51, no. 3 (September 1957): 613-50.

25. Carr, *Spain, 1808-1939*, p. 566.

26. Ibid., pp. 574-81.

27. Stanley G. Payne, *Falange* (Stanford, Calif.: Stanford University Press, 1961), p. 7.

28. *Spain, 1808-1939*, p. 580.

29. "The Spanish organization may be described as follows: The trades and professions of the country were classified into twenty-seven groups or *Corporaciones*. In each of them the organization comprised: locally a *comité paritario* composed of five employers and five men elected by their respective unions and a chairman appointed by the government. These committees had power to regulate conditions of work, such as hours, rest, individual or collective labor contracts, to deal with conflicts, to organize labor exchanges and a trade census. Mixed commissions were also created locally in order to coordinate the work of the committees of connected trades. The competence of these commissions covered mostly matters of technical education, advice, study, and reform. The mixed commissions, however, did not participate in the more general organization of the corporative system of the state. The corporation was defined as the sum total of all the *comités paritarios* of the same trade in the nation. Each of them was governed by a corporation council composed of eight employers and eight men elected by the committees. The council watched over national conditions in the industry covering the same ground locally entrusted to the committees. It was expected that they would also act as authoritative advisers to the government on matters concerning their industry and that they would engage in codifying the laws, by-laws, regulations and customs of their trade. At the apex of the organization, the *Comisión Delegada de Consejos*, presided over by the Director-General of Labor, brought together delegates (one employer and one man) from all the Corporation Councils of the nation." De Madariaga, *Spain*, p. 350.

30. For a chilling history of self-slaughter among the forces of the Left during the Civil War, see George Orwell, *Homage to Catalonia* (Boston: Beacon Press, 1955).

31. *The Spanish Labyrinth*, p. 83.

32. *Spain, 1808-1939*, p. 599.

33. It is a stunning irony that two years later and again five years later General Sanjurjo would be one of the major conspirators against the very republic whose birth he had assured.

3
The Second Republic

The Second Republic has received good press in Western Europe and in the United States, possibly better than it deserves. Perhaps this praise is a manifestation of the myths talked about earlier. Perhaps this posthumous benediction is expiation for the abandonment of the Spanish republic in its death throes when its government sought help from the United States, Great Britain, and France to put down the military uprising and was rejected. By comparison, the German republic of the 1920s has surely not been idealized as has the Spanish republic, which it resembled in many ways. Possibly Weimar is looked at differently because its collapse led to Hitler, who was defeated, whereas the decomposition of the Second Republic led to Franco, who ruled for almost forty years.[1] Moreover, in its last months Weimar did not behave as a republic should. The German republic "turned" to Hitler; the Spanish republic "fell" to Franco. Weimar expired condemned by the world whereas the Second Republic died a martyr's death.[2] These are inaccurate, emotional, and all too universal appraisals of both republics. Weimar and the Second Republic in Spain died simply because each was beyond the political capacity of its people.

Even if a political system is judged by the intentions of its participants (leaving aside any evaluation of the efficiency or accomplishments of the political process), the Second Republic cannot escape harsh evaluation. The early euphoria following the municipal elections in April, 1931, was deceptive, springing from a negative consensus based on the rejection of a corrupted king. Seen in retrospect, the republican vote (which itself was misleading since the small towns and rural areas voted against a republic) was the expression of widespread disgust with the monarchy; it was not an overwhelming endorsement of republicanism. It must be admitted that the elections were the freest in all Spanish history up to that time, yet equally free elections for the Constituent Assembly, which took place two months later in June, revealed that

59

there was little consensus about the kind of republic that should be created. The polity fractionalized into over twenty parties fanning from Left to Right, each desirous of a republic tailored to its own ideological nature and each unaware of or unconcerned with the procedural consensus that transforms political rhetoric into effective democracy.[3] In observing the British political system, which he considers to be a model of stable democracy, Harry Eckstein writes: "In essence the British invest with very high affect the procedural aspects of their government and with very low affect its substantive aspects; they behave like ideologists in regard to rules and like pragmatists in regard to policies. Procedures to them are not merely procedures but sacred rituals."[4] This notion—so absolutely essential to effective democracy and to the maximization of viable outputs—would have been beyond the ken of the vast majority of representatives who were returned to the Cortes. In fact, the reverse concept would have characterized most of the men of the Second Republic.

As a consequence of their pentecostal approach to politics, the constitution the deputies created was considered to be invalid by a large but splintered minority of the Spanish people—primarily on the Right—whose representatives were outvoted in December, 1931. At that time the constitution was ratified, the Constituent Assembly was transformed into the first regular parliament, and the provisional government became the first cabinet of the new republic. Ironically, when this same rightist minority returned in a majority coalition as a result of new parliamentary elections held two years later in 1933, the former leftist majority that had governed Spain since 1931 considered this new coalition to be illegitimate and condemned its program designed to reorient the constitution to the advantage of the Right.[5] From the very beginning, then, the consensus needed to restructure the Spanish system—and more importantly to have that restructuring nationally sanctioned—was nonexistent. The cleavages that divided Spaniards into political enemies not only separated the Right from the Left in the classical continental European pattern but also fractured the two major blocs into warring factions whose animosity toward one another was as bitter as that which bisected the two major blocs themselves.[6]

The division was deeper among the forces on the Left. On the Right, all groups were united in their disapproval of the constitution created by the Left; many abominated the Republic itself. The degrees of their alienation separated them into factions, but they all held repudiative emotions in common. On the Left, the anarchists, increasingly under the apostolic control of the F.A.I. (Iberian Anarchist Federation), anathematized the Republic outright. A republic, irrespective of how favorably it might treat the proletariat, was still a government, and all governments by their very nature were illicit. Their commitment to doctrinal purity compelled the anarchist leaders (almost a contradiction in terms) to urge their followers to boycott elections since casting a ballot would admit the tacit acceptance of the political system. Moreover, they excoriated all the other forces on the Left and called them bourgeois collaborationists for running for political office. In their hatred of the Republic, the anarchists were matched only by the extremists on the Right. Within the politically participant Left, the socialists were divided into two camps. The majority followed Largo Caballero, the collaborator with Primo de Rivera, who had become gradually more militant since the fall of the monarchy and who after 1934 became thoroughly radicalized as a result of a brief prison sentence during which, for the first time in his life, at age sixty-six, this socialist patriarch read Marx! The more moderate socialists followed Indalecio Prieto, between Largo Caballero and whom was deep personal enmity. The Communists also took part in republican politics but remained weak until just prior to the Civil War; after its outbreak their strength grew enormously in proportion to the aid rushed into Spain from the Soviet Union, whose cause remained more sacred to many Spanish Communists than did Spain's. Communist loyalty to the Spanish republic was, therefore, always suspect.[7]

The feud between Largo Caballero and Prieto was equaled by the enmity between Manuel Azaña and Alejandro Lerroux. Azaña was the most significant personality in the Second Republic. It was he who shaped the constitution; he founded and headed the strongest and largest nonsocialist party on the Left—Acción Republicana (Republic Action);[8] he was prime minister for a longer period of time (twenty-five months and nineteen days) than any other person in the eighteen governments that presided over the Republic; he became president of Spain in May, 1936. Azaña was dedicated to intelligent, systemic change, but he was unable to overcome his personal, almost esthetic, repugnance for the coarseness and vulgarity in the man with whom a parliamentary alliance might have placated both the Right and the Left and might have spared Spain the agony of the Civil War—Alejandro Lerroux, the founder and still chief of the Radical party. This was the same Lerroux who, the reader will recall, early in the century spoke to the bloodlust of the Barcelona proletariat.[9] But time, circumstances, and expediency had cooled him and his party so that at the birth of the republic the Radicals were right of center with a program that could have easily meshed with that of Republican Action, a progressive middle-class party left of center, and thereby could have created a strong centralist fulcrum on which to balance extremist contention. It was unfortunate for the fledgling republic that its most important men on the Left—Largo Caballero, Prieto, and Azaña—were caught in conflicts of personality that obstructed good judgment and made cooperation almost impossible. Pique is not a Spanish monopoly. It seems congenital in all politicians in all political systems, but only stable systems can afford the luxury of its indulgence among their leaders.

The Second Republic suffered from several structural faults that doomed it from its conception. The insights of Harry Eckstein will be applied to the following analysis of Spain in this period. The Republic was dominated by the legislature, which constitutionally had pre-dominant power. Because of the political fractionalization of the Cortes, however, the power was primarily negative, particularly after the first biennium, able to harrass and cripple but unable to create and give direction, a situation much like that which existed in the lower house in the French Third and Fourth Republics. The government was presided over by a prime minister appointed by the president, but the prime minister in turn had to assemble a cabinet acceptable to the Cortes, and both had to resign if they failed to maintain the confidence of the deputies. Had there been stable majorities with established leadership in the Cortes, the president's appointive power would have been forced to become a rubber stamp of legislative will; given the proliferation of parties, however, the prime minister was the pawn of both the president and the Cortes. The president was chosen by the Cortes itself for a period of six years and was constitutionally prohibited from immediately succeeding himself. He had the power to choose the prime minister and to dissolve the Cortes, but the power of dissolution could be used safely only once during his tenure. After the second dissolution and subsequent elections, the returning Cortes had the right to replace the president if it could muster the votes.[10] A disruptive legislature could, therefore, hamstring both executives, the president and the prime minister. Probably the most effective weapon the president possessed but never used was the right to have the Cortes reconsider legislation that had emerged from that body not earmarked as urgent. (An urgent bill demanded immediate promulgation.) The suspensively vetoed legislation then had to be repassed by a two-thirds majority. The proper use of this authority would not have furnished the direction that the government needed, but possibly it could have tempered impetuous legislative action.

The constitution did not provide for a Senate; consequently that classic institutional avenue of legislative restraint was nonexistent. The elimination of an upper house had long been one of the planks in the program of the European Left. It was a leftist coalition that controlled the Constituent Assembly in Spain, and it rejected the creation of the Senate recommended by the Commission of Jurists appointed by the assembly to prepare a draft constitution.[11] There are those who argue hypothetically that a Senate would have had the same impact on the Second Republic in Spain that the French Senate had on the Third Republic in France and would have acted as a conservative brake on the Cortes during its *radical* first two years thereby preventing the alienation of the Right. But there are others who make the equally valid conjecture that a conservative Senate would have collaborated with the Cortes during its *reactionary* second biennium and would have snuffed out democratic institutions.[12]

The electoral law of the Second Republic further reflected the political inexperience of the Spanish leaders. The law was designed to achieve stability and to benefit those parties or coalitions of parties that were the strongest. The law worked in the following way: Each constituency returned a large number of deputies, but each elector was allowed to vote for no more than four candidates for every five seats. In addition, the party or an electoral coalition of parties that won a majority could take four out of the five seats irrespective of how large the minority might be. The party or coalition able to win the most votes in Madrid, for example, took thirteen out of the city's total of seventeen seats, and in Barcelona sixteen out of the total of twenty seats. The law was created by the Left when it felt its muscle during the provisional government and during the first two years of constitutional government after December, 1931. Unfortunately for the Left, the electoral formula tailored to its majoritarian advantage operated to the profit of the Right in the parliamentary elections of 1933. Unfortunately for the Right, the law worked once again to the advantage of the Left in the next national elections in 1936. Neither bloc was willing to change the law because the coalition controlling the legislature in each biennium had won because of the law's operation. As a result, the Republic was wrenched from Left to Right to Left in its brief lifetime of four and one-half years, with one major bloc pitted uncompromisingly against the other and with smaller political groups left to rage and conspire. Electoral mechanics to produce legislative stability do not work in nonconsensual polities torn by ideological strife.[13]

This electoral hybrid produced artificial majorities within the Cortes that did not reflect political reality within the country. The governments that emerged from these majorities came to be called the Red Biennium (December 9, 1931, to December 3, 1933), the Black

Biennium (December 3, 1933, to February 16, 1936), and the period of the Popular Front (February 6, 1936, to July 17, 1936—the day the Civil War began). The Red Biennium should in reality be dated from July 14, 1931, rather than December 9, because the coalition that dominated the first biennium also dominated the Constituent Assembly and formed the provisional government. These artificial majorities were deceptive to those outside Spain, particularly those in the Western democracies who thought they saw in the provisional government and in the first biennium an overwhelmingly positive national response to systemic change. More significantly, the majorities within the Cortes also deceived themselves by assuming a popular mandate that—if the opinions of all Spaniards were to be heeded and not just the opinions of those whose parties or coalitions had won because of electoral mechanics—was far more conservative than the crusading Left was able to see in 1931 and far more progressive than the moralistic Right cared to see in 1933. As a consequence, the Left shaped a constitution and for two years gave to the nation a government too radical for the Spain of the 1930s. In turn, the Right, when it came to power in 1933, responded with a program too reactionary. Neither the Left nor the Right had the national mandate necessary to create the kind of Spain each bloc envisioned. Only a revolution could have brought that about. As the anarchist Juan Peiró said: "The Republic came in without blood; therefore, it was not a true revolution. It always lived insecurely as a result."[14]

The Red Biennium

The Republic under the domination of the Left during the Constituent Assembly and during the first biennium mishandled the Church, the schools, the army, the autonomous regions, and land reform. Moreover, the Left allowed its passions to manage its intellect, and eventually Spain paid a terrible price for this self-indulgence.

In the name of abstract liberty, the Left (either through the constitution or through subsequent legislation) declared freedom of religion, abrogated the Concordat of 1851,[15] abolished the state clerical budget that paid the secular clergy (i.e., those clergy not members of religious orders), closed all Catholic schools except seminaries, forbade any religious to teach in any school, outlawed the Jesuits and confiscated their property, legalized divorce, and abolished religious burial unless specifically provided for by the deceased. These actions were an outburst of anticlericalism as blind and irrational as clericalism itself, and many of these enactments were contemptibly petty—

particularly the laws about Christian burial. Needless to say, the uproar was deafening not only from the Church but also from the faithful as well. True enough, the proletariat had long since become de-Christianized, but even within that class its women still practiced their religion, and within the middle and upper classes church ritual was a major part of the daily life of both sexes.

Admittedly the Spanish Church was corrupt; its hierarchy was venal and unresponsive to the problems of the poor; many of its members from bishops to sacristans were woefully uneducated and often militantly ignorant. But no institution with the power, the authority, the awesomeness, the tradition, and the sheer longevity of the Catholic Church can be uprooted by constitutional fiat unless that decree is overwhelmingly sanctioned by an entire society. Moreover, the Republic in its formative years lost a fine opportunity to gain supporters among the rank and file of the clergy. The vast majority of the secular clergy had a standard of living much like that of its parishioners[16] and would have benefitted from the socioeconomic change programmed by the Left, but the precipitous denial of its livelihood turned its members into bitter opponents of republicanism. The outlawing of the Jesuits was meaningless, particularly since the Society of Jesus, sensing the wind, had been the most vocal spokesman for republicanism in the Spanish Church. The Jesuits have been expelled from too many countries for too many years not to be experts at survival. Their major wealth was no longer in real estate; their fortune was carefully concealed in dummy corporations or held under assumed names. Expropriation of their landed property touched only a tiny portion of their possessions but turned them into dogged enemies of the Republic.

Closing Catholic schools exacerbated an already staggering national problem. In 1931 illiteracy was more than 30 percent in Spain;[17] even officially only 50 percent of school-age children received an education,[18] and of that percentage, half was educated by the state and half by the Church. To forbid the Church to educate was to deny a large percentage of Spanish children any learning at all. The educational program of the Left was ambitious and admirable in theory, and the government of the first biennium claimed to have built 13,570 school rooms between 1931 and 1933, but anyone who has lived in the South in the United States, for example, does not have to be told that the number of school rooms, the number of teachers and students in them, and the quality of education given and received are not necessarily positively related.

The reform of the army was designed to reduce the number of officers and modernize the military—an admirable goal naively approached.

This observation is especially valid knowing, as Spanish leaders should have known, that the army would tolerate no direct threat to its integrity irrespective to the origins of that threat. The recent example of Primo de Rivera should have sufficed as a warning. In 1930 there were 22,208 officers, including reservists, in an army of approximately 130,000 men.[19] The provisional government under Azaña's leadership offered to all of the generals and to most of the lower-ranking officers, including those on reserve, the opportunity to retire on full salary. Almost half of those to whom the offer was made accepted,[20] and many of these then used their well-paid free time to plot against the republican regime. Stanley Payne comments:

> Thus, the post-1931 officer corps was composed, for the most part, of bedrock professionals who stayed on by choice and narrow-minded incompetents who would have had difficulty adjusting to another profession or style of life. These men were not political reactionaries, but they were in a difficult position vis-à-vis Republican progressivism. It was not so much what Azaña had done to the officer corps, but the way in which he had done it. The Republican leader completely lacked a politician's tact, and gloried in being able, as he put it, to "pulverize" *(triturar)* the Army. The supercilious tone of his speeches, in which he gloated over the discomfiture of the old military hierarchy, raised the hackles of hundreds of military men. To them, reform had soon ceased to be a "reform," but was rather a revolutionary attack—an attempt to weaken, humiliate, and degrade the old Army spirit. And so, in a sense, it was.[21]

The Left's response to regional autonomy was especially indicative of its misunderstanding of how the game of democratic politics should be played. It is essential to know that by the 1930s the Left and the Right had switched positions on home rule. In the nineteenth century and into the twentieth, the progressives had been fervid centralists while the conservatives had been equally avid federalists. With the coming of the Second Republic, the Left, in the name of libertarian self-determination, became the defenders of regional rights, while the Right, in the spirit of pure opposition, became dedicated nationalists. The majority leftist coalition that governed Spain during the Constituent Assembly and during the first biennium of the Republic enthusiastically granted autonomy to Catalonia. The promise of home rule had been made in the Pact of San Sebastian;[22] moreover, Catalonia had become zealously republican following the debacle of Primo de Rivera when the dictator had abrogated the weak but powerfully symbolic statute of Catalan self-determination granted in 1912.[23]

The autonomy of the Basque country was a different matter, however, and its handling demonstrated the hypocrisy of the Left and its unwillingness to play by its own rules when those rules did not operate to its advantage. The Basque provinces, including Navarre, were ultraconservative and devoutly, even fanatically, Catholic and were fiercely opposed to the anti-Catholic provisions in the constitution. At one point, the deputies from these provinces had stormed from the legislature when the antireligious provisions were adopted by the Constituent Assembly. They eventually returned to the Cortes, however, and, taking advantage of the Left's commitment to regional autonomy, made their claim for self-determination in the Basque provinces and in Navarre. The leftist coalition governing the Republic turned them down! The Socialist Prieto claimed that the area would become a Vatican Gibraltar. Paradoxically when the conservative Catholic rightist coalition came to power in 1933, it also rejected the Basque and Navarrese claims not because of the political orientation of these provinces but because the Right now supported unrestricted national sovereignty. In 1936 when the leftist Popular Front was organized and won the parliamentary elections in February, the plot became even more complex. Navarre chose religion over autonomy and supported the rightist coalition (and in the Civil War the Navarrese fought with the rebel Nationalists). The Basque provinces chose autonomy over religion and supported the Popular Front, which in October, 1936, rewarded them with autonomy (and in the already erupted Civil War, the Basques fought with the Republic). The Basques' devotion to Catholicism had not weakened, but their commitment to self-determination had grown stronger.

The key to the restructuring of Spanish society was the redistribution of land, particularly the breakup of the inefficient large estates owned primarily by absentee landlords and concentrated in Extremadura, western Andalusia, La Mancha, and Salamanca, where working conditions and living standards for the peasant were just above those of peonage. Article 44 of the constitution allowed for the expropriation of land with compensation unless decided otherwise by statute. The Agrarian Reform Law passed in September, 1932, expropriated the land of all the Spanish grandees (the noblemen) without compensation and provided that the remaining land to be redistributed would be paid for by the state in accordance with the land's evaluation by its owners for tax purposes. Unfortunately, the law was grossly maladministered by the newly created Institute of Agrarian Reform, whose chief was an incapable political spoilsman, a journalist with no experience outside his profession. The institute did too little to satisfy the legitimate land hunger of the peasants abused for centuries but did too much not to enrage the major landowners—particularly the powerful and influential nobility. Before the leftist coalition was voted out of office in December, 1931, only 117,837 hectares (about 290,000 acres) of land had been either expropriated by the state or temporarily occupied by the peasants. At that rate, given the total amount of land available for redistribution, it would have taken over one hundred years to have completed land reform.[24] Franz Borkenau comments:

> Instead of putting agrarian reform before everything the Government immediately got itself into trouble with the Church about religious matters. The creation of the secular state was the pet idea of the radical intellectuals, and at the same time an easy way of escaping for the moment the urgent problems of economy and administration. . . . The Government introduced legislation to separate Church and State. When, many months later, after the ecclesiastical question had created a Government crisis, a split in the republican camp, and an attempt at armed rising in Navarra, the Government at last turned to the agrarian question, the reaction had rallied again. Now the agrarian problem which could have been solved peacefully in April and May [1932] could only be solved with blood and iron. The civil service, deeply implicated with the interests of the large landowners, sabotaged the reform and the only way left to make it effective would have been to appeal to the peasants to take their claims into their own hands which would have meant social revolution. The republicans were far from wanting that.[25]

Ramón Tamames, the Spanish historian–political scientist–economist, returns over and over to the theme that the leftist coalition by decree could have and should have made desperately needed socioeconomic changes, particularly land reform, during the early months of the Republic when almost anything might have been tolerated by the confused but still optimistic Spanish people.[26]

The Left proved much more adept at stirring passions (witness the religious legislation) than it was at producing meaningful outputs (witness land reform), and it was repudiated at the polls in December, 1933. Ironically, the Left lost the election largely because of one of its few dispassionate legislative achievements, the enfranchisement of women. As predicted, women, with their use of the ballot for the first time in Spanish history, overwhelmingly supported the Right in the parliamentary elections allegedly because of vengeful priestly influence within the confessional. The Left helped to defeat itself, however; in the name of doctrinal purity the anarchists refused to go to the polls, almost guaranteeing by their boycott the success of the Right.

Gerald Brenan appraises the first biennium:

> What was the cause of the failure? Briefly that the Republic had alienated large sections of the middle classes without giving satisfaction to the peasants and factory workers. Had it, as Lerroux desired, contented itself with being a continuation, in a somewhat more enlightened form, of the Monarchy, it would have drawn all the middle classes around it. But it would then have united all the working class against it and since their claims could no longer be denied, a revolutionary situation would have developed. If, on the other hand, it had gone deeper, throwing open all the large estates to the peasants and to the political organizations that controlled them, it would have risked initiating a social revolution and being carried out of its depth. The Army would then have intervened "to restore order." It chose therefore a middle course—which in Spain, one must remember, is always the line of greatest resistance.[27]

To its discredit, the Left, during the first biennium, used the constitution as a weapon and not as a tool, failing to comprehend that a constitution, unless it is framed to legitimize a revolution, must reflect the customs and traditions of a society. The American Constitution, for example, was viable because it institutionalized and formalized the enduring political beliefs of the people. It was far from a revolutionary document. The American Revolution had been a revolution in the sense of a breakaway; it was not a revolution in the sense of a restructuring of a polity. The Constitution reflected the prevailing attitudes of the new country; in fact, the first ten amendments had to be added because the charter did not sufficiently reflect the political mentality of the entire society. By contrast, the Spanish constitution of 1931 did not mirror the political thinking of the majority of Spaniards. Because of this failure, the constitution was artificial, mandating changes (in divorce, marriage, education, and property rights) for which the nation was not ready. The Leftists who fathered the constitution were dogmatists emerging from a doctrinaire society, and their liberalism was illiberal in spirit and in application.

To its credit, however, the Left, during the first biennium, did not resort to coercion to implement the constitution during the early euphoric months in 1931 and 1932 when the Spaniard was still stunned by the traumatic birth of the Republic and still unfocused in his expectations of the new political system. An exquisite paradox lies here: orthodox Liberals used a liberal constitution illiberally as a weapon to destroy those forces that the Liberals had hated for so long—the Church, the army, and the great landowners. But orthodox Liberals were prevented by their ideological commitment from using the one weapon that most likely would have guaranteed their success—force.

The Black Biennium

The Right governed from December 3, 1933, to February 1, 1936—the Black Biennium. It was dominated by two major parties: the right-of-center Radicals under the leadership of the chameleonic Alejandro Lerroux, and the conservative Catholic Confederación Española de Derechas Autónomas—C.E.D.A. (Spanish Confederation of Autonomous Rightist Parties)—whose chief was José María Gil Robles. Given the play of forces within a working democratic polity, when parties or coalitions are returned to office, they seek to implement their own program. As a consequence, during the Black Biennium, the Right sought to undo much of the legislation passed or begun by the Left during the Red Biennium. Clerical reform, antireligious legislation, land reform, military reorganization, social legislation, educational reform, and regional self-determination were all either reversed or retarded in their application. Whether or not this policy was wise, considering the explosive political atmosphere and considering, too, the undeniable suffering of countless Spaniards, depends on one's own ideological persuasion. Irrespectively, the action of the Right lay within its mandate as the majority that had won the 1933 election. This statement does not contradict the earlier observation that no party or coalition ever had a sufficient mandate from the people to remake Spain according to its own vision, but the voice from the citizens in the elections of November, 1933, did reflect deep-seated unease with the program of the Left during the Red Biennium. As a consequence of that disquiet, the parties of the Left dropped from 265 seats in the Cortes to 98; the parties of the Right rose from 219 seats to 386. *Still, paradoxically, there was never present any positive expression from the people for or against a clear-cut leftist or rightist program.*

The actions of the Right were reactionary in the popular usage of the term, but they were reactionary also in the sense that the Right was *acting against* what it considered to be abuses of the Left, yet the response was within the provisions of the constitution. These actions were condemned by the Left in the Cortes, a posture understandable and defendable. That is the way constitutional government is designed to work. But in October, 1934, when C.E.D.A. was brought into the governing coalition for the first time,[28] leading nonsocialist figures on the Left in the Cortes, including the former prime minister Manuel Azaña, communicated to the president of Spain that they were breaking all association with the existing institutions of the country.[29] They did not content themselves with declaring their opposition to the *program* of the Right, a stance within the concept of loyal democratic opposition; they declared themselves against the *existing institutions of the country*—institutions they themselves had established and whose rules they themselves had created. In a situation similar to the refusal to grant home rule to the Basque provinces and to Navarre, the Left abandoned the game when the rules worked to its disadvantage.

The catalyst for this behavior was Gil Robles, the chief of C.E.D.A. The accusations hurled against him by the Left (many of whom were consumed with an almost paranoiac hatred of the man) simply did not materialize. He was accused of being a fascist, of being a Spanish Dollfus.[30] Undeniably his political philosophy, which he labeled "accidentalism," did not swear allegiance to the Republic. By "accidentalism" Gil Robles meant that by its outputs and not by its labels did one judge a political system. Yet, neither he nor his political party ever stepped beyond the limits of the constitution, and no one can be judged and condemned politically for what he might have done—not in a democracy, at least.

Gil Robles aside, however, the most inept and the most ominous move made by the rightist government during the Black Biennium was to pardon General José Sanjurjo for his abortive, bloodless, short-lived coup in August, 1932. This was the same general who had acted as midwife to the Republic by refusing to bring the Guardia Civil to the defense of Alfonso in 1931, but by the summer of 1932 the leftist direction of the government during the Red Biennium prompted Sanjurjo to rise up in the name of "real" Spain against "legal" Spain— the antique rationalization used by all insurgents.[31] The coup was instanty quashed because the pronunciamiento had little active support either in the military or in the police, otherwise it could not have been so easily suppressed. The Left had the good sense not to martyrize Sanjurjo by having him shot but put him in jail instead. The Right, when it came to power in 1933, should have had the equal good sense to have left him there, but instead he was pardoned and released, though banished to Portugal. Irrespective of how well-meant the amnesty may have been (interpreted by some as a device on the part of the moderate Right in the Cortes to placate a potentially restive army, particularly since the government had already conciliated the Church) to the parliamentary Left, the action was interpreted to mean that, in the eyes of the Right, violence was condoned not only against the Left's program but more significantly against the constitution and against the Republic itself. The validity of the logic of the Left cannot be denied.

By this time, however, no practical analysis of the Second Republic can be meaningfully concerned only with what was taking place *within* the Cortes. By autumn 1934, political reality had moved into the city streets and into the countryside. In October the nonparliamentary Left (the trade unions primarily) warned the president of Spain that if either C.E.D.A. or its chief, Gil Robles, were allowed to take part in any government at any time, the Left would revolt. The fact that in a legal, parliamentary election the Right had won 386 out of 484 seats in the Cortes and that C.E.D.A. had won 113 out of the total 386 on the Right, gaining 33 seats more than the second largest party on the Right, the Radicals, and 74 seats more than the third largest party on the Right, the Partido Agrario (Agrarian Party), was of absolutely no consequence to the forces on the Left.

In spite of the threat, when the cabinet was reshuffled on October 1, 1934, C.E.D.A. was awarded three portfolios—Agriculture, Justice, and Labor—not one of which went to Gil Robles and none of which was pivotal to either political or military power, as posts with control over the armed forces or the police would have been.[32]

The Left exploded in what Stanley Payne has accurately labeled "the most intensive, destructive proletarian insurrection in the history of Western Europe to that date."[33] The rebellion broke out principally in Madrid, Barcelona, and Oviedo (in Asturias in northwestern Spain, the major mining center of the nation) but was quickly put down in Madrid and Barcelona. In Oviedo the armed revolt lasted two weeks with over 30,000 workers taking part. In some Asturian towns, revolutionary committees were set up, and the dictatorship of the proletariat was declared: "Union of Proletarian Brothers!" With strategy planned by Franco from the War Ministry in Madrid, the insurrection was crushed by Moroccan troops and by the Foreign Legion. But the operation cost over 4,000 casualties, and the rightist government had made a serious psychological misjudgment when it sent Africans to Asturias, the one region in Spain the Moors had never reached and the location of the holy city of Covadonga, the birthplace of the Reconquest.[34]

It is dangerous to stoke historic memory, but the government cannot be condemned for putting down an armed revolt against the Republic. It can and should be condemned, however, for allowing the grisly orgy of mutilations, torture, and rape unleashed by the Moroccan troops against the defeated miners and their families. Furthermore, as de Madariaga posits, *"With the rebellion of 1934, the Left lost every shred of moral authority to condemn the rebellion of 1936."*[35] Practically speaking, the Civil War began in October, 1934, for the alignment of forces that later fought in the war coalesced in the Asturian revolution. The alliance of all of the groups on the Left—the Alianza Obrera

(Workers' Alliance)—had given the insurrection its extraordinary impetus. The massive force had come from the U.G.T. under the messianic influence of Largo Caballero, but so powerful was its vortex that even the anarchists were pulled in, and for the first time they fought with their fellow workers.[36]

In the months following the suppression of the rebellion in Asturias, the cities and the countryside of Spain became battlegrounds of terror. Long-existing paramilitary units sprang into the open: from the Right, Falangists were organized nationwide; Requetés (resembling the Camelots du Roi in France) were active in Navarre; from the Left, Escamots, and the shock troops of the socialist, communist, and anarchist trade unions roamed Catalonia and spread throughout the country. The Communists had also organized, apart from the terrorist union thugs, the Milicias Anti-fascistas Obreras y Campesinas (Antifascist Workers' and Peasants' Militias). About these Payne writes: "It was the only well-organized, well-led paramilitary group in the country (with the possible exception of the Carlist Requetés) thanks to the expert assistance from the Comintern."[37] The militias had been organized since 1933 but came into their own in the spring of 1936. These vigilantes fought and killed each other in open combat in the city streets and on country roads and were either aided or attacked by the police and military forces, depending upon these officials' political orientation: the Guardia Civil (Civil Guard), the national, primarily rural, police force, and the Carabineros (Frontier Customs Guards), whose leadership was sympathetic to the Right; the Guardia de Asalto (Assault Guards), the national police force created by the government during the first biennium because the loyalty of the traditional police was suspect, and the Mozos de Escuadra (Young Squadmen) in Catalonia, whose commanders were sympathetic to the Left. Brian Crozier appraises the second biennium:

> Thus ended the *Bienio Negro*. It had been a period that brought little credit to any Spanish politicians who lived through it. Gil Robles' party had been denied its logical and democratic right to rule, though it had participated in the Centre-Right coalition. Legislatively, the *Bienio* had been a desert of negatives: nothing of value had been achieved, though the trend of Azaña's rule had been reversed (if only temporarily). There had been a premature revolution from the Left, and a brutal repression from the Right. The trend towards political extremism and violence had been accentuated, and the two years had ended in scandal and the annihilation of the Centre. If Azaña's revolution had shown the absurdity of parliamentary democracy in Spain, the anti-Azaña government that followed had demonstrated that lunacy was hardly too strong a word for a

system which neither national temper nor historical tradition justified.[38]

The demands for new elections to resolve the conflict became irresistible. Or more accurately, the only ones who by then made opinion, the extremists, clamored for elections not to resolve the conflict but hopefully to intensify each bloc's claim to be the Moses of the people. The elections were held on February 16, 1936. They were not the therapy for survival but the death rattle of a moribund republic. Moreover, there was a strong odor of hypocrisy about the elections, for many of the leaders on both sides had no intention of abiding by their outcome. The Left, coalesced politically and electorally for the first time in the Frente Popular (Popular Front), won 272, and the Right won 212 out of a total of 484 seats in the Cortes. Once again, however, as in 1931, there was no overwhelming mandate from the people (whose opinion by this time appeared to have been totally ignored by the political elite) for revolutionary change from either the Right or the Left. The most interesting and unique analysis of the political meaning of the vote comes from Salvador de Madariaga.[39] He breaks the figures and their meanings into the following classification: Marxist Left (i.e., anticlerical, antimilitaristic), 1,793,000 votes; Non-Marxist Left (i.e., anticlerical, antimilitaristic), 3,193,000 votes; Parliamentary Right (i.e., anti-Marxist, clerical, nonmilitaristic, 3,783,000 votes; Anti-Parliamentary Right (i.e., anti-Marxist, nonclerical, militaristic), a few thousand. In an even more provocative appraisal, de Madariaga synthesizes that "Spain pronounced herself: (1) By two to one against Marxism; (2) By two to one against Clericals and Militarists; (3) By eight to one against a Socialist revolution; (4) Almost unanimously against a military rebellion."[40] Payne concludes:

> The situation was not so radically defined in the minds of most voters as it was in the minds of militants. Evidence of all the diversity of opinion among the Spanish public at that time leads one to the conclusion that the majority of those who cast their ballots for the conservative *National Front* on February 16, 1936, were not voting for an authoritarian regime but for the defense of religion and of property and that the majority of those who opted for the *Popular Front* were not supporting violent revolution but endorsing individual freedom and social reform.[41]

The Popular Front

The electoral program of the Popular Front was not excessively extremist since all the forces of the Left (republican and socialist) had to find room under its umbrella. Had politically intelligent leadership emerged in the Cortes, Spain may have been able to have avoided civil war, but the word "may" is the operative term because by the spring of 1936, Spain was perhaps beyond a peaceful solution to her problems. The platform called for, among other things, the reinstatement of land reform and the extension of social legislation, but it did not include the extremists' demands for nationalization of the land and of the banks. But the Left showed its incredible inability to learn from experience by repeating what the Right had done when it pardoned Sanjurjo, thereby setting afire in the Right in the spring of 1936 the same sentiments the Right had ignited in the Left in the spring of 1934! The Popular Front went to the electorate "guaranteeing complete amnesty for the insurrectionists of 1934 and for all those accused of politicosocial crimes since 1933, but prosecution of all those guilty of 'acts of violence' in repressing political crimes."[42] Except for this incredibly egregious blunder (or deliberate flouting), the program would not have been impossible for Spain to live with. Payne comments:

> This was mostly a social democratic reformist program. Contrary to many assertions it did not go beyond the original left Republican position in some respects but steered clear of the anticlerical obsession that had exhausted so much energy in the past. . . . It was understood that after a Popular Front victory the next government should be formed by the middle-class left alone though the other members of the electoral coalition would support that government with their votes in parliament at least until it had carried through the minimal program espoused in the electoral agreement.[43]

The fate of the Republic lay with the Socialists, the largest and strongest party in the coalition with 88 out of the 272 seats on the Left. Its attitude could have shaped the behavior of the other parties in the coalition, but the Socialists were rent by the conflict between the charismatic and increasingly revolutionary Largo Caballero and the moderate but less popular Prieto. Their inability to reconcile differences, due almost exclusively to the compelling rigidity of Largo Caballero, condemned the Popular Front to ineffective leadership and doomed the Republic to the precipitous sweep to the Left inside the Cortes and to the insurgence of the Right outside. The moderately conservative de Madariaga says flatly: "What made the Spanish Civil War inevitable was the Civil War within the Socialist party."[44] The leftist Ramón Tamames writes: "Because of his ability, knowledge, and information at all levels, his facility to get to the bottom of problems, Prieto would have been the best leader *(gobernante)* of the Republic."[45] Brian Crozier comments:

In 1933 Communist propaganda was still dubbing Largo Caballero as
a "Social Fascist." But in December of that year Moscow launched the
policy of alliances between communist and other "non-fascist" parties
that came to be known as the "Popular Front." And Largo Caballero's
new revolutionary policy made him and his Socialists receptive to Communist overtures. It was shortly after this—and not by coincidence—that
Moscow's propaganda machine started flattering Largo by calling him
"the Lenin of Spain." Ideally, from Moscow's point of view, the
Communists should have been preaching revolution, with Largo
Caballero trailing along. But the increasing violence of Largo's speeches
forced them to take an even more incendiary line. Largo's personal
responsibility for the Civil War is thus a particularly heavy one, heavier
perhaps than that of any other individual.[46]

The streets were already at war by early 1936. Murder and assassination were nearly a daily occurrence. The Right, fearing that Spain was
on its way to a leftist revolution *through the Cortes*, began its plot
against the regime. In the very beginning there appears to have been no
single revolutionary ringmaster. Many of those who would have logically numbered among the antigovernmental conspirators, the older and
higher-ranking members of the military, were initially reluctant to
commit themselves. For most good bureaucratic officers like the ones in
Spain, war—particularly civil war—is a terrible threat to personal and
family security, to life, and to pension. Moreover, as Payne comments,
"The ferocious propaganda of the Left made it clear that in any radical
confrontation, defeated army dissidents would not be treated so easily as
in an earlier generation."[47] But as unchecked civil strife swept the
country, the insurrectionists began to weave the pattern of revolt. The
rebels included: in the army, the generals Sanjurjo (who became the
titular commander-in-chief of the conspiracy and who from exile in
Lisbon furnished the conduit for the intrigue), Quiepo de Llano,
Fanjul, Goded, Yagüe, and Mola (who after March became the director
of the uprising and its creative, motive force); the Carlist leader Fal
Conde, from Navarre, the one region in the country where there was
broad popular support for rebellion against the leftist Republic; from
his prison cell in Alicante, where he had been jailed on March 14, José
Antonio Primo de Rivera, the chief of the Falange;[48] in the Cortes, the
monarchist José Calvo Sotelo, by now the leader of the strident
parliamentary Right. (Gil Robles, whom the Left had feared and
excoriated so passionately during the Black Biennium, remained
committed to the Republic but had released his fellow members of
C.E.D.A. to follow their consciences.) Among the very last to commit
himself was Franco, who finally joined the conspirators after his

warnings to the prime minister about smoldering discontent in the army had been ignored.[49]

Franco had been involved in the intrigue since February, but he did not commit himself to rebellion until July. What he had sought early in the year had not materialized. He had urged the caretaker government (acting between the collapse of the rightist coalition cabinet and the election of the new parliament) to place political power in the hands of the army to maintain order before the results of the second balloting would almost surely award power to the Popular Front. This would have satisfied Franco's unorthodox sense of constitutionality (since the Spanish constitution provided for emergency contingencies). In Franco's mind this would have obviated a pronunciamiento. His plan was, of course, rejected and the Popular Front came into office. Franco's commitment to the uprising had been wary in the early months of the new government because such action would go against the constituted authority that Franco respected and that as a soldier he had sworn to uphold, but as chaos piled upon chaos, and order (the first commandment in Franco's doxy) almost disappeared in Spanish public life, his reluctance began to erode, and by July he had made up his mind to join the conspirators.

The event which activated the rebels took place on the Walpurgis Night of July 12, when Calvo Sotelo was taken from his home and murdered by the Assault Guards, the republican police force, allegedly in retaliation for the killing earlier in the day of one of its lieutenants by three Falangists. "Never before in the history of a western European parliamentary regime had a key opposition leader been sequestered and murdered in cold blood by the state police. To many it seemed to indicate that revolutionary radicalism was out of control and the constitutional system at a complete end."[50] Brian Crozier comments:

> It is hard perhaps to convey the enormity of this deed, for it is almost impossible to transpose it to other countries and different circumstances. Sir Alec Douglas-Home kidnapped and murdered by Special Branch detectives? Senator Robert Kennedy kidnapped and murdered by the F.B.I.? Unthinkable, one might say. And that is the point: in Spain in the summer of 1936, the unthinkable had become normal.[51]

The military uprising that was to become a civil war and was to last until April 1, 1939, began in Morocco on July 17, 1936, and spread to the peninsula the next day.

The Collapse of the Second Republic: An Analysis

The Second Republic collapsed because the Spanish people were not prepared to make it work. The statement is not an indictment; it is not a condescendence. The Spaniards were not ready because they were ignorant not just of the nuances of the art of democratic living, they were ignorant of the fundamentals as well. The society remained deeply conflictual; no political consensus was ever reached either about ends or about means. The system was neither legitimate nor efficient to a large enough majority of the people for a long enough period of time to fulfill the criteria of stability, if by stability we mean, with Harry Eckstein, "persistence of pattern, decisional effectiveness, and authenticity."[52] In fact, it can perhaps safely be said that the Second Republic was counter or antipolitical when politics is defined by Bernard Crick as "the activity by which differing interests within a given unit of rule are conciliated by giving them a share in power in proportion to their importance to the welfare and the survival of the whole community."[53] On the contrary, the contending groups in Spain were not conciliated; they opposed one another in the *à outrance* sense spoken of by Alfred Grosser when he distinguished *Opposition* from *opposition*. "The first implies a rather precise role in the pluralistic political system clearly defined by constitution and custom. The second suggests a variety of attitudes and behavior of which the only common characteristic is hostility to power."[54] Stanley Hoffmann, writing about Frenchmen, could have been writing with equal insight about Spaniards:

> As Raymond Aron remarked, Americans tend to believe that man fulfills himself when he adjusts to society, and cooperates with it as a good citizen who does not challenge its basic values. Frenchmen, on the contrary, think that man is himself only when he rebels and says no to all the conventions or established beliefs that threaten his personality. Here we find the key to our subject: In France protest is the norm.[55]

Elena de la Souchère sees the Spaniard as an actor on the stage, at once a part of and distant from his audience—an impossible political role in a democratic society.

> This somewhat dramatic conception of social life, by which a man considers himself the principal actor in a play, either drama or comedy, confers upon the interlocutors and witnesses a secondary role: that of satellites of the "self." The term "satellite" should not be taken as referring to a social hierarchy. If the action by which a man seeks to assert himself is political, he will undoubtedly look for subordinates in the social sense of the term. If the action is rather literary or artistic the individual may wish for ministers, princes, kings to praise and patronize his achievements. But no matter how eminent the social position of the

witnesses, they inevitably play a secondary role in any action involving the "self." This tendency constitutes a predisposition to intolerance. Indeed, while he pays his respects to another through the formulae of refined courtesy custom demands of him, at that very moment the Spaniard is miles away from even conceiving of the other person's point of view. This mental impermeability turns every dialogue into a misunderstanding not likely to be resolved because each party to it— walled within himself and speaking for his own benefit—pays very little attention to the arguments which are opposed to him. If he were to accord awareness to the disagreement which places him in opposition to others, he would be as offended by it as by an attack upon his inner world, his personality, and certainly he would be right in thinking an insult had been offered to all that he holds most dear: to the illusion that is indispensable to him. The world must be as his vital need of the world depicts it.[56]

V. S. Pritchett, in describing a heated but amicable discussion among Spanish strangers traveling in a compartment on a train, writes:

> The whole performance illustrated the blindness of Spanish egotism. The speaker stares at you with a prolonged dramatic stare that goes through you. He stares because he is trying to get into his head the impossible proposition that you exist. He does not listen to you. He never discusses. He asserts. Only *he* exists.[57]

These evaluations can be made more tangible by using and applying to Spain the analytical devices of Harry Eckstein and Lucian Pye. Eckstein suggests, as a general hypothesis, that "a government will tend to be stable if its authority pattern is congruent with the authority pattern of the society of which it is a part."[58] He then expands and loosens his definition into a more workable concept.

> Government will be stable (1) if social authority patterns are identical with the governmental patterns, or (2) if they constitute a graduated pattern in a proper segmentation of society, or (3) if a high degree of resemblance exists in patterns adjacent to government and one finds throughout the more distant segments a marked departure from functionally appropriate patterns for the sake of imitating the governmental pattern or extensive imitation of the governmental in ritual practices.[59]

In short, a democratic government must function within a democratic society where democratic socialization is a part of everyday living. Eckstein sees contemporary Great Britain as the model of congruence.

He finds the ideal type present not only in the government but everywhere in society.

> In nonpolitical adult organizations from friendly societies and clubs to business organizations . . . one finds in these organizations at least a great deal of imitation, if only as ritual, of the governmental pattern. Even small-scale neighborhood clubs . . . generally have their relatively inconsequential elections and stable oligarchies, their formalities, petty constitutionalisms, and ritualistic annual meetings; and still more is this true of larger clubs and friendly societies, like the famous snob clubs of Pall Mall and that holiest of holies, the Marylebone Cricket Club. It may be easier in such small organizations to participate in decision-making, if they wish, but the essential forms and actual patterns of authority do not differ very much from the great political associations.[60]

The key to the congruence is this: "Throughout this structure operate norms typical of all public authority in Great Britain: that decision-making must be carried out by some sort of collective leadership, which is both responsive to the mass of the organization and, to a large extent, autonomous of it, which is expected to behave according to some code well-understood in the group but normally not explicitly defined and which although resting to some extent on an elective basis enjoys great tenure of office, often for as long as the leaders want to keep their position."[61]

At the opposite end of the measure Eckstein sees Germany during the Weimar Republic.

> Democracy, in interwar Germany, was, for all practical purposes, isolated at the level of parliamentary government, but at that level it was organized in an almost absurdly pure and exaggerated manner. . . . The Weimar constitution was proclaimed in its day as the most perfect of all democratic constitutions, and for good reasons.
>
> This unalleviated democracy was superimposed upon a society pervaded by authoritarian relationships and obsessed with authoritarianism. . . . That the Germans should have been deeply preoccupied with naked power, large and petty, is hardly very surprising in a society democratized on its parliamentary surface but shot through with large and petty tyrants in every other segment of life. Compared with their British counterparts German family life, German schools, and German business firms were all exceedingly authoritarian. German families were dominated more often than not by tyrannical husbands and fathers, German schools by tyrannical teachers, German firms by tyrannical bosses. Insolence, gruffness, pettiness, arbitrariness, even violence were so widespread that one could certainly not consider them mere deviations from normal patterns.[62]

Like Germany during the Weimar Republic, Spain during the Second Republic was a noncongruent polity. Democracy existed only within the parliamentary halls, yet within those halls, it existed primarily in the mind of each deputy and was personally defined to suit his individuality. Even the spirit of democracy was misconceived. The much bruited equality among Spaniards is an equality not based upon the concept that each man is as good as the next; it is based upon the conviction that each man is better than the next. Both notions will arrive at a kind of democracy since the latter will admit of no superiors at least as each person looks at himself. Thus in a house of kings no one takes precedence even as each man holds the next in contempt. Spanish democracy as practiced in the Second Republic was not unlike the Congress of Vienna, where the delegates sat at a round table within a round room with doors equal to the number of seats at the table so that all participants could enter simultaneously, obviating the necessity of hierarchy and protocol. One must admit that this was a democratic solution to a delicate dilemma, but national legislatures in democratic polities are not aristocratic conferences, and elected representatives to a republican Cortes are not delegates from the individual principality of each constituent's ego.

Moreover, even if we were to allow ourselves to label the Second Republic democratic for the mere sake of discussion, democracy was nonexistent in almost every other facet of Spanish life.[63] True enough male suffrage had existed since the Second Restoration in 1875, but its effectiveness had been perverted through collusion; from a practical point of view, before the Second Republic most Spaniards had never cast a meaningful vote. Society was deeply classridden. The Church was authoritarian (in Spain one is almost tempted to call it totalitarian); the army was despotic and infected with scandal, particularly in Morocco;[64] the school system if run by churchmen or churchwomen was as authoritarian as the Church itself, and if run by the state was as corrupt and featherbedded as the state itself; the civil service was a spoils system ripened to the point of putrefaction;[65] the family was ruled by a paterfamilias who brooked no opposition. Even organizations made up of the long-suffering poorer classes—primarily the labor unions—were undemocratic in organization. One of the reasons given for the early lack of support of the Socialist party and its union, the U.G.T., was their authoritarian structures. Only the anarchists seemed to live the libertarian life, but anarchists are not what one would call good material for a functioning, effective democratic polity; moreover, the moral code of the anarchists was so rigid that one's freedom of choice was strongly circumscribed if not by rules and regulations then by peer pressure.

Eckstein could have been describing Spain when he wrote about Germany: "The trouble was not that the Germans were so one-sidedly authoritarian; the trouble was rather that they were—and perhaps had always been—so remarkably two-sided (i.e., incongruent) in their political beliefs and social practices. Profound ideological commitment to governmental democracy is not a sufficient basis for stable democracy; in fact it can be worse, in the long run, than a more qualified commitment to democracy."[66] In the same vein Gabriel Almond and Bingham Powell write:

> All political systems have mixed political cultures. The most primitive societies have threads of instrumental rationality in their structure and culture. The most modern are permeated by ascriptive, particularistic, and informal relationships and attitudes. They differ in the relative dominance of one against the other and in the pattern of mixture of these components. Secularization is a matter of degree and of the distribution of these "rational" aspects. . . . The modern societies have been presented as secular and rational. Their cultures have been presented as embodying attitude patterns which treat individuals in universalistic fashion according to personal relationships and attitudes. The bureaucrat looks with equal favor upon all applicants for services; he does not favor his brother or his cousin. Traditional societies, on the other hand, have been viewed in terms of ascription of particular statutes, and diffuse and particularistic relationships. That is, individuals attain position according to criteria other than their merit (such as status of parents) and personal relationships and informal communication patterns permeate the political process.[67]

By these criteria, Spain at the time of the Second Republic, was a mixed political system but with the traditional culture strongly dominant over the modern. Spain, under the Second Republic, was caught between modernity and traditionalism. By contrast, the dictatorship of Primo de Rivera was almost purely traditionalistic with adornments of modernity. The Second Republic succumbed to the intimately interrelated developmental crises that Lucian Pye calls the crises of identity, legitimacy, penetration, participation, integration, and distribution.[68]

The crisis of identity. Spain at the beginning of the Second Republic was once again back where she had been centuries earlier. She was still a people in search of a nation, a nation in search of a state, particularly after the great agglutinative force of religion had, since the middle of the nineteenth century, cleaved Spain and turned class against class so that faith no longer offered a common sense of nationality. Both horizontal and vertical identity were threadbare: exemplified horizontally not only by deep alienation between the upper and lower classes but also by fratricidal hatred among the lower classes themselves; exemplified vertically by regional and subcultural estrangement in Catalonia, the Basque country, Navarre, and Galicia.[69]

The crisis of legitimacy has already been sufficiently talked about in this chapter. The animosity between the Left and the Right over the range and impact of the constitution was the most serious trauma of the Second Republic.

The crisis of participation was almost self-inflicted. Intransigent stands on doctrinal purity kept the anarchists as a group away from the polls. In the elections in 1931, individual anarchists did vote and did so en masse in the elections of 1936, but the anarchist organizations were philosophically committed against electoral participation, and the intensity of their boycott helped to guarantee the success of the Right in 1933. Women, for all practical purposes, bloc voted for the Right after 1933. This may have been a legitimate expression of their opinion and, therefore, theoretically irreproachable, but bloc voting—irrespective of how legitimate or necessary from the voter's point of view—is indicative of systemic malfunction.[70]

The crisis of penetration. Because of the impossibility of establishing the legitimacy and identity of the Second Republic, the effectiveness of the government in motivating changes in values and habits was abortive. Changes that were initiated during the first (the Red) biennium (in religion, land tenure, organization of the military, education, and regional home rule—to name the primary ones) were repudiated during the second (the Black) biennium, and the attempts to reinstate these changes after the electoral success of the Popular Front in February, 1936, was the catalyst which brought on the Civil War.

The crisis of integration. If, according to Pye, a system that has weathered successfully penetration and participation has by that dual achievement become integrated, "relating popular politics to governmental performance,"[71] then Spain, during the Second Republic, remained almost totally disintegrated. The wildly contradictory demands made upon the system—epitomized by the almost two dozen parties articulating those demands from 1931 to 1936—were incapable of being integrated without *revolution*. Democracy is weak in giving direction. Dispassionate politics, which must characterize democracy, is realizable only when the range of choices is narrow. Democracy is successful when it demands very little of the citizen and does not compel him to make painful choices. Only revolution can pull deeply divergent and antagonistic peoples into the magnetic field of rational, compromising political action, in other words, can integrate the polity, and even then only long after the passions of revolution have cooled and the new consensus allows the polity to enjoy the luxury of political pragmatism within the newly established limits of tolerance.[72]

The crisis of distribution was symbolized in the failure of land reform but was repeated in all the other changes attempted. All reform fell between doing too little to rectify the great inequalities separating the classes but doing too much not to force the possessing class into reaction against the dispossessed. Raymond Carr summarized it well when he wrote about "the Republican New Deal" in Spain:

> The weakness of republican legislation, both in the spheres of finance and of labor, was that it threatened fundamental change which the government lacked the will or the desire to implement. Like Blum's legislation in France, none of its provisions was incompatible with orthodox capitalism but altogether they caused capitalists to lose confidence. The railway legislation disrupted the old board of directors but stopped short of nationalization; the Banking Law, while it gave the government a control over the discount rate . . . left the banks almost as powerful as before. Savage control of foreign exchange operations was held to hamper the flow of trade. Income tax was raised—the top rate on fortunes over one million pesetas was 7.7 per cent—but without any radical reform of a tax system which Primo de Rivera had stigmatized as "undemocratic" and unjust. The capitalist classes were alarmed, but their power was untouched.[73]

All the crises broke out simultaneously. Spain resembled France and Italy and Germany, where at similar times in their histories the great revolutions of religion, regime, and economics erupted together, interconnecting and interinfecting so that a relatively peaceful resolution became impossible, unlike England, where the major crises arose, were met, and were resolved each in turn thus insuring relative stability.

Notes

1. For comparative purposes see Arthur Rosenberg, *A History of the German Republic (1918-1930),* trans. Ian F. D. Morrow and L. Marie Sieveking (London: Methuen and Co., Ltd., 1936); William J. Halperin, *Germany Tried Democracy* (New York: Thomas Y. Crowell Co., 1946); Erich Eyck, *A History*

of the Weimar Republic, trans. Harlan P. Hanson and Robert G. L. Waite (Cambridge, Mass.: Harvard University Press, 1962).

2. By the same logic, Germany's defeat in World War II has in part expiated the "sins" of the Germans for their corruption of democracy and for their acceptance of Hitler.

3. The following schematic of parties comes from Ramón Tamames, *La República, la Era de Franco* (Madrid: Alianza Editorial Alfaguara, S.A., 1973), pp. 15-16.

I. The Left

    A. Republican Parties
        1. Acción Republicana (Republican Action) and Izquierda Republicana (Republican Left)
        2. Partido Radical-Socialista (Radical Socialist Party)
        3. Unión Republicana (Republican Union)

    B. Regional Autonomous Parties
        1. Esquerra Catalana and Estat Català (Catalan Left and Catalan State)
        2. Partido Catalanista Republicano (Catalan Republican Party)
        3. Organización Regional Autonomista Gallega [O.R.G.A.] (Autonomous Regional Gallegan Organization)
        4. Partido Nacionalista Vasco (Nationalist Basque Party)

    C. Workers' Parties and Organizations
        1. Partido Socialista Obrero Español [P.S.O.E.] (Spanish Socialist Workers' Party) and the union associated with it, Unión General de Trabajadores [U.G.T.] (General Union of Workers)
        2. Partido Comunista de España [P.C.E.] (Communist Party of Spain)
        3. Partido Obrero de Unificación Marxista [P.O.U.M.] (Workers' Party of Marxist Union)
        4. Partido Sindicalista (Syndicalist Party)
        5. Confederación Nacional de Trabajo [C.N.T.] (National Confederation of Labor, the Anarchist trade union)
        6. Federación Anarquista Ibérica [F.A.I.] (Iberian Anarchist Federation, not a party officially)

II. The Right

    A. Republican Parties
        1. Partido Radical (Radical Party)
        2. Derecha Liberal Republicana (Liberal Republican Right), Partido Progresista (Progressive Party), Partido Republicano Conservador (Conservative Republican Party)
        3. Partido Agrario (Agrarian Party)
        4. Partido Liberal Demócrata (Liberal Democratic Party)

5. Confederación Española de Derechas Autónomas [C.E.D.A.] (Spanish Confederation of Autonomous Rightist Groups)

B. Autonomist Parties
   1. "Lliga" Regional de Cataluña (Regional League of Catalonia)

C. Monarchist Parties
   1. Renovación Española (Spanish Renovation)
   2. Comunión Tradicionalista (Traditionalist Communion)
   3. Acción Española (Spanish Action)

D. Authoritarian Parties
   1. Partido Nacionalista Español (Spanish Nationalist Party)
   2. Juntas Ofensivas Nacional Sindicalistas [J.O.N.S.] (National Syndicalist Offensive Groupings)
   3. Falange Española (Spanish Phalanx)

4. Harry Eckstein, *Division and Cohesion in Democracy* (Princeton, N.J.: Princeton University Press, 1966), p. 265.

5. The reader must bear in mind that when the author uses words like "condemn" and "illegitimate," he does so with the full impact of these terms intended. This is not the condemning of one party by the others that takes place within the tempered intemperance of the British parliament, for example. This is condemning done with the force of ostracism or, more typically for Spain, with the force of an auto-da-fé.

6. For an explanation of the term "enemy" in this context, see William Ebenstein, *Today's Isms* (Englewood Cliffs, N.J.: Prentice Hall, 1961), pp. 106-107. For basic concepts of the continental European systems, see Gabriel A. Almond, "Comparative Political Systems," *The Journal of Politics* 18 (August 1956): 391-409.

7. Among the best accounts of the Communists in Spain is the study by Burnett Bolloten, *The Grand Camouflage* (New York: Praeger Publishers, 1961).

8. After the overwhelming defeat of the Left in the elections of November, 1933, Acción Republicana collapsed; to replace it Azaña created Izquierda Republicana (Republican Left), which had great success in the elections in February, 1936 as part of the Popular Front.

9. See pp. 37-38 this study.

10. This is precisely what happened after the electoral success of the Popular Front in February, 1936. The conservative Catholic president Alcalá Zamora was voted out of office and replaced by Manuel Azaña.

11. The coalition was dominated by the Partido Socialista Obrero Español (Spanish Socialist Workers' Party) and Acción Republicana (Republican Action) under the leadership of Manuel Azaña.

12. For a comparison to the French Senate in the Third Republic, see David Thomson, *Democracy in France*, 5th ed. (New York: Oxford University Press,

1964), pp. 91-101.

13. For an in-depth analysis of the relationship between electoral mechanics and systemic stability, see Maurice Duverger, *Political Parties* (London: Methuen and Co., Ltd., 1954), Book II, "Political Systems."

14. Brenan, *The Spanish Labyrinth*, p. 260.

15. See p. 24 this study.

16. This statement about clerical poverty might be difficult for the average American to accept. If he is a traveler and has been to Spain only as a tourist, the Catholic Church to him is the great cathedrals, monasteries, and convents and their staggering treasuries filled with gold, silver, and jewels. This he cannot equate with penury. If he is not a traveler, and, therefore, believes that all clergy everywhere lives like American clergy (both Protestant and Catholic), then he is simply wrong. The American Catholic clergy, whether secular or ordered, lives comfortably or at the very least never, ever knows want. The Spanish clergyman who does not have a fashionable parish or who is not a member of a rich order even today lives humbly. In most parishes, he lives poorly. He lived even more poorly in the 1930s. The class structure in Spain still applies and applied then to religious as well as to lay society.

17. Exact figures for illiteracy for 1930 are difficult to come by. *Whitakers's Almanac* (London, 1936), p. 65, gives the figure at 44 percent but does not state the source of its statistics.

Figures based on the Spanish census for 1920 put illiteracy at 44 percent out of a population of 16,700,750 and for 1940 at 23.2 percent out of a population of 20,870,455. Around 1930 primary school enrollment per 100 children from ages five to fourteen was 45. From United Nations, Educational, Scientific, and Cultural Organization, *World Illiteracy at Mid-Century*, 1957, pp. 103 and 166.

18. Given the extent of child labor in Spain, where even today, with compulsory education to the age of fourteen, the state shuts its eyes to the illegal employment of school-age children in the full-time work force, this percentage was probably inflated.

19. Stanley G. Payne, *Politics and the Military in Modern Spain* (Stanford, Calif.: Stanford University Press, 1967), p. 241. The officer-soldier ratio was about twice as great as that in the French army.

20. Ibid., p. 268.

21. Ibid., p. 275.

22. See p. 54 this study.

23. See p. 53 this study.

24. De la Souchère, *An Explanation of Spain*, p. 146.

25. Franz Borkenau, *The Spanish Cockpit* (London: Faber and Faber Ltd., 1937), pp. 48-49.

26. Tamames, *La República, la Era de Franco*, p. 178.

27. *The Spanish Labyrinth*, pp. 259-60.

28. After the elections in November, 1933, C.E.D.A. supported the rightist Radical government, but C.E.D.A. deputies had occupied no cabinet seats until October, 1934. Initially none of the cabinet posts was offered to Gil Robles, the bete noire of the Left.

29. "Four Republican leaders, Azaña, Felipe Sánchez Román (head of the most moderate of the small Left Republican groups), Diego Martínez Barrio (leader of the most liberal part of the Radicals . . .) and Miguel Maura all dispatched virtually identical notes to the president condemning the action and announcing that they broke off all association with the 'existing institutions' of the country. This *pronunciamiento* of the middle-class left and liberals was designed to place pressure on Alcalá Zamora [the president] to withdraw confidence from Lerroux [the prime minister] and call new elections. Its promulgators evidently expected support from a Socialist general strike. With even middle-class liberals unwilling to tolerate the functioning of parliamentary democracy under the constitution, the extremists swung into action." Payne, *The Spanish Revolution*, p. 149.

30. Englebert Dollfus proclaimed himself dictator of Austria in March, 1933, dissolved the legislature, outlawed political parties, and abolished civil rights. He did this, he claimed, to preserve Austrian independence against nazism. He was assassinated by Austrian Nazi rebels in July, 1934.

31. "Legitimacy is denied in the name of opposition of a 'true' majority against a 'false majority.' The distinction which everyone admits in theory between the *pays légal* (the majority that expresses itself through electoral and institutional devices) and the *pays réel* (a true but invisible majority) is very old. Formulated in these terms on the extreme right . . . it has often been utilized by others." Alfred Grosser, "France: Nothing But Opposition" in Robert Dahl, ed., *Political Oppositions in Western Democracies* (New Haven, Conn.: Yale University Press, 1966), p. 284.

32. In a subsequent reorganization of the cabinet in May, 1935 (seven months after the October revolution), Gil Robles became minister of war, yet no coup took place against the Spanish Republic as the Left had predicted Gil Robles would engineer if he were given a position of power.

33. *The Spanish Revolution*, p. 155.

34. According to Brian Crozier, however, those same troops had been called in by Azaña to put down the Sanjurjo uprising in 1932. *Franco* (Boston: Little, Brown and Co., 1967), p. 142.

35. *Spain*, p. 435. Emphasis added.

36. Borkenau, *The Spanish Cockpit*, p. 56.

37. Stanley G. Payne, "The Army, the Republic and the Outbreak of the Civil War" in Raymond Carr, ed., *The Republic and the Civil War in Spain* (London: Macmillan and Co., Ltd., 1971), p. 89.

38. Brian Crozier, *Franco* (London: Eyre and Spottiswoode, 1967), pp. 153-54.

39. *Spain*, p. 447.

40. Ibid., p. 448.

41. *The Spanish Revolution*, p. 181.

42. Ibid., p. 176. The present author is fully aware that pardoning a general whose oath demands allegiance to legally constituted civilian authority is of different significance from pardoning civilian insurrectionists of varying degrees of complicity. But in the eyes of the opponents of each pardoning, the

action was symbolic of contempt for the political system.

43. Ibid., p. 177.

44. *Spain*, p. 455.

45. Tamames, *La República, la Era de Franco*, p. 238.

46. *Franco*, pp. 137-38.

47. "The Army, the Republic and the Civil War," in Raymond Carr, ed., *The Republic and the Civil War in Spain*, p. 95.

48. José Antonio (as he was and still is referred to without the surname attached) was the son of the dictator General Miguel Primo de Rivera. He was imprisoned when the Popular Front outlawed the Falange in March, 1936.

49. Crozier, *Franco*, pp. 167-86.

50. Payne, "The Army, the Republic and the Civil War," in Raymond Carr, ed., *The Republic and the Civil War in Spain*, p. 96.

51. *Franco*, p. 165. Given revelations in the United States since Watergate about the F.B.I. and the C.I.A., this author will let the irony reverberate. Still, Crozier's statement is a chilling thing to read.

52. Harry Eckstein, *Division and Cohesion in Democracy* (Princeton, N.J.: Princeton University Press, 1966), p. 229.

53. Bernard Crick, *In Defense of Politics* (Baltimore, Md.: Penguin Books, 1964), p. 21.

54. Alfred Grosser, "France: Nothing But Opposition," in Robert Dahl, ed., *Political Oppositions in Western Democracies*, p. 284.

55. Stanley Hoffmann, "Protest in Modern France" in Morton Kaplan, ed., *The Revolution in World Politics* (New York: John Wiley & Sons, 1962), p. 69.

56. *An Explanation of Spain*, pp. 29-30.

57. V. S. Pritchett, "Spain," *Holiday* 37 (April 1965):63.

58. *Division and Cohesion in Democracy*, p. 234.

59. Ibid., pp. 239-40.

60. Ibid., p. 244.

61. Ibid., p. 243.

62. Ibid., pp. 248-49.

63. For interesting, if somewhat limited, views of Spanish society see Michael Kenny, *A Spanish Tapestry, Town and Country in Castile* (Bloomington: Indiana University Press, 1961) and J. Pitt-Rivers, *People of the Sierra* (London: Weidenfeld and Nicolson, 1954).

64. See Stanley G. Payne, *Politics and the Military in Modern Spain*, chaps. 12 and 14 and by the same author, "The Army, the Republic and the Outbreak of the Civil War," in Raymond Carr, ed., *The Republic and the Civil War in Spain*, pp. 79-107. See also Julio Busquets, *El Militar de Carrera en España* (Barcelona: Ediciones Ariel, 1967).

65. Gerald Brenan has a marvelously insightful footnote in *The Spanish Labyrinth* (p. 20) describing indirectly the quality of the Civil Service well into the twentieth century: "Romanones in his *Notas de Una Vida* (p. 71) [which covers the period 1868 to 1912] remarks that elections in Spain are won by offering jobs and by possessing friends. In explanation of this, he gives the following extract from one of the daily papers:

Today the Alcalde [the mayor] of Madrid, the Conde de Romanones has resigned. Tomorrow a special train will leave for Guadalajara [Romanones' home town] with employees of the municipality who were appointed by him and are now being replaced!

This notice, which was published to annoy him, in fact did him, he says, a great deal of good."

66. *Division and Cohesion in Democracy*, p. 252.

67. Gabriel A. Almond and G. Bingham Powell, *Comparative Politics* (Boston: Little, Brown and Co., 1966), pp. 32-33. The authors define secularization of culture as "the process whereby traditional orientations and attitudes give way to more dynamic decision-making processes involving the gathering of information, the evaluation of information, the laying out of alternative courses of action, the selection of a course of action from among these possible courses, and the means whereby one tests whether or not a given course of action is producing the consequences which were intended." Ibid., pp. 24-25.

68. Lucian W. Pye, *Aspects of Political Development* (Boston: Little, Brown and Co., 1966), pp. 62-67.

69. I have not spoken before about the Gallegan subculture with its own language (not dialect) and literature nor have I spoken about Gallegan home rule because not every fact can be detailed in a short monograph. Moreover, the Gallegans were the weakest regionalist group, yet they were sufficiently strong and vocal to be represented by a leftist political party that returned delegates to the Cortes during the Constituent Assembly and during the first biennium, the Organización Regional Autonomista Gallega—O.R.G.A. (Gallegan Autonomist Regional Organization).

70. Because the hybrid electoral system in the Second Republic was neither a proportional nor a plurality one, exact analysis cannot be made, but interesting observations about bloc voting (or "crystallized majority") can be read in A. J. Milnor, *Elections and Political Stability* (Boston: Little, Brown and Co., 1969), pp. 25-26.

71. *Aspects of Political Development*, p. 65.

72. For example, only now can the Soviet Union allow a certain amount of thawing of the rigid revolutionary doctrine, its leaders relatively secure in the knowledge that the range of options will lie within the limits of Communism. The United States has been the quintessentially pragmatic polity because the range of choice in the overwhelming majority of circumstances has always kept within the confines of liberal democracy.

73. *Spain, 1808-1939*, pp. 614-15.

PART 2
THE CIVIL WAR

¡Viva la Muerte!
Long Live Death!
    —*José Millán Astray*

We are going to exalt national sentiment with insanity, with paroxysms, with whatever need be. I prefer a nation of lunatics.

    —*Ernesto Giménez Caballero*

4
The Two Camps

An analysis of the internal politics of the two camps after the start of the Civil War may help to indicate why the Loyalists (as the republican defenders came to be called) lost and why the Nationalists (as the Rebels preferred to call themselves) won. Before the analysis is presented, however, certain facts about the war should be made clear.

The Setting

It should be understood that the Civil War was a Spanish event erupted from causes uniquely Spanish, dramatically but only peripherally associated with the larger political issues of Europe in the 1930s. The European powers became involved in a Spanish crisis; Spain was not acting out its version of a larger European drama irrespective of Franco's pose as the savior of Western civilization. Had there been no communist Russia, no nazi Germany, no fascist Italy, there still would have been the Spanish Civil War. This statement does not ignore the fact that the totalitarian powers had keen interest in the events taking place in Spain and that already before the war began they had been in touch with those Spanish forces that afterward were to find themselves on opposite sides of the trenches. Nor does it ignore the fact that, without the intervention of Germany and Italy on the side of the Rebels and of the Soviet Union on the side of the Loyalists, the war may have had a different ending. But the ending would still have been a Spanish phenomenon.

It should also be understood that the involvement of the Germans, the Italians, and the Russians, and the noninvolvement of the British and the French (and the Americans, for that matter) had everything to do with their own domestic and international politics and little to do with a disinterested concern for the plight of the Spanish belligerents. When the Spanish hostilities erupted, those European powers that later be-

came the major aggressors in World War II saw an opportunity to maneuver for strategic geographic advantage on the Iberian peninsula even
while those who became the major victims preferred to think that
noninvolvement in the Spanish conflict could prevent the inexorable
European Armaggedon. Britain and France, for domestic and international reasons just as self-serving as those of Germany, Italy, and the
Soviet Union, denied to the Republic the aid it sought and formalized
that denial in the Non-Intervention Pact designed to keep all material
assistance not only from the Rebels but from the Loyalists as well. The
pact was signed in August, 1936, by France, Great Britain, the Soviet
Union, Germany, and Italy. It assuaged the French and particularly the
British, who wanted peace above all else and who thought that by
refusing to help Spain the European war already smoldering could in
some way be prevented. The pact was doggedly complied with by the
French and the British in the face of its blatant flouting by the Germans,
the Italians, and the Russians, who cynically respected the pact when the
Spanish side each was aiding temporarily needed no assistance but who
ignored it when once again help was sought. Hugh Thomas, in
speaking of the committee created to oversee the operation of the pact,
comments: "Thus was born the Non-Intervention Committee, which
was to graduate from equivocation to hypocrisy and humiliation and
which was to last out the Civil War."[1]

Finally, it should be understood that the charade of nonintervention
made purely academic the issue of the rightness or wrongness, legality or
illegality of aid given to the Rebels. If, under international law, the
legitimate Spanish government had the right to seek aid from other
governments for its survival, why, then, was that assistance denied by
major powers who proclaimed their respect for international law—
Great Britain, France, and the United States—while at the same time
help was granted to the Rebels by those nations who proclaimed their
contempt for it—Germany and Italy?

The Republican Camp

The blow dealt by the rebel generals in July, 1936, shattered republican Spain into myriad, contentious pieces. For the duration of the war,
much of the energy of the republican central government was spent in
trying to put back together those antagonistic and independent shards.
Immediately following the pronunciamiento, independent self-governing juntas proliferated throughout republican Spain in villages, towns,
cities, and provinces. Each junta was independent of the other, and all
were independent of Madrid, which was unable to maintain national

unity because it had no effective armed forces to carry out its orders.[2] In addition to the juntas, committees sprang up in the factories and on the farms, which ceased to be private property and became the possession of collectives. Even small independent farmers, shopkeepers, and family entrepreneurs—men little more than peasant or proletariat themselves —were forced to give up their holdings and join the collectives, often becoming employees on their own property and as a consequence becoming silent but intransigent foes of the chaotic Republic. The committees and juntas would brook no interference in their dogmatic rule, and they indulged in what de Madariaga calls "the two ruling passions of the Spaniard: separatism and dictatorship."[3] Discipline was maintained within these autonomous units by militias loyal not to republicanism but to the ideology that inspired the particular local governing body—here communist, there socialist, or anarchist. Order ceased to exist as the masses yielded to orgies of destruction—wrecking churches and pillaging their treasuries, celebrating parodies of the mass and dressing in ceremonial religious garments (the classic masquerade among Spanish revolutionists), killing priests and nuns and members of the old elite, and burning public records, particularly deeds to land and property.[4] Republican Spain witnessed an explosion of idealism and violence from the lower classes, who saw the military uprising as the occasion for the revolution that would change forever the political, economic, and social structure of the country. Behind the republican lines another civil war erupted that was oftentimes as deadly as that being waged between the Rebels and the Loyalists. About the social revolution within the war, Hugh Thomas asks and answers:

> Who were the killers? In general they can only be understood as the final explosion of a mood of smouldering resentment which had lain beneath the surface in Spain for generations. In fact, many of the killers . . . were butchers of the sort that all revolutions spawn; many actually enjoyed killing and even gained from it near-sexual pleasure. But most were not of this kind. The Socialists and Communists who formed part of murder groups seem to have killed members of the *bourgeoisie* as part of a military operation, thinking that the battle was being fought on all fronts all the time and that he who did not strike first would himself be struck. The Anarchists of the F.A.I. and C.N.T. were different once more. They killed as if they were mystics, resolved to crush forever all the material things of this world, all the outward signs of a corrupt and hypocritical *bourgeois* past. When they cried "Long live Liberty" and "Down with Fascism," while some unjust steward was dying, they voiced deep passion of fearful sincerity. Many of those captured in Barcelona were taken thirty miles down the coast to be shot overlooking the superb Bay of Sitges. Those

about to die would pass their last moments on earth looking out to sea in the marvelous Mediterranean dawn. "See how beautiful life could have been," their assassins seemed to be saying, "if only you had not been a *bourgeois*, and had got up early and had seen the dawn more often—as workers have had to do."[5]

Thomas then adds a trenchant but macabre footnote: "If the Anarchists had not spent so much petrol driving future victims to beautiful places to die, and trying to burn churches to the ground, the task of their armed forces against the Nationalists in Aragon in August would have been a good deal easier."[6]

At issue in this civil war within the Republic inside the larger Civil War between the Republic and the Nationalists was the question of priorities. Which should be pursued first—the larger or the smaller civil war? Should all the energies be used to defeat the Rebels, delaying the revolution until the war was won, or should the revolution be carried on simultaneously with the larger Civil War and given precedence over it if necessary? The moderates—primarily the moderate socialists and the republicans—believed that the larger war should be pursued to the utmost. The extremists—particularly the anarchists in the F.A.I. and the C.N.T.—fervently believed that the revolution should take place while the larger war was being waged, delaying the pursuit of the latter if the former could not be achieved. The moderate leaders knew that radical change would alienate all those elements in republican Spain that saw the Civil War not as the catalyst of revolution but as the defense of liberal democracy. They also believed that revolution within the Republic would frighten away support from the Western democracies. Moreover, the moderate elements within the Republic were well aware that the constitution of 1931 was still in force. The Rebels had repudiated it, but the existing Republic was still being governed under its provisions. The revolution demanded by the extremists would be unconstitutional. If profound systemic change did take place for which there was no mandate from the people, the constitution would become a dead letter and the Republic itself would cease to exist. If this were to occur, there would be no sovereign government and no rebel band but merely two forces of equal legitimacy (or equal illegitimacy) fighting to create a new nation-state.

To the moderate voices in the Republic was added that of the Communist party—a paradox that makes sense only if the international stratagem of the Soviet Union during the mid-1930s is understood. The Kremlin leaders had ordered the Communist parties within the European democracies to join with socialist and bourgeois republican parties to form popular front governments as a defense against fascism. When the military rebellion took place in Spain, the Russian leaders realized that the Republic to which the Spanish Communist party was theoretically allegiant could not wholeheartedly and successfully fight the Rebels while torn by fratricide. They realized, too, that the collapse of the Republic would turn Spain, if not into an ally of Mussolini and Hitler, then at least into a supporter of their anticommunist policy. If, on the other hand, the Republic were victorious—particularly with indispensable Russian aid[7]—postwar Spain would be communized, the revolution would take place automatically and effortlessly, and the Soviet Union would have a totally dependent ally in Western Europe. Following directives from Moscow, the Spanish Communist party supported the all-out war against the Rebels, delaying the revolution until victory. For this, the Communists were branded as counterrevolutionaries by the militant socialists and by the anarchists. The latter had been enemies of the Communists since the split between Marx and Bakunin in the First International.[8] The hatred had deepened after the creation of the Soviet state in the 1920s, which in the eyes of the anarchists was no less repugnant because it was proclaimed in the name of the people. The state qua state was an ideological aberration. Thus, any policy which had its origins in Moscow was anathema to the anarchists irrespective of its logic, and the logic, if not the spirit, of the Communists during the Spanish Civil War was unassailable.

Because the anarchists sought immediate revolution and because they were the dominant force in the early, bohemian months following the rebellion, certain relatively moderate elements within republican Spain swelled the ranks of the Communist party because at that point it appeared to represent stability and caution, an absurdity that has confounded world opinion to this day. Raymond Carr writes:

> The Jacobin paradox—that a party whose revolutionary credentials and ultimate revolutionary intentions are above reproach is best equipped to risk a policy of temporary social conservatism—brought the Communist party a flood of recruits. Its membership rose from perhaps 40,000 in July, 1936, to 250,000 by March, 1937, and in the process it almost ceased to be a workers' party.[9]

The Spanish Communist party gradually became the major force within the Republic primarily because it was the sole conduit for the aid coming from the Soviet Union, whose leaders parceled out their generosity in proportion to the Party's control of republican politics. The civil war within the Civil War was relentlessly ground down by the

Communists as they reestablished the authority of the central government and built a republican army to replace or absorb the militias that were more loyal to their parent organizations (like the U.G.T., the F.A.I., the C.N.T., for example) than they were to the Republic. The Communists were never completely successful, however. The party's heavy-handed tactics dictated from the Kremlin offended Spanish national pride and alienated even ardent supporters like Largo Caballero, whom the Communists had made prime minister and whom they later removed from that post when he became too independent, too "Spanish." It became obvious to some leaders of the Republic that Soviet international policy was taking precedence over national Spanish needs. Moreover, international animosities within the Communist world infected the Spanish scene. This was particularly true in Catalonia, where dissident Trotskyite sympathizers had organized their own anti-Stalinist Marxist party, the Partido Obrero de Unificación Marxista (Workers' Party of Marxist Unification). The methods used by orthodox Communists to purge communist heretics within the Republic were as draconian as the methods used against the rebel enemy.[10]

As de Madariaga writes, the Republic "was a true revolutionary hydra with a Syndicalist, an Anarchist, two Communist, and three Socialist heads, furiously biting at each other."[11] The third socialist head, in addition to the moderate and radical ones within the major socialist party (the Democratic Socialist Workers' party) was the Partido Socialista Unificado de Cataluña (Unified Socialist Party of Catalonia) affiliated wtih the Communist Third International. The second Communist head was the Communist affiliate in the Catalan party.

The Nationalist Camp

The symbolism of the hydra could be applied appropriately to the Nationalist camp as well as to the Loyalist with one essential difference: the heads knew who the enemy was. Each of the groups supporting the rebellion had different ideas about the kind of Spain that would succeed the Republic, but each knew that first of all the Republic had to be destroyed. Perhaps had the rebellion been initially successful, the many hydra heads of Nationalist Spain would have attacked one another in the same way as did those of the Republic, but this possibility was foreclosed by the conversion of the rebellion into civil war and by the unity imposed upon the Rebels by Franco.

Military unity was achieved as of September 30, 1936. Before the uprising, the rebel generals had thought that Spain would fall easily into their hands following the pattern of the pronunciamientos in the nineteenth century. When their plans did not materialize (and the word "plans" is in reality misused because there were few plans in the sense of a carefully thought out strategy since immediate victory had been taken almost for granted), it became obvious that the rebellion would turn into civil war. To be successful the war would require the order and discipline achieved only through unity of command. Thus the Junta de Defensa Nacional (Junta of National Defense), which had been in command of the rebellion since July 24, would be inadequate for the task. General Sanjurjo, who should have become the commander in chief, had been killed on July 20 in the crash of the plane flying him from exile in Portugal to join the Rebels in Spain. General Mola, who had set up the junta and who had been the creative force behind the rebellion, logically should have been Sanjurjo's successor, but the fates decreed otherwise and smiled instead upon Franco.

The rise of Franco has something of the touch of fortune about it. Perhaps it was for this reason that, as Crozier states, Franco—at forty-four years of age the youngest general in Europe—allowed himself to accept what his wife, Carmen Polo de Franco, already believed: "That a divine hand had guided his destiny; that God had chosen him as saviour of Christian Spain."[12] By September, 1936, Franco was in a position that made his choice as supreme commander seem inevitable yet totally fortuitous. In the spring of 1936 the republican government had reassigned several officers whose loyalty to the regime seemed questionable. Mola was transferred from Morocco to Pamplona. Goded was restationed in the Balearic Islands, and Franco was posted to the Canaries. When the rebellion broke out, Franco was flown from the Canary Islands to Morocco, where he took command of the finest fighting units in the Spanish army—the Regulares, made up of Moorish recruits, and the Tercio Extranjero, the Spanish Foreign Legion. Between July 29 and August 5 these troops were flown into Spain in German aircraft[13] and under Franco's leadership established important bridgeheads in Andalusia and Extremadura and began the march to Madrid. (How different would the situation have been had Mola not been transferred to Pamplona from Morocco, where it would have been he and not Franco who commanded the Moroccan army? How different would the situation have been after the uprising had the crucial decision not been made by Hitler and Mussolini to lend pilots and aircraft to transport that army to the mainland?) Mola had no battlefield successes in northern Spain to match those of Franco in the South, nor could his troops compare to the tough and seasoned soldiers from North Africa. His inability to take Madrid particularly weakened his initial advantage. In short, Franco commanded the most powerful army in Nationalist Spain. Moreover, the other generals who were members of the original conspiracy and who could have been Franco's competitors for leadership were dead. Sanjurjo was dead already in July. Goded, who flew from the Balearics to take command in anarchist-controlled Catalonia, was captured, tried, and shot in August. Fanjul, in command in Madrid, vacillated before the revolutionary populace, and was captured, tried, and executed a few days following the death of Goded. From those who met in Salamanca in late September, 1936, to choose the commander in chief, Franco emerged the leader. With ease his fellow officers chose him to be generalissimo. It was his political title that caused dissension. Would Franco be chief of state or head of government? Among others, Mola, who nourished political ambition, resisted the designation of Franco as chief of state, but he lacked the leverage—particularly military superiority—to impose his will. After negotiations that to this day remain unclear,[14] Franco was named "head of government of the Spanish state" but with a provision that made the restrictive title "head of government" meaningless and that allowed Franco to become, in power if not in name, head of state. The provision granted him "all of the powers of the new state."[15] In addition he was declared "generalissimo of the national land, sea, and air forces."[16] Franco officially took power on October 1, 1936, in Burgos (though he had already claimed it the day before in Salamanca) and kept it intact until his death on November 20, 1975.

In April, 1937, Franco moved to consolidate the power granted to him in the previous October. The Rebels were deeply divided over the political future of Spain. Even though they were in agreement that "communism" and "liberalism" had to be rooted out, their political differences, unless resolved, would weaken the Nationalist cause. Many army officers preferred some kind of military rule for postwar Spain, patterned perhaps after that of Miguel Primo de Rivera in the 1920s. The monarchists loyal to Alfonso XIII awaited his restoration or, if that were impossible, the restoration of the Alfonsine branch of the Bourbon house under some form of constitutional monarchy. The Carlists continued to support their pretender and championed a conservative, authoritarian state that would defend regional rights and the purity of Catholicism. The Falangists called for an authoritarian, syndicalist state that would enforce national unity and bring about socioeconomic reform, which in its sweep would resemble the revolution sought by the Left. The Falangists were divided among themselves, however. The major cleavage was along the line of seniority in the party. The camisas viejas (the old guard, literally the "old shirts") had joined the Falange in its early days before its massive growth following the elections of February, 1936. The *camisas nuevas* (the new guard, literally the "new shirts") comprised men of a variety of right-wing ideological persuasions and were looked upon by the old guard as opportunists. Yet the *camisas viejas* were themselves divided. One faction, the larger, followed Manuel Hedilla, the political heir of the founder of the Falange, José Antonio Primo de Rivera, jailed in Alicante (and secretly executed there on November 20, 1936).[17] The other faction claimed to represent a purer version of the doctrines of José Antonio, now called *el Ausente*—the "absent one," gone, perhaps to return, perhaps dead, but who nevertheless lived as the holy spirit of Falangism.

It was around this spirit of José Antonio—this charisma once removed—that Franco created his own party (or Movement as he preferred to call it; to the insurgents, the word "party" was part of the perverted vocabulary of liberal democracy). The techniques used by Franco to accomplish this seemingly impossible task are revelatory of the approach he took to politics throughout his career, an approach that goes far to account for his political longevity. Franco was aided in his task by Ramón Serrano Súñer, his brother-in-law and political advisor during the early years of his rule. But it was Franco's power alone that made the accomplishment possible, and thus it was Franco who can be considered to be the creator of the new party. This statement, too, is revelatory. In the almost forty years of Franco's regime, there was never a gray eminence working its will through Franco. If any man appeared to aspire to that position, he was done away with—not executed but dropped or, a favorite tactic of Franco, promoted.

The nucleus of Franco's movement was the fascist Falange Española de las Juntas de Ofensiva Nacional-Sindicalista—a fusion of the Falange Española (Spanish Phalanx), created by José Antonio, with the Juntas de Ofensiva Nacional-Sindicalista (National-Syndicalist Offensive Juntas, the J.O.N.S.), the product of the merger of two fascist groups, one founded by Onésimo Redondo y Ortega and the other founded by Ramiro Ledesma Ramos.[18] It is difficult to encapsulate the ideology of the final political amalgam, but Hugh Thomas describes the thinking of José Antonio, who became the leader and spokesman of the new Falange Española de las J.O.N.S.: "His speeches and writings leave the impression of a talented undergraduate who has read but not quite digested an overlong course of political theory."[19] It is safe to say that José Antonio (and by extension, the Falange Española de las J.O.N.S.) was romantic and poetic and dreamed of a unified, Catholic Spain, condemned class warfare and proselytized an authentic national syndicalism, anathematized liberalism, socialism, capitalism and traditional conservatism, yet called for revolutionary economic reform in language usually associated with the Left and not with the Right, all the while extolling violence and bloodshed and worshipping the dark goddess of eternal Spain—death.

The Falange was fascist in it extreme nationalism, its violence, its dreams of glory, its historic atavism, and most particularly in its irrationalism, the perfervid romanticism that degenerates into emotional excess. Yet it was not fascist in the pattern of the German or Italian parties because it professed a belief in God and in Catholicism with that religion's respect for the inviolability of man. The party and its ideology were uniquely Spanish. The appeal of the hybrid Falange was weak before the election of 1936, in which it failed to win even a single seat. Its early support by economic conservatives crumbled when the extent of the party's social and economic reformist program became clear. The party's distrust of the military (springing in large part from José Antonio's memories of the army's abandonment of his father in 1929)[20] and its fundamental antimonarchical sentiments (an aspect of its anticonservatism) alienated these two classic forces on the Right. Yet after the victory of the Popular Front in February, 1936, the Falange became the most militant antigovernmental force, and its ranks swelled with those panicked by their fear of the Left. Payne estimates that party membership doubled between February and the beginning of the war.[21] On March 14, 1936, the party was outlawed by the Popular Front government, and its leaders, including José Antonio, were jailed. The mystique was established.

This mystique Franco decided to turn to his own political use. He was aware that a war is more enthusiastically fought when the people have a cause around which to rally. The old conservative parties were in disrepute because of their parliamentary association. The Falange was now the only force on the Right with sufficiently wide appeal to symbolize the Nationalist crusade. The Carlists, united officially in the Comunión Tradicionalista (Traditionalist Communion), had a mystique superior to the Falange, but it was too narrow and too local. In an action which parallels in its impact and bravado the assumption of complete military and governmental power in September, 1936, Franco "captured" the two political groups, the Falange Española de las J.O.N.S. and the Comunión Tradicionalista, and forced them into an unnatural union called the Falange Española Tradicionalista y de las Juntas Ofensivas Nacional-Sindicalistas—the F.E.T. y de las J.O.N.S. It was proclaimed by decree on April 19, 1937, and became the only legal party in Nationalist Spain. (All political parties had been outlawed by the junta in July, 1936.) It remained the only party in Spain—with modifications in name and statutes—until 1976. Both the Falangists and the Carlists were incensed by Franco's extortion, but they were powerless to act. They could not revolt against him because the larger enemy still remained the hated Republic, a war against which would suffer because of internecine struggle within the Nationalist camp. Moreover, to forestall the possibility of rebellion, Franco imprisoned Hedilla (who had refused a proffered position within the new party) and exiled Manuel Fal Conde, the leader of the Carlist Comunión Tradicionalista. Once again, the fates smiled upon Franco. There was now no one left who could be his political rival. The return of José Antonio would have presented Franco with an impossible dilemma, but fortunately for Franco, José Antonio was dead. He was quickly transformed into a cult figure the dedication to whom spilled over to Franco, who encouraged the devotion. Even the co-founders of the Falange Española de las J.O.N.S. were dead. Onésimo Redondo was killed in July, 1936, fighting in the first campaign of the war, and Ledesma Ramos was executed in prison later the same year.

Articles 1 and 2 of the decrees of April 19, 1937, reinforced Franco's power as head of state and named him chief of the Movement, as the party was called. Franco was now head of government, head of state, generalissimo of the armed forces, and head of party. His control over Nationalist Spain was total. Following the end of the war, the Statutes of the F.E.T. y de las J.O.N.S., which had been approved for Nationalist Spain by Franco on August 4, 1937, were revised and officially approved for the entire nation on July 31, 1939. Chapter XII, Article 47, of the Statutes is particularly significant:

> The national Chief of the *F.E.T. y de las J.O.N.S.* who is supreme *Caudillo* of the Movement, personifies all values and honors. As author of the historic era in which Spain is gaining the possibility of achieving its destiny and thereby the deepest aspirations of the Movement, the Chief assumes full and absolute authority.
> *The Chief answers to God and to History.*[22]

By these provisions, Franco, now called the caudillo, was placed above the law where he remained until his death. The Statutes were modified by the Law of May 17, 1958, but Franco's power remained untouched.

The Two Camps Compared

It would be presumptuous to think that one could give definitive reasons for the outcome of a war. Suggestions have been offered here. Perhaps now some comparisons might be in order.

With few exceptions—token assistance given by Mexico, airplanes purchased in France at the very beginning of the war, and intermittent aid by way of France throughout the war—the Republic received no aid other than that from the Soviet Union. The famed International Brigades, although often manned by heroic idealists from around the world, were almost exclusively Communist in organization, their Communist origins many times disguised but obvious to those who looked with care. Russian aid was never wholehearted, however, and it was always linked to Comintern dominance within the republican government. Hugh Thomas comments: "With crablike caution . . . Stalin seems to have reached one conclusion, and one conclusion only, about Spain; he would not permit the Republic to lose, even though he would not help it to win. The mere continuance of the war would keep him free to act in any way. It might even make possible a world war in which France, Britain, Germany, and Italy woud destroy themselves with Russia, the arbiter, staying outside."[23] When it became obvious to the Russian leaders that such a war was not to take place in the way they had hoped, aid to Spain was drastically reduced. After the agreement in Munich in September, 1938, international events drew Soviet attention away from Spain and toward a reappraisal of its relationship with nazi Germany. Spain was no longer useful, and the Republic was abandoned.

The Communists had brought a large measure of unity to the Republic, but it was artificial, achieved not by Spaniards but by foreigners, or if by Spaniards, then by natives—men like Largo Caballero and Juan Negrín, who succeeded him and became the last prime minister of the Republic—subservient to a foreign power. Republican unity was a Russian accomplishment not an indigenous one, yet Communism had never been strongly attractive to the Spanish until the war began. In the first republican elections in July, 1931, the Communist party received not one seat in the legislature; in the elections in November, 1933, the party received one seat. In the elections of February, 1936, the Communists won 17 of the 272 seats on the Left out of a total of 484 seats in parliament.[24] The Communism associated with the Soviet Union was a weak force until the outbreak of the Civil War, when its power grew for reasons already seen. In short, the Communists, who had the greatest strength within the Republic after 1936, were either of foreign origins or of foreign inspiration.

The anarchists were the most powerful indigenous force on the Left within the Republic after the rebellion began, but the tragic flaw in anarchist doctrine precluded the very organization needed to achieve positive goals. Organization was contrary to anarchist thought.

Anarchism is primarily a state of mind unable to be made manifest. As a consequence, that most Spanish of ideologies was unable to engender the strength of its commitment in so many Spanish souls.

Regionalism—another powerful, indigenous force—also worked counterproductively to the republican cause. The Basques, in exchange for their support of the Popular Front coalition, finally were awarded their statute of home rule by the government on October 10, 1936— almost three months after the Civil War began, an unpropitious time for the beginning of decentralization. Moreover, the Basques were caught in a painful but self-created moral dilemma: These deeply Catholic people were fighting with the Loyalists, who were determined to rip the Church out of Spain. In Barcelona the regional government, the Generalitat, almost declared Catalan independence during the early euphoristic months of separatism following the near collapse of central governmental authority in Madrid after the outbreak of the war. The Generalitat went far beyond the powers awarded to it under the statute of home rule granted by the Republic in 1931. Moreover, the social revolution within the larger Civil War was especially fierce in Catalonia because of the strength of the anarchists and because of the internecine struggle among the Communists. In time Catalonia came to follow the lead of Madrid in the pursuit of the war, but it was neither a stable nor a tranquil relationship. Unfortunately for the Republic, the strongest indigenous forces fighting in its ranks represented the fissiparous elements of Spanish society.

The Nationalist cause, on the other hand, reached wellsprings that were indigenously Spanish and that were able to be effectively channeled. True enough, it tapped the dark waters of the Spanish source, but they were native waters nonetheless. Unity, order, hierarchy, nationalism, Catholicism are beliefs natural to Spain. The war against "liberalism," "communism," "Freemasonry," "atheism," "capitalism" was a crusade against concepts that many, many Spaniards considered to be aberrative and perverse. The Nationalists used as the instrument of unity the historic, deep-seated Spanish hatred for foreign ideas and ideologies. Nor did foreign intervention seem to compromise those sentiments. The assistance from nazi Germany and fascist Italy was no less self-serving than that from Communist Russia. Hitler and Mussolini were in Spain solely for whatever advantage might accrue to their countries—particularly influence in or, more desirably, control over the nation guarding access to the Mediterranean and lying astride the roads to North Africa. German influence on Franco was strong particularly through Serrano Súñer, an admirer of the nazi system. But once unity under the single command of Franco was achieved between

October, 1936, and April, 1937, there was no chance for the foreigners to play off faction against faction in the Rebel camp. Nor was either German or Italian aid able to be linked to direct *political* control within Nationalist Spain even though, as Donald Detwiler writes, "By the end of the Civil War, German *economic* interests had penetrated Spain and Spanish Morocco as never before, thanks to a ruthless policy of exacting contractual concessions from the Nationalists as the price of continued support."[25] Moreover, there was no German or Italian equivalent to the Comintern, no organized international movement to take precedence over Spanish interests and appear to be mortgaging Spanish birthrights. It is not possible to say precisely why Hitler and Mussolini continued to aid an associate as noncommittal and as ungrateful as Franco proved to be, but the aid continued throughout the war, and in Franco's mind it appeared to be accepted on his (i.e., Spanish) terms. Thus the forces fighting for the Nationalists represented indigenous, centripetal elements in Spanish society. The strongest centrifugal element—the intensely regional Carlists from Navarre—had made the choice between their religion and their autonomy and were committed, albeit reluctantly, to national unity.

The tragic victims of the war were the moderates in Spain. Those who found themselves behind the Nationalist lines learned to be silent if they were fortunate enough not to *be* silenced. Those who found themselves behind the Republican lines were caught in a viper's tangle in which all the ideologies were militant except liberal democracy, which was crushed. The Rebels, in repudiating the Republic, rejected liberal democracy along with it. The Loyalists, while professing to be fighting in democracy's name, lost sight of it completely as it drowned under the flood of more exigent doctrines. Perhaps it is for this reason that democracy has taken such a long time to regerminate in Spain: The seeds had been almost destroyed along with the plant and the roots during the Civil War.

Notes

1. Hugh Thomas, *The Spanish Civil War* (New York: Harper and Row, Harper Colophon Books, 1963), p. 264.

2. Most army officers who were able to do so defected to the Rebels. The Guardia Civil also went over to the Rebels. Only the Guardia de Asalto remained loyal to the Republic. There were, of course, exceptions in individual units of the police and the other armed forces.

3. *Spain*, p. 490.

4. For a vivid picture of this period see Part II, "A Diary in Revolution,

1936," in Franz Borkenau's, *The Spanish Cockpit*, pp. 64-170.
   5. *The Spanish Civil War*, p. 179.
   6. Ibid., p. 179.
   7. The Soviet Union was the only major nation in the world willing to help the Loyalists. Mexico—which could hardly be considered an important country in 1936—proffered little more than token assistance.
   8. See p. 39 in this study.
   9. *Spain, 1808-1939*, p. 661.
   10. See George Orwell, *Homage to Catalonia*, and Burnett Bolloten, *The Grand Camouflage* (London: Hollis and Carter, 1961) for an account of the Communists' attempted takeover.
   11. *Spain*, pp. 524-25.
   12. *Franco*, p. 219.
   13. This was the first airlift in history made necessary because, except for few craft, the navy, under the control of mutinous sailors who had killed their commanders, remained loyal to the Republic. The sea route from Morocco to Spain was closed.
   14. See Brian Crozier, *Franco*, p. 213, and Hugh Thomas, *The Spanish Civil War*, p. 403, for conflicting interpretations.
   15. Decree 138, September 29, 1936, Articles 1 and 2.
   16. Ibid.
   17. See p. 76 in this study.
   18. For a history of the Falange, see Stanley Payne's now classic study, *Falange* (Stanford, Calif.: Stanford University Press, 1961).
   19. *The Spanish Civil War*, p. 70.
   20. See p. 53 in this study.
   21. *Falange*, p. 98.
   22. "Falange española tradicionalista y de las Juntas ofensivas nacional-sindicalistas" in *Fundamentos del Nuevo Estado* (Madrid: Ediciones de la Vicesecretaría de Educación Popular, 1943), p. 36.
   23. *The Spanish Civil War*, p. 216.
   24. Tamames, *La República, La Era de Franco*, p. 54.
   25. "Spain and the Axis During World War II," *Review of Politics* 33 (January 1971): 36. Emphasis added.

PART 3
THE FRANCO REGIME

For the Spaniard it is not enough to have heaven guaranteed for himself; he must also have hell guaranteed for his neighbor.

—Anonymous

5
The Philosophical Foundations of the Franco Regime

The Thoughts of Franco

In order to understand the political evolution of the Franco regime, it is necessary to know the perspective from which Franco saw the Civil War. His view not only shaped the system he created, but it also placed him within the context of Spanish history, thereby beginning the long process of legitimization that was not finished, at least to Franco's satisfaction, until the third decade of his era. Calling this "the Franco era" is not meant to treat Franco hagiographically, much less to exalt him beyond the saints as would his idolators, but the period of his rule must be called "the Franco era" because it belonged almost exclusively to him alone. Not only did he govern longer than most of the rulers of Spain, but he also governed more personally with fewer influences from fewer people than did almost any leader except the ascetic, monastic autocrat Philip II, who, like Franco, governed from outside Madrid away from the everyday life of his subjects.

To Franco the war was a crusade to free Spain from her contamination by everything non-Spanish, and he saw himself as a fighter-monk who would lead the battle. "The spirit of criticism and reservation is a liberal thing which has no roots in the soil of our Movement, and I repeat to you once again that its tone is military and monastic, and to the discipline and patriotism of the soldier must be added the faith and fervor of the man of religion."[1] He spoke in medieval cadence and resembled nothing so much as a man from the Reconquest, ridding Spain not of the Moor and of the Jew, but of the republican, the liberal, the capitalist, the communist, the Freemason, and the atheist. The echoes of ¡Santiago y Cierre España! come thundering to the ears. Nationalist Spain was waging a revolution! "Doesn't a century of defeat and decadence demand a revolution? It does indeed—and a revolution in the Spanish sense that will destroy an ignominious century of foreign-inspired doctrines that have caused our death. . . . In the name of liberty, fraternity, equality and all such liberal trivia, our churches have been burned and our history destroyed."[2] In his speech celebrating the creation of the F.E.T. y de las J.O.N.S., he recalled the Carlists in the nineteenth century as defenders of ideal Spain against "the bastardized, frenchified, europeanized Spain of the liberals."[3] Franco envisioned a "Spain free of bastardy, treason, lodges [Freemasons], and internationals."[4] "We fight to free our people of the influences of Marxism and international communism. . . . By this struggle we wish to save the moral, spiritual, religious, and artistic values created by the Spanish people down through their glorious history, values which represent the foundation of our national and individual existence."[5] He spoke of "the triumph of truth over occult international forces."[6] He called his native Galicia "that simple and traditional Spain guarding our spiritual treasures without contaminating itself with democracy and liberalism." He spoke of a "new Covadonga"[7] (the city in Asturias where the Reconquest began). Franco rhapsodized about the future as the recapturing of a distant past: "The new Spain will be faithful to her ancient tradition, but she will develop progressively. We will not have our future regime based on democratic systems totally unsuited to our people. . . . We will found it on ideals more faithfully democratic and better fitted to the unique character of the Spanish race."[8]

Franco condemned both capitalism and communism. "Bourgeois capitalists spill more blood while making fabulous profit from Spanish lives. Foreign lodges and international committees may fight the sentiments of Nationalist Spain; they will achieve nothing against the strength of our ideals, the justice of our cause, the valor of our youth."[9] "We do not want a Spain dominated by a single group . . . either capitalist or proletarian."[10] Our victory constitutes "the triumph of economic principles in conflict with old liberal theories by whose myths colonialism was established over many sovereign states."[11] "The liberal world is dying, a victim of the cancer of its own errors, and with liberalism is crumbling commercial imperialism with its financial capitalism and its millions of unemployed. The happiness offered by the French Revolution was bartered for 'economic man' [*hombre mercancía*] and for commercial competition with its miserable workdays and its abandoned, neglected masses. Increased wealth was not accompanied by equitable distribution, and an important part of humanity now struggles against new forms of misery."[12] "They fool themselves who dream of establishing liberal democratic systems in Western Europe face to face with Russian communism. They err who speculate about liberal peace and bourgeois solutions; the world is marching along a different path."[13]

Franco saw the Civil War in a perspective larger than Spanish. Over and over during the early years of his regime, he harkened back to the theme of Spanish redemption of the West. "Just as Spain saved the world civilization at the battle of Lepanto, so today she has undertaken a similar historic act against the equally dangerous present threat."[14] "Once again Spaniards are given the glory of carrying, on the points of their bayonets, the defense of civilization, Christian culture, and the Catholic faith, and maintaining them like Don Quixote, marching with the courage, inspiration, and virtue that are the heart and sinews of Spain today."[15] "I want international opinion to know that our Spain is battling not only to achieve her own ends and survival but also to safeguard the rights and ideals of humanity, to save the immutable principles of Christian civilization and [to preserve] justice, progress, and work."[16] "I want . . . to convince France, Europe, and America—countries with religious people—that our war is not a civil war, a war of parties, a war of pronunciamiento, but a crusade of men who believe in God, who believe in the human soul, who believe in the good, in ideals, in sacrifice, who battle against men without faith, without morals, without nobility."[17]

To Franco, the enemy was communism. "In doing battle against communism, we believe we are aiding Europe because communism is a universal danger. If we go under, the threat will be greater for the rest of the world."[18]

> We are faced with a war that more each day takes on the character of a crusade, of historic greatness, of a transcendental struggle of peoples and civilizations—a war that, once again in history, has chosen Spain as the battleground of tragedy and honor on which to resolve itself and to bring peace to a world gone mad.[19]

Franco's words not only summarized his sentiments about the war but also functioned to place him in the perspective of Spanish history. It is not possible to know whether his words were carefully crafted or whether they flowed spontaneously from his facile and baroque Spanish rhetoric. If the former, they represent an astute political maneuver, if the latter, an extraordinary fortuity. Irrespective of their genesis, on them were built the first pillars of legitimacy for the uprising and for the man who was its leader. One can deduce that Franco reasoned in the following manner. Spain's destiny began with the Reconquest, whose pursuit created the unified nation-state. That solidarity in turn focused and released the national energies with which a new world was discovered and Catholicism was universalized. According to Franco's perspective, this was the first phase in the evolution of modern Spain, or as he called it, "the ideal and normative phase"[20] of Ferdinand and Isabel, Charles V, and Philip II, which was the model for all subsequent Spanish history. The second phase, which began in the eighteenth century and continued into the twentieth, was an ignoble period disfigured by foreign ideologies and foreign masters and by internal disintegration and corruption. Only the Carlists in the nineteenth century had kept alive authentic Catholic, hispanic values. The third phase, the present era, in which the united nation-state was once again established, began with the dictatorship of Miguel Primo de Rivera and was followed by the formation of the J.O.N.S. and of the Falange Española. Their merger and the subsequent merger of that union with the Comunión Tradicionalista to create the F.E.T. y de las J.O.N.S. marked the completion of the quest for solidarity; the price paid to protect the new life of the reunified Spanish nation-state was the Civil War.

What was the significance of Franco's philosophy for Spain's political future? With his words and deeds Franco began to build a foundation of legitimacy for the new regime. In his mind, the Nationalist Movement resumed the authentic evolution of Spanish history that had been interrupted generations earlier. The Second Republic had been the culmination of the illegitimate evolution of anti-Spain born of foreign contamination. Franco openly repudiated most of Spanish history back to the Golden Age, but he was careful not to condemn the institution of the monarchy, which, along with the Church, had maintained historic continuity. Yet he was equally careful not to announce when Spain would again become a monarchy. It was the unity of Spain that was traditionally legitimate and not its transient governmental form.

> If the time for the restoration should arrive, the new monarchy would of course have to be very different from that which fell on April 14, 1931: distinct or different not only in its content but also in the person who embodies it. If the moment should arrive, the monarchy would be a tie between . . . the youth who are now fighting and the glorious traditions of Spain.[21]

In the meantime, the Nationalist Movement would embody eternal Spain, and Franco would be his country's paladin.

The Organic Concepts

The political regime created and bequeathed by Franco is called an "organic democracy" and was institutionalized over a thirty-year period in the seven Fundamental Laws of the State, which together make up the Spanish constitution. Organic democracy sees man not as a solitary individual but as a member of several permanent, natural communities that magnify his being and define his existence. Inorganic (or what Franco and his followers disparagingly called "liberal") democracy treats man as an isolated entity. In theory he is politically free to act alone or to join with others, but in practice he is vulnerable to whimsical majorities or selfish minorities ultimately destructive not only to the integrity of the individual but also to the order and security of the state (the latter an abstraction existing apart from its citizens at a particular historical moment). Inorganic democracy gives one man one vote and allows him to be one in a majority with little commonality except an impermanent membership in a numerical preponderance. Organic democracy does not give one man one vote but instead offers him representation in a group with which he shares common experiences and values: the family, the municipality, and the syndicate. A Spaniard of organic persuasion once explained that when a man is asked to identify himself to a stranger he does so by giving three pieces of information: his name (above all his surname, his family name, since his given name alone does not adequately demarcate him); his place of residence (which in less mobile societies is usually the place of his birth and most probably of his death); and his occupation. Thus, according to that Spaniard's reasoning, man sees himself organically as a part of larger units and therefore should be represented politically in the same manner in which he identifies and delimits himself in time and space. Article 8 of the Law on the Principles of the National Movement, considered to be the most basic of the Fundamental Laws, enshrines the organic concept:

> The representative character of the political system is the basic principle of our public institutions. The participation of the people in the legislative and other functions of general interest shall be implemented through the family, the municipality, and the trade union [the syndicates] and other organically representative bodies recognized by law for this purpose. Any political organization whatever outside this representative system shall be deemed illegal.[22]

This way of considering political man is predemocratic, if by democracy one means liberal individualism, the eighteenth-century concept brought into Spain from France following the Revolution of 1789. It is not predemocratic, however, if one argues, along with Franco, that through the *fueros*[23] Spaniards had been practicing true democracy centuries before it was discovered in France or enjoyed by the rest of the world. Moreover, Franco associated authentic, organic democracy with the power and prestige of Spain at the height of her Golden Age and associated un-Spanish, unauthentic, inorganic democracy with the nadir of her shame and disgrace reached in the Second Republic.

> If one examines what we lost under the sign of inorganic democracy with its regimes of political parties and what we attained under unity and the organic system, we can compare their products. Under the first, Spain passed from the zenith of her glory, well-being, and power to the lowest point in her history, on the brink of falling apart. Under the second . . . we conquered international communism.[24]

Under the new regime created by Franco, Spain would recapture her past splendor, structured organically once again as she had been centuries earlier in the days of her hegemony. Moreover, Spain would serve as an example to the world and offer a method of sociopolitical organization that was a middle way between what Franco considered bankrupt liberal democracy and pernicious Soviet Communism:

> The people of the world are faced with the following dilemma: either to continue their divisions and revolutions, and the patching and mending of a system crumbling to pieces or to fall to communism . . . as the only viable solution for unity, authority, continuity, discipline, and efficiency.
> I am so bold as to affirm that between the worlds of Soviet enslavement and inorganic democracy can be found modern democratic solutions that are more just and efficient. Our regime—satisfying the longings for social justice, economic progress, and an improved standard of living— exemplifies an optimal solution that, while saving the essentials of our liberties, allows our nation mobility in a regime of unity, authority, continuity, and efficiency where democracy comes from man's natural organizations.[25]

The organic axioms have roots deep in the Spanish sociopolitical tradition, and it is in large part for this reason that they possess at least *theoretical* legitimacy for many Spaniards with the exception of those who are the philosophical heirs to the more recent liberal and Marxist traditions. These Spaniards, however, share the older organic tradition with their countrymen in much the same way that all Americans share the Puritan ethic (especially those who reject it most passionately) and in the same way that all Frenchmen inherit the Revolution of 1789. Traditional Spanish society was Catholic, layered, corporative, authoritarian, patrimonial, elitist, stratified, and hierarchical. To a great extent Spanish society remains that way.

The following extensive excerpts are from a study by Howard J. Wiarda. Mr. Wiarda is writing about Latin America and is looking back to Spain in an attempt to explain why the Spanish sociopolitical heritage in Latin America has been so tenacious (and so difficult to understand for the non-Iberic Latin).

If modern political analysis in the Northern European and Anglo-American tradition was to lead to the glorification of the accomplished fact and of political pragmatism, to materialism and the success theory, and to a unilinear, stage-by-stage conception of development which was also derived principally from the experiences of these nations, then Iberic Latin culture can surely claim as its basis a moral idealism, a philosophical certainty, a sense of continuity, and a unified organic-corporate conception of the state and society. This conception derives from Roman Law (one can still profitably read Seneca for an understanding of the Iberic-Latin tradition), Catholic thought (Augustine, Aquinas), and traditional legal concepts (the *fueros* or group charters of medieval times, the law of the *Siete Partidas* of Alfonso the Wise). In comprehending the Iberic-Latin systems, one must think in terms of a hierarchically and vertically segmented structure of class and caste stratifications of social rank orders, functional corporations, estates, judicial groupings and *intereses* (interests)—all fairly well defined in law and in terms of their respective stations in life—a rigid yet adaptable scheme whose component parts are tied to and derive legitimacy from the authority of the central state or its leader. The foundations for these systems lie in what Morse has called the "Thomistic-Aristotelian notion of functional social hierarchy,"and they find their major expression in the political thought of Spain's Golden Century.

.   .   .

Vitoria and Súarez stand as the great systems builders on which the Spanish empire and Iberic-Latin society were constructed. Their genius lay in fusing the older Thomistic conception and the system of juridical estates derived from Spanish customary law with the newer concept of absolute, state-building royal authority. There were important differences among the several writers mentioned, to be sure, but what is more striking are the common, unifying themes. All assume an ordered universe, all adopt the Thomistic hierarchy of laws, and all base their theories of state and society on Christian assumptions. All share, furthermore, a disdain for the common man; what they mean by popular government is feudal and aristocratic, based upon a restoration of the privileges or *fueros* of the Middle Ages, the power of the traditional estates, dominated by "natural elites", and without popular suffrage. Their view of society and the state is an organic one—the government is natural, necessary, and ordained by

God for achieving harmony among men. This conception is an almost inherently conservative one. In contrast to contract theory which, except in Hobbes, is individualistic, democratic, liberal, and progressive, organic theory subordinates human law to natural and divine law, is more tolerant of authority, slights the individual in favor of group "rights" or a superior "general will", accepts and justifies the status quo, reserves extensive powers for traditional vested interests, and leads inherently toward a corporate system which subordinates man to some allegedly higher end and unity.

The best form of government, therefore, is an enlightened monarchy or an all-powerful executive; there can be no "separation of powers" or "checks and balances" on the U.S. model. Rather, a monistic structure is required to keep peace and maintain the "natural" order. Extensive powers are also reserved for such corporate entities as the church, the municipalities, the landed and commercial elites, the guilds, the military hierarchy, and other vested and chartered interests. Organic theory in both church and state rejects liberal individualism and materialistic and secular conceptions that accompanied development in Northern Europe.[26]

The totality of power in the hands of Franco, the manipulative techniques by which he maintained it, and the devices of its perpetuation which he institutionalized in the Fundamental Laws were all precise manifestations of the organic concepts of society and politics analyzed by Wiarda. Ronald Newton, in describing the state in six-teenth-century Spain, could have been talking about the state as conceived and structured by Franco, each state an entity "with a remarkable stability, a stability achieved through the delicate balancing of opposing and ultimately antagonistic forces."[27] Franco's balancing was a way of achieving order, or from the viewpoint of organic theory, perhaps a way of preserving order conceptualized as a preexistent phenomenon to be discovered and maintained.

Careful students of British politics would have insights into organic theory, for similar ideas are a part of the intricate fabric of British sociopolitical thinking. What Samuel Beer calls Old Tory and Old Whig concepts of representation are organic in nature.[28] In Old Tory theory, the monarch embodied the state and represented the community as a whole above and apart from the three estates—King, Lords, and Commons. But the early Old Tory view of society was for all practical purposes absorbed by that of the later Old Whig.

> Nor . . . were the Whigs rugged individualists. Their conception of the society was not only hierarchic but corporate. Individuals were seen as members not only of the various ranks and orders of men but also of the local communities of villages and household, borough and shire, and it

was such bodies rather than isolated individuals that were regarded as the legitimate bases of representation in Parliament. Thus Burke, writing at the height of Whig ascendancy, attacked the philosophy of natural rights because it proposed "personal representation" and failed to recognize corporate personality.[29]

But England moved beyond Old Tory and Old Whig theories as she progressed toward modern, popular democracy. It could be said that Franco, in clinging to the ideas of organic democracy, tried to freeze Spain into a sociopolitical mold similar to that discarded by England a century and a half ago. It could also be said that the opponents of Franco and of his successor want to accomplish in Spain what the opponents of Old Tory and Old Whig ideas accomplished in England—the move toward political modernization and popular democracy.

Notes

1. *Palabras del Caudillo* (Madrid: Ediciones de la Vicesecretaría de Educación Popular, 1953), p. 317. All translations of Franco's works cited here are mine.
2. Ibid., p. 54.
3. Ibid., p. 11.
4. Ibid., p. 72.
5. *Pensamiento Político de Franco* (Madrid: Servicio Informativo Español, 1964), p. 33.
6. *Palabras del Caudillo*, p. 75.
7. Ibid., pp. 135-36.
8. *Palabras del Caudillo*, p. 365.
9. Ibid., pp. 26-27.
10. Ibid., p. 56.
11. Ibid., p. 118.
12. Ibid., pp. 524-25.
13. Ibid., p. 527.
14. *Pensamiento Político de Franco*, p. 34.
15. Ibid., p. 35.
16. *Palabras del Caudillo*, p. 376.
17. Ibid., p. 395.
18. *Pensamiento Político de Franco*, p. 38.
19. *Palabras del Caudillo*, p. 9.
20. Ibid., p. 11.
21. Ibid., pp. 346-47.
22. *Fundamental Laws of the State: The Spanish Constitution* (Madrid: Ministerio de Información y Turismo, 1972), pp. 43-46.
23. See pp. 14-16 in this study.

24. *Pensamiento Político de Franco*, p. 250.

25. Ibid., p. 254.

26. Howard J. Wiarda, "Toward a Framework for the Study of Political Changes in the Iberic-Latin Tradition: The Corporative Model," *World Politics* 25 (January 1973): 210-214.

27. Ronald Newton, "On 'Functional Groups,' 'Fragmentation,' and 'Pluralism in Spanish American Political Society,' " *Hispanic American Historical Review* 50 (February 1970): 12.

28. Samuel Beer, *The British Political System* (New York: Random House, 1974), ch. 9.

29. Ibid., p. 160.

6
The Political Evolution of the Franco Regime

The political evolution of the Franco regime can be divided roughly into four phases, each identified by basic systemic change: The first phase is almost coterminous with the Civil War, 1936-1939; the second extends from 1942 to 1947; the third from 1953 to 1958; and the fourth from 1959 to the death of Franco on November 20, 1975.

The First Phase: 1936-1939

Politically the war years witnessed (1) the creation of the F.E.T. y de las J.O.N.S. and the consolidation of absolute executive authority; (2) the initiation of the institutionalization of the Nationalist regime; (3) the proclamation of the Fuero de Trabajo (Labor Charter), a kind of social Magna Carta—the first of what would become the Leyes Fundamentales (Fundamental Laws) of the new Spanish state; and (4) the enactment of legislation, by decree of Franco, reestablishing the position of the Catholic Church in Spanish society, denationalizing confiscated property, instituting rigid press censorship, and restricting civil rights.

The Twenty-six Point Program and the Statutes[1] of the F.E.T. y de las J.O.N.S. formed the ideological bases of the new organic Spanish state, which, according to their provisions, would be unitary and Catholic and governed by a single executive responsible to no other than God and History.[2] Article 6 of the Twenty-six Point Program was fundamental. The state was declared to be a totalitarian instrument in the defense of the fatherland; all political parties and interest groups were abolished, and *inorganic* suffrage (i.e., universal suffrage, one person with one vote) was to be replaced by *organic* participation through the family, the municipality, and the syndicate. No legislature was created, however. Article 39 of the Statutes did provide for a National Council of the Movement (i.e., of the F.E.T. y de las J.O.N.S.), but its only function was to make recommendations to the caudillo in the event that he should seek them. It had no other power; moreover, all of its members were appointed by Franco and could be removed at his will. Neither the program nor the Statutes contained enabling legislation; as a consequence, their prohibitions were self-enacting but their provisions remained to be fulfilled.

The first steps toward governmental institutionalization were taken early in 1938. After October 1, 1936, when Franco was awarded supreme command, he had governed wth the aid of a provisional Junta Técnica (Technical Junta), whose duties were primarily military rather than political. When it became obvious that the rebellion had turned into a civil war that would last indefinitely, it also became clear that Nationalist Spain would require day-to-day political leadership. On January 30, 1938, Franco established the first permanent departments of state to be headed by full-time ministers appointed by the caudillo and responsible to him alone.[3] There still was no legislature. The government was to be composed of a prime minister (who was the caudillo) and his cabinet. This was not a collegial body, nor was the prime minister first among equals. In order to underscore this fact and to demonstrate that in his capacity as head of state the caudillo was responsible to no one, Franco was given the authority to make law: *"la suprema potestad de dictar normas jurídicas de carácter general"* ("the supreme power to dictate juridical norms of a general character").[4] Thus, as of January 30, 1938, Franco was not only head of state and head of government (power he had acquired on April 19, 1937), but also chief and sole legislator.

On February 1, 1938, Franco created his first cabinet. There were twelve cabinets during his near forty-year regime, and all displayed the pluralism that was characteristic of Franco's political technique.[5] Pluralism may appear to the reader to be an inappropriate term to describe what is popularly thought to have been a totally monolithic dictatorship, but pluralism did exist. It was not the pluralism of a democratic society in which each group theoretically is able to enter and compete freely within the political arena. The Franco regime operated within a relatively closed arena entry into which was possible but difficult, yet within the arena a variety of forces competed for a share of the spoils of power centered in Franco. Franco's authority was absolute until the moment of his death, but the authority was used to balance or mix those groups or institutions without whose support he would have been unable to rule: the army, the monarchists (both Alfonsine and Carlist), the hierarchy of the Catholic Church in Spain, the Movement, the great landowners, the powerful business interests, certain members of the aristocracy, and later the Opus Dei, a sociopolitical religious group. These groups and institutions set the limits of the Spanish political game. Within these perimeters Franco used his awarded powers with skill sufficient to keep any group from permanent ascendancy, thereby keeping his own authority superior and indispensable to the stability of the polity. Under Franco's manipulative control, the potentially antagonistic groups within the arena were kept in perpetual maneuver away from the permanent base of power, which was always the caudillo, yet sufficiently near to it so that from time to time each group could replenish its store of energy and patronage. Once the equilibratory mechanism had been put into motion during the war years, when each group feared the Republican enemy more than it distrusted its Nationalist allies, no one group could afford to jeopardize the operation of the mechanism without risking its own security. The groups together could have changed the entire structure of power, but that would have required more dispatch and unanimity than existed among rivals who tolerated but contemned one another. Moreover, once the structure were tampered with, those elements excluded from its operation either would have to be accommodated or would have to be resolutely suppressed. In fact, as the Franco regime began to age, those societal elements not within the perimeters of power did indeed begin to seek either entry into the enclosure (the growing middle class and the technocrats of the new industrial Spain, for example) or reorganization of the entire system (the working classes and the left-wing intellectuals, primarily). A discussion of these developments will be presented in Chapter 10. For now, it is important to see in operation the technique that kept Franco in power for almost four decades and from which Spain drew great benefit—if by benefit one is willing to accept peace and profound socioeconomic improvement without concomitant political growth and liberalization.

The elements conciliated in Franco's first cabinet were primarily the party (within it, both *camisas viejas* and *camisas nuevas*), the monarchists (both Alfonsine and Carlist), and the army. The oligarchy was conciliated by provisions in the Labor Charter, discussed in the next section of this chapter, and the Church was conciliated by legislation discussed in the last section of the chapter. Within the balance of the first cabinet were both German and British sympathizers. These sentiments were not important to appointments in the cabinets after 1945, but they are included in this analysis in order to give evidence of the extent of Franco's political adroitness in keeping the maximum number of factions allegiant and relatively content. Also included in the first cabinet were men of no political affiliation appointed because of their technical skills rather than the necessity to balance their power or demands. Men of this sort were to play a part in all subsequent cabinets. It should be clarified at once that by a man's political affiliation is meant that man's group identification. After April 19, 1937, there was only one party in Spain. Consequently, everyone in every public position had to be a Falangist, but a man was considered to be a Falangist for the sake of the blend or balance of forces only if his primary political identification was with the F.E.T. y de las J.O.N.S. The party will be discussed in Chapter 8, but it can be said here that Franco's Spain was never a party state nor was the Falange a state party. The F.E.T. y de las J.O.N.S. was only one of the groups within the limitedly pluralistic Spanish political system.

The *camisas nuevas* were conciliated by giving the Ministry of the Interior to Ramón Serrano Súñer, Franco's brother-in-law, a major voice in the creation of the F.E.T. y de las J.O.N.S. and a militant pro-German. The post traditionally controls internal security and would have put the Falangists (and in particular the *camisas nuevas*) in a position to infiltrate the police forces within Nationalist Spain, but Franco balanced this potential disturbance to his power fulcrum by creating for the duration of the war a special Ministry of Public Order headed initially by a military man, General Severiano Martínez Anido. The *camisas viejas* were conciliated by making Raimundo Fernández Cuesta, a colleague of José Antonio, secretary-general of the Movement.[6] Fernández Cuesta was also made minister of agriculture, a position of lesser importance within the governmental structure that diminished the prestige accompanying his appointment as secretary-general. (Franco gave and took away with the same hand.)

The Foreign Ministry and the position of deputy prime minister were given to the Count of Jordana. This appointment was splendidly intricate and plurally conciliative. Jordana was a general and an aristocrat. He was also sympathetic to Great Britain at a time when Franco's major support came from Germany, whose staunchest champion in Franco's entourage was Serrano Súñer. The army could feel conciliated because a post that traditionally should have gone to a civilian (and considering the times should have gone logically to a pro-German Falangist) went instead to a soldier respected by the democracies. Moreover, Jordana was an Alfonsine monarchist. The Ministry of Defense went to another military man who was also an Alfonsine monarchist, General Fidel Dávila Arrondo. (It is interesting to note that each of these generals differed in background and temperament, illustrating yet another aspect of Franco's amalgam: Jordana was a titled statesman; Martínez Anido, a feared and ruthless policeman who had crushed dissident groups in the early 1920s and had been named minister of the interior by the dictator Primo de Rivera; Dávila Arrondo, a simple soldier with no political affiliation but a man fiercely loyal to Franco.)

The Alfonsine monarchists were conciliated by the appointments of Jordana and Martínez Anido and by the appointment of another monarchist as minister of finance, Andrés Amado y Reygonband. The Carlist monarchists were conciliated by the appointment of the Count of Rodezno as minister of justice. The Carlists would also have liked the Ministry of Education with its vast potential for socialization, but that post went to another Alfonsine monarchist, Pedro Sainz Rodríguez. The Carlists did not have to be accommodated to the same extent as did the Alfonsine monarchists because the former were a smaller, less powerful group defending what was in reality a moribund cause. But they could not be ignored because their militiamen, the Requetés, were, along with the Moroccan troops, the finest soldiers in the Nationalist army. Moreover, the Carlists were the most militantly Catholic group in Spain, and Catholicism was Franco's strongest instrument of unity.

Adroitly, Franco allowed no group to control more than one or two vital centers of power. Moreover, these centers were often administered by the most intense rivals—for example, the army and the Falange, or the Falange and the monarchists, or the Alfonsine and the Carlist monarchists. Those who might have been potential threats to Franco's power were, for all practical purposes, prechecked by rivalry among the factions. Franco, therefore, except on rare occasions, was able to use and then discard an overly ambitious man without having to resort either to permanent exile, imprisonment, or execution because the threat could be considered to have been made not against Franco's *personal* power, but against the power of a rival faction. This was Franco's adaptation of "divide and conquer."[7]

The Fuero de Trabajo (Labor Charter) was decreed on March 9, 1938. After World War II it was officially converted retroactively into a Fundamental Law by Article 10 of the Law of July 26, 1947.[8] The name of the charter is significant. It invoked the ancient laws of Spain, those mythologized mountain *fueros* predating the Reconquest and those later *fueros* that came into being during the seven-hundred-year crusade. Franco, in choosing to revive this terminology, was once again, as in his speeches exhorting unification, invoking the hallowed names of the past, attempting to imbue the decree with legitimacy by association.

The charter was designed to secure for the working masses an honored place in the new Spain being created by the Nationalists. This warranty was necessary because the overwhelming majority of the laboring classes—proletariat and peasant—was pro-republican. Like so many of the early decrees, however, the Fuero was not accompanied by enabling legislation; its prohibitions were self-enacting but its provisions took years to be implemented. The Fuero guaranteed to each man the right to a job (i.e., stable employment) with a salary sufficient to maintain a family and working conditions in keeping with Christian dignity. It also provided for annual paid holidays and Sunday rest. The peasant was promised a small family farm and work during periods of unemployment. The guarantee of employment was of paramount importance because it was intended to compensate for the worker's being legally forbidden to unionize, to demonstrate, to engage in any form of what was called "worker resistance" (slowdowns or sitdowns, for example), or to strike. Strikes were considered to be offenses against the sovereign power of the state (*delitos de lesa patria*) and were punishable under the law.

The charter spoke to more than the workers, however. It guaranteed to the possessing class that private property would be respected, that capital was an instrument of production, and that the firm (the *empresa*) was the hierarchical unit of production under the leadership of its owner (the *patrón*). The enterprise had to contribute to the well-being of the entire national community, however, and the state had the right to fix the terms of employment and remuneration and to intervene in the development of the economy where private initiative was insufficient. Both employer and employee were to be included together in vertical syndicates set up for each occupation, but as shall be seen later, the syndicates harnessed the employees but were circumvented by the employers, particularly the large and powerful ones.[9]

When the Labor Charter in its original form, written in 1938, is compared to its revised form, the form in which it has appeared in all official publications since it was rewritten in 1947, an interesting transformation in diction appears. The original wording was extremist, reflective of the early anticapitalist and anticommunist bias of the Nationalist ideology. As the regime moved away from its initial totalitarianism, however, Franco eliminated all totalitarian references in official documents in order to make Spain more acceptable to the world, particularly after 1945. More evidence of this will be shown, but for the moment compare the introductory passage in the original Fuero to that in the official version rewritten in 1947 and amended by the Organic Law of the State of January 10, 1967. The original version reads as follows:

Reviving the Catholic tradition of social justice and of the lofty sense of humanity which inspired our imperial legislation, the national state, as a totalitarian instrument in the service of the integrated and syndicalist Fatherland and as a representative of the reaction against liberal capitalism and Marxist materialism, undertakes the task of realizing, with a militant, constructive, and deeply religious air, the revolution which Spain has had pending and which once and for all will return to the Spaniards the Fatherland, Bread and Justice.[10]

The revised version reads as follows:

Following the Catholic tradition of social justice and the high sense of human values that informed the legislation of our glorious past, the State assumes the task of offering to every Spaniard the guarantee of a country, the means of survival and justice.

Following the Labor Charter, other legislation was enacted by Franco's decree. In March, 1938, civil marriages were banned. Henceforth, all marriage ceremonies were to be performed in the Catholic Church under its requirements, provisions, and prohibitions. Divorce was made illegal retroactively to the Republican divorce laws enacted in 1932. Religious education was made compulsory in all schools. On May 3, 1938, the Jesuits were allowed to return to Spain. Already in July, 1937, the Spanish episcopate had signed a letter supporting the rebel cause, and in October of the same year the Vatican established diplomatic relations when Pope Pius XI appointed a nuncio to Nationalist Spain. In April, 1938, the Servicio Nacional de Reforma Económica y Social de la Tierra (National Service of Economic and Social Reform of the Land) was established to begin the return to the original owners most of the land nationalized during the Republic's agrarian reform program. That same month, on the twenty-second, the Press Law was decreed requiring that every publication in Spain be submitted to prior censorship. Under the provisions of this law, the state regulated the number and conditions of publications, took an integral part in the appointment of the managerial personnel in all publishing institutions (which remained nonetheless private property), and regulated the journalistic profession by licensing its members. Only certain publications of the Catholic Church were exempt from these requirements. To the Spanish Church was granted the closest approximation of freedom of the press to exist in Spain between the Press Law of 1938 and the new Press Law of 1966.

The most overtly totalitarian law of the new state was decreed on February 9, 1939, a few weeks before the end of the Civil War, the retroactive Ley de Responsabilidades Políticas (Law of Political

Responsibilities). This order made criminally liable all those who had contributed to what was called "red subversion" since 1934 (the year of the uprising in Asturias)[11] and all those who had actively opposed the Nationalist Movement. The decree of July 20, 1939, forbade all unauthorized public meetings with the exception of Catholic ceremonies and meetings held by legitimately established associations in accordance with their statutes. On March 1, 1940, all Masonic, communist, and anarchist organizations were outlawed. The right of association was defined and limited by the decree of January 25, 1941, which required all organizations to be approved by the Ministry of the Interior with the exception of official governmental, syndicalist, and party associations and Catholic associations with exclusively religious aims.

The Second Phase: 1942-1947

In this period Franco began his retreat from the totalitarianism that had blazoned so proud a banner during the Civil War and during the first three years of World War II when the Axis powers were sweeping invincibly through Europe. In the original Labor Charter, the national state was called "a totalitarian instrument in the service of the integrated and syndicalist Fatherland."[12] Article 6 of the Twenty-six Point Program of the F.E.T. y de las J.O.N.S. declared the state to be a totalitarian instrument in the defense of the unity of the fatherland.[13] Over and over, Franco used the word "totalitarian" to describe the new state even though the term was never defined with ideological precision. "Spain will be organized within a fully totalitarian concept through those national institutions that assure her totality, her unity, and her continuity."[14] "While efforts are being made to accomplish the definitive organization of the totalitarian New State, the national yearnings . . . of the components of the Spanish Phalanx will be fulfilled."[15] On the second anniversary of the rebellion, Franco proclaimed in his message to the Spanish people that "in the place of a neutered state with no ideals will be substituted a totalitarian state with the mission to give direction to the people."[16] Franco did insist, however, that Spanish fascism and totalitarianism would be different, adapted to Spanish customs and traditions. In a statement made to an envoy of the United Press, Franco said that "[Spain] will follow the structures of the totalitarian regimes, like Italy and Germany," but he emphasized that structure in Spain would be a "suit cut to Spanish measure."[17] In an interview published in *The New York Times Magazine,* Franco reiterated: "Spain has its own traditions, and the majority of modern formulas which were discovered in the totalitarian countries can be found already incorporated in our national past."[18] To the questions asked by the *New York Times* reporter about popular participation in government and about the practicality of democratic republicanism in Spain, Franco gave the following answer:

> Five years of experience with that kind of government which was the cause of the Civil War has proved in Spain the false democracy of republican parlimentarianism. But our new state will be a totalitarian instrument in the service of national unity. All Spaniards will participate in it through the carrying out of their municipal and syndicalist functions, but they will not participate as representatives of political parties because we have totally abolished the old parliamentary system with its well-known ills: inorganic suffrage and conflict among hostile groups.[19]

Franco did reject, however, the word *dictatorship* because it was "incompatible with the desires and aspirations of our nation which furthermore could never shape itself along foreign lines."[20] Moreover, he felt strongly that Spain's unique Catholic tradition made Spanish fascism essentially different from the German or Italian models.

> We are Catholics. In Spain one is Catholic or one is nothing. Even the Reds who deny their faith still remain Catholic if for no other reason than to be *anti*-Catholic . . . for everywhere, in Burgos as well as in Valencia, in Salamanca as well as in Barcelona, it is still the same people, the same race. We find our unity and fraternity within Catholicism. . . . There, too, we find our conception of what the world and life is. This Catholic characteristic would be enough to distinguish our Spanish revolution from Mussolini's statism and Hitler's racism, our revolution which is a complete return to the true Spain, a total reconquest.[21]

Irrespective of the disclaimers of the difference between Spain on the one hand and Germany and Italy on the other, it seemed clear that Franco had plans to turn Spain into a totalitarian regime. The scheme appeared definitive when Spain joined the Anti-Comintern Pact on March 21, 1939, four days before the end of the Civil War. On the day of final victory, March 31, Spain signed a secret treaty of friendship with Germany whereby both nations would proffer diplomatic assistance in the event of external danger. In the event either nation went to war, the other would do nothing to disfavor it nor do anything to aid the enemy. When Germany invaded Poland in September, 1939, Spain cautiously declared her neutrality (but left her air and sea ports open to German and

Italian warcraft). As the war swept so spectacularly to the advantage of the Axis, Franco moved from neutrality to nonbelligerency on June 12, 1940. Under this more active status, Spain maintained her noninvolvement but gave diplomatic and economic assistance to her friends. Irrespective of nonbelligerency, however, in June, 1941, Franco sent a voluntary air division, the División Azul (Blue Division), to fight with the Germans against the Soviet Union. It would appear to anyone who could reason that Franco had become an enthusiastic supporter of the New Order envisioned by the Axis powers and would reap advantage from his alliance with those he then considered to be the inevitable victors.

Within Spain, the career of Serrano Súñer gives evidence to Franco's apparent totalitarian commitment. On August 2, 1939, Franco appointed his second cabinet. The pro-British Jordana was replaced in the Foreign Office by Juan Beigbeder Atienza, who in turn was replaced on October 17, 1940, by Serrano, who until May 5, 1941, continued as minister of the interior. From March, 1940, to November, 1941, he was also in almost complete control of the Movement.[22] This convergence of power put the militantly pro-Axis Falangist simultaneously in charge of internal security, the party, and foreign affairs for an extended period during 1940 and 1941 at the height of the Axis domination of Europe.

After the German invasion of Russia on June 22, 1941, the tide of war gradually but inexorably began to run against the Axis, and Franco started his strategic retreat from totalitarianism. In Spain, on September 3, 1942, Jordana again became foreign minister, replacing Serrano Súñer, who retired permanently to private life. His forced withdrawal signaled the end of the fascist, totalitarian period of the Franco regime. On October 3, 1943, Franco moved from nonbelligerency back to neutrality and in the same month withdrew the Blue Division from Germany. This gradual disengagement from the Axis alliance was paralleled by changes in the political system designed to make Spain more acceptable to those nations that, already in early 1942, Franco either perceptively or fortuitously saw would be the ultimate victors in the war. There was still no representative body in Spain; the National Council of the Movement could make recommendations to the caudillo if he should request them, but the council was an institution of the party not of the government. On July 17, 1942, Franco decreed the creation of a parliament through the Ley Constitutiva de las Cortes (Constitutive Law of the Cortes).[23] It was not a parliament recognizable by democratic criteria, however. Members of parliament (called *procuradores*, once again an ancient term revived) were of three types: (1) ex officio; (2) elected; and (3) appointed. Ex officio representatives sat automatically in the Cortes because they occupied certain posts outside the parliament, most of which were filled by Franco. Elected representatives were chosen indirectly from the syndicates, municipalities, and corporate bodies, the majority of whose officials were also appointed by Franco. The third group of parliamentarians was appointed directly by Franco. There were no *procuradores* elected directly by the people.

Article 1 of the Constitutive Law of the Cortes reads:

> The Cortes is the highest organ of participation of the Spanish people in the workings of the state. The principal mission of the Cortes is the elaboration and approval of the laws—without prejudicing their sanction which belongs to the Chief of State.[24]

In other words, the cabinet, appointed by Franco and responsible to him and not to the Cortes, would present bills to the legislature, which would discuss, amend (not in substance but in form), and approve them, and turn them into laws that would be promulgated by the caudillo. It would be useless not to approve the bills submitted for deliberation because the chief of state had full authority to govern through decree-laws in matters of urgency defined by him alone. The Law of the Cortes is a Fundamental Law, the second in order of promulgation in what is considered to be the Spanish constitution, but the organ it created was vestigial from conception.

On July 17, 1945, Franco proclaimed the Fuero de los Españoles (Charter of the Spanish People), a document akin to a bill of rights.[25] The charter was the third Fundamental Law. Until its promulgation the Spaniards had lived under the provisions of the Statutes and of the Twenty-six Point Program of the F.E.T. y de las J.O.N.S. modified in part by the Labor Charter. There were, however, no constitutional guarantees to prevent in theory the total submission of the citizen to the dictates of the party. The Charter of the Spanish People was designed to provide that protection, but in spirit similar to that of the Law of the Cortes, qualifications and restrictions prevented the charter from being a democratic instrument. Moreover, once again, as in the first two Fundamental Laws, its provisions were merely declarations of principle requiring ordinary legislation for their implementation. Freedom of speech was guaranteed unless it threatened or undermined the "fundamental principles of the state."[26] The exercise of all the civil rights enumerated in the charter was guaranteed unless that enjoyment threatened or undermined the "national, spiritual, and social unity of Spain."[27] What constituted a threat and what were meant by fundamental principles and the unity of Spain were not spelled out.

Moreover, Spaniards were forbidden collectively to petition the government, and the basic guarantees (contained in Articles 12, 13, 14, 15, 16, and 18) could be partially or totally suspended by decree-laws, decided, of course, by Franco.[28] Spaniards were forbidden to divorce.[29] Under the provisions of Article 6 of the charter, Catholicism became the official religion of Spain protected by the state, which guaranteed the freedom of all other religions by "effective legal guidance"[30] (*"eficaz tutela jurídica"*), a qualification of sufficient ambiguity to allow it to be interpreted as Franco saw fit.

On October 22, 1945, Franco promulgated the Ley del Referendum (Referendum Law), the fourth Fundamental Law.[31] It was designed to give to all Spaniards over twenty-one years of age—men and women alike—a participatory role in governmental matters of transcendental importance determined by the caudillo, who still preserved for himself the legislative powers contained in the laws of January 30, 1938, and August 8, 1939.[32] The Referendum Law was curious. If inorganic electoral participation were unsuitable for Spain under ordinary circumstances, why then was it deemed appropriate for the passage of extraordinary legislation? Moreover, if, under ordinary circumstances, only male heads of family could vote at the first step in the indirect elections for the Cortes and women could not vote at all, why were all men and women over twenty-one considered sufficiently capable politically to decide upon extraordinary issues? It could be argued that the Referendum Law was a denial of the basic organic concepts upon which the whole political structure of the new Spanish state was built.

On July 6, 1947, Spain was declared a monarchy in the fifth Fundamental Law, the Ley de Sucesión en la Jefatura del Estado (Law of Succession in the Headship of State).[33] The law was submitted to the people by referendum and was approved by 73 percent of those voting, who constituted 82 percent of the electorate. Until this date the government had no constitutional status. The country was ruled by a dictator whose succession was provided for only in the Statutes of the F.E.T. y de las J.O.N.S. promulgated on July 31, 1939. Article 40 of the Statutes stated that the caudillo would secretly designate his successor who would be proclaimed by the council of the party at his death. In the Law of Succession, Franco declared Spain to be a monarchy but did not designate who the monarch was to be. The chief of state remained Franco with his full panoply of powers intact. "The Chief of State is the Caudillo of Spain and of the Crusade, Generalissimo of the Armies, don Francisco Franco Bahamonde."[34] Under the provisions of the Law, Franco could at any time submit for the approval of the Cortes the name of the man who would be king, but Franco could later change his mind even after the Cortes had approved his nominee and made the designation. The Law created two new bodies to aid in the transition and to take part in the governing of Spain *when a king should one day sit on the throne*—the Council of the Regency and the Council of the Realm, both of which will be discussed in Chapter 7. Finally, the law declared that the Fuero de Trabajo, the Ley de Cortes, the Fuero de los Españoles, the Ley del Referendum, and the Ley de Sucesión en la Jefatura del Estado were Fundamental Laws and could be repealed or modified only with the approval of the Cortes followed by the approval of the people in referendum.[35] Yet, new fundamental laws could be added to the constitution at any time without the formality of either of these processes. This meant that Franco could decree new fundamental laws when and if he chose, which is exactly what he did in 1958 when he promulgated the Ley de Principios del Movimiento Nacional (Law of the Principles of the National Movement).

Irrespective of the transparency of the true nature of the Fundamental Laws, the referendum approving the Law of Succession was of profound significance to the legitimacy of the new regime. Until the plebescite, the Franco government rested upon the dubious, if incontrovertible, legality of "might makes right." Franco had sought to imbue his decisions and actions with traditional legitimacy by attempting to link his regime in the mind of Spaniards with pre-eighteenth-century Spain, the Golden Age of *Hispanidad* (Spanishness). Furthermore, he had attempted to transfer to himself some of the charisma of the martyr-hero, José Antonio, the Cid of Falangism. But both of these contrivances were only partially successful. Moreover, such psychological legitimacy must exist in the hearts and minds of the people and remains difficult if not impossible to determine. The referendum approving the Law of Succession was the first manifestation of popular support of the regime and the first step toward the establishment of an identifiable and measurable rational-legal legitimacy. The referendum not only approved the restoration of the monarch and the succession to the throne but also retroactively ratified the basic laws, all of which were converted into Fundamental Laws and made part of the Spanish Constitution.[36] It is essential to understand, however, that the referendum was not an outpouring of enthusiasm for the monarchy. Fernando Súarez writes:

> We have been told by no less a person than José María Pemán: "The truth is that the referendum was arranged in such a way that it was an acclamation for the present not an approval for a future succession. He who voted 'yes' voted for Franco, for the law which Franco had proposed to him. He who voted 'no' also voted for Franco because in no way was he concerned about the monarchy and the succession. The truth is that all the

propaganda for the great electoral mobilization was built on a present-day emotion not on some future succession."[37]

If the Fundamental Laws decreed between 1942 and 1947 were designed in part to win for the Franco regime the approval of the democracies, they were futile creations. On June 19, 1945, the United Nations meeting in San Francisco voted to deny a seat to Spain. At the Potsdam Conference held from June 17 to August 2, 1945, and again in the United Nations on February 9, 1946, the Spanish government was condemned. On December 13, 1946, the General Assembly of the United Nations passed a resolution recommending the withdrawal of all ambassadors to Spain. Of the major nations only Argentina refused to recall her emissary when all the other ambassadors left Madrid. Paradoxically this condemnation by the nations from which he sought approbation worked domestically to the enormous advantage of Franco. On December 9, 1947, during Spain's trial by opinion taking place throughout the world, hundreds of thousands of Spaniards demonstrated in the Plaza de Oriente, across from the royal palace in Madrid, roaring their approval of Franco—or perhaps their approval of Spain and of themselves as Spaniards, united against universal hostility. Since, like it or not, Franco and Spain were now one, the people's shouts of "Franco! Franco! Franco!" came from the voices of Spaniards demonstrating their support of the government for the first time since the Civil War ended, telling the world to go hang. Eyewitnesses say the demonstration was too emotional, too authentic to have been completely orchestrated. It may have been arranged to begin with, but at the end it was a manifestation of Spanish pride from which Franco reaped great profit. Six months later the referendum on the Law of Succession took place; its results can in part be interpreted as an expression of this galvanic spirit.

Spain was declared a pariah nation by that vain and fickle spectre, world opinion, which did not forget the early words of Franco that had branded him as a totalitarian and as a fascist ally of Hitler and Mussolini. It is a paradox that so cautious a man as Franco, who characterized his own policy as one of *habil prudencia* (skillful prudence), should have been trapped by the excesses of his own rhetoric. We shall perhaps never know if Franco truly meant what he said between 1936 and 1942. Part of those secrets lies locked in archives that may never be made public; part lies locked forever in a crypt in the Valle de los Caídos (Valley of the Fallen).[38] If we take Franco at his word—and if some of his words are used to condemn him, other words must be accepted to redeem him—he said over and over during the Civil War that he was not beholden or grateful to the Axis powers for their assistance. "Spain is free of a future mortgage that would limit her sovereignty."[39] "We would cease to be nationalists if we ceded one inch of our territory."[40] "Germany provided us with the material we lacked to fight against the Russian war machine the Reds [the Loyalists] had at their complete disposal. But we paid for it all, and we paid for it in cash. Thanks to our agricultural riches, to our industrial activity and thanks to the state of our finances we have not had to go into debt to anyone."[41] Donald Detwiler writes:

> The fact is that Franco felt less obligated to Hitler and Mussolini than might have been expected. This was because the Spanish civil war did not represent for him what it did for them. He and a great number of his followers fought the civil war in the sign of the cross as a struggle to preserve Western Christiandom from atheistic Bolshevism in sinister alliance with Asiatic barbarism. . . . In Spanish Nationalist perspective Hitler had actually been participating in a Holy War not a business enterprise. . . . Consequently they [the Nationalists] tended to regard themselves not as military rebels or reactionary conspirators but rather as soldiers of Christ and as such they felt more or less the same gratitude for Hitler's and Mussolini's support as the pastor does for the Sunday collection.[42]

If after the Civil War Franco did not support Hitler and Mussolini out of gratitude, then he must have supported them out of conviction. If he supported them out of conviction, then his totalitarian and fascist words were a reflection of his true belief, and the democratic world judged him accurately. Yet, his defenders say he gave nothing to the Axis, made no concessions to Germany, particularly when Hitler was plotting Operation Felix, the plan to seal the western Mediterranean by capturing Gibraltar and controlling North Africa. This operation, which might have given a different ending to World War II had it been carried out, would have necessitated a march across Spain, a tactic Franco refused to allow. In the meeting between Hitler and Franco at Hendaye on the Spanish-French border on October 23, 1940, Franco stood firm in his demands and his refusals, and Hitler later remarked to Mussolini that he would prefer to have several teeth pulled out than to go through another session with Franco.

Did Franco gamble and win or did he gamble and lose? Franco presented exorbitant terms in exchange for Spanish participation in Operation Felix: hundreds of thousands of tons of wheat, heavy equipment, military hardware, and territorial acquisition. Franco demanded Gibraltar and African colonies that would be taken from

England and France. None of these demands was met by Hitler, and Franco refused all military cooperation with the Germans. Did Franco make no concessions to Hitler because he could get none in return? Did he gamble and lose the opportunity to create a new Spanish empire? Or did he purposely make his demands so unreasonable that he knew Hitler could not agree to them? Did Franco give the appearance of willingness to cooperate with the Germans knowing he would not have to do so, all the while remaining within the terms of the treaty of friendship signed in 1939? Did he gamble and win, keeping a starved and devastated Spain out of another war?

The Third Phase: 1953-1958

Until the early 1950s Spain was drawn within herself nursing the near mortal wounds of the Civil War. A poor nation made infinitely poorer by the conflict and unaided by the countries that had ostracized her from the community of nations, she regressed, appearing not to be a part of the modern world. A visit to Spain in the late 1950s, after her recovery was already under way, unveiled a country still deeply affected by the war that had been over for almost twenty years.

It will never be possible to know how many Spaniards perished in the war. In the 1970s the gathering of statistics is still a relatively undeveloped science in Spain. For the Republican period, data are sketchy; for the period of the Civil War, they are little more than the results of intelligent speculation. The mortality figures most quoted by non-Spanish scholars are those of Gabriel Jackson and Hugh Thomas. Jackson estimates that 580,000 people died as a direct result of the war, even though he himself feels that his figure for battlefield deaths—100,000—is too low.[43] Hugh Thomas calculates that approximately 110,000 men were killed in battle on the Nationalist side and 175,000 on the Republican. He conjectures that approximately 600,000 Spaniards died as a direct result of the war.[44] The Spaniard Ramón Tamames believes that Thomas is closer to the true figure than Jackson, but goes further than either Thomas or Jackson and offers an appraisal of the total human and material cost of the war. He estimates that during the last months and immediately following the war approximately 300,000 men fled into exile, most of them men in their prime, many of them skilled and educated. This figure added to 600,000 equals approximately 900,000 Spaniards lost to the nation through death or emigration. Comparing prewar and postwar demographic statistics, he deduces that during the conflict the population fell another 500,000, more or less, because of a decline in the birth rate. He further calculates that 875,000 productive man-years were lost in prison. Tamames states that from 1939 to 1950 at least 300,000 men were jailed as political prisoners with sentences of varying lengths.[45]

To this incredible human loss he adds the following material devastation: (1) the equivalent of $575 million worth of gold spent by the Republicans to finance the war; (2) military outlays alone of almost 300,000 million pesetas calculated by the value of pesetas in 1963 which Tamames calls "the greatest sterile investment in all our history";[46] (3) the complete destruction of 250,000 dwellings and the partial destruction of 250,000 more out of a national total of approximately 6 million; (4) over 192 towns and cities more than 60 percent destroyed; (5) approximately 50 percent of all railway rolling stock and 30 percent of all merchant ships destroyed; (6) approximately 34.2 percent of cattle, 32.7 percent of sheep and goats, and 50.4 percent of pigs destroyed; (7) agricultural production down by approximately 21.2 percent, and industrial production down approximately 31 percent; (8) gross national income down by approximately 25.7 percent and per capita income down by approximately 28.3 percent.

After the Civil War, Franco attempted to cope with these losses by initiating a policy of autarchy, a governmentally regulated program of national self-sufficiency geared to minimum subsistence goals based on small-scale production and cheap labor—an understandable and unavoidable solution but one ill-adapted to full economic recovery and postrecuperative modernization and growth. Given Spain's international ostracism and isolation, however, there were perhaps no alternatives. The cold war was the catalyst that brought Spain readmission to the community of nations and started her economic recovery. Commercial agreements were signed with Great Britain and France in 1948. Credit was opened by the Chase Manhattan Bank in 1949 and by the Export-Import Bank in 1951. The sums of money advanced were relatively small, but the negotiations that brought them into being marked the beginnings of the thaw in diplomatic relations between the democracies and Spain. Franco's predictions about Soviet Communism appeared to be coming true, and, as a result, the prophet gained stature in international opinion. The Korean War accelerated the process of acceptance, and on November 4, 1950, the General Assembly of the United Nations reversed its decision made in 1946 regarding diplomatic relations of member nations with Spain and gave indications that Spanish petitions to join the specialized agencies of the U.N. would be favorably regarded. In 1951 Spain became a member of the World Health Organization and in 1952 of the United Nations Educational, Scientific, and Cultural Organization. These negotiations paved the

way for the two most important international agreements of the Franco regime: The concordat signed with the Vatican on August 27, 1953, and the agreement signed with the United States less than a month later on September 26. By the very act of treating, Franco's Spain was recognized as an equal by the world's most powerful democratic nation and by the world's most powerful spiritual institution. The symbolism of this dual recognition was not lost on the free world. On December 15, 1955, Spain was admitted to the United Nations.[47]
Nations.[47]

In the case of the agreement negotiated with the United States, Franco could boast that the American leaders came to him not he to them. He could and did claim that Spain did not have to beg or make concessions; thus the prestige of his regime was strengthened domestically and internationally. Spain reaped enormous benefit from the agreement, but once again—as with the aid and assistance that came from nazi Germany and fascist Italy during the Civil War so with the aid and assistance that came from democratic America seventeen years later—Franco made clear that Spain owed gratitude to no one. The Americans came to Spain for their own advantage just as the totalitarians had come to Spain for theirs. If Spain earned profit, so much the better for Spain. There was neither humility nor contrition. The fates continued to smile on Franco. American aid came at a time when his policy of autarchy had exhausted its limited potential and the regime desperately needed money and foreign investment. Once again, Spain's strategic location became a prize to be courted.

The Concordat with the Vatican

By the terms of the concordat, the Spanish Church got more than the Spanish state, but the state retained final control over the appointments of bishops and archbishops. This privilege confirmed a practice that had already been established in the convention signed in 1941. Under this system (which is a modification of the ancient "right of presentation" belonging to the monarchs of Spain), the Spanish head of state submits to the Holy See a list of six episcopal nominees. From this list the Vatican eliminates three, then from among the remaining three the Spanish head of state makes the appointment. In exchange for this right, the Church received extraordinary privileges. Catholicism was declared the official state religion (theoretically without prejudice to other religions) to be subventioned by the state. The state was to subsidize parishes, seminaries, and schools of higher learning for religious study, and to provide to the clergy adequate remuneration adjustable to the cost of living. All church property, including the educational establishments, and all contributions and legacies made to the Church were exempt from taxation. The clergy would have special legal status and immunities, and in the event of court action would be tried in semisecret. If convicted and sentenced to prison, a clergyman would be jailed in special facilities. All clergymen were exempt from military service. Marriage was to be regulated by the Church, and annulments and separations would be granted by ecclesiastical tribunals. Religious instruction was to be given in all schools, public and private (with the theoretical right of parents to reject it for their children). The Church was given the right to censor all publications and public spectacles in order to guard the purity of Catholic dogma and morals. Most of the provisions contained in the concordat had already been set forth in agreements made between the Vatican and Spain since the end of the Civil War, but the concordat brought them all together, modified where necessary, and gave them the status of a treaty. The agreement reaffirmed in the most tangible form possible the support of the regime by the Catholic Church.

The Agreement with the United States

The governments of Spain and the United States concluded three bilateral agreements designed "to strengthen the capabilities of the West for the maintenance of international peace and security."[48] The three agreements covered (1) the construction and use of military facilities in Spain by the United States, (2) economic assistance, and (3) military and item assistance. Under the terms of the agreements, Spain became eligible for American economic, technical, and military assistance under the Mutual Security Progam. The United States was authorized to develop, build, and use jointly with Spanish forces certain military airfields and naval facilities in Spain. The agreement would be effective for ten years to be extended automatically for two successive periods of five years each unless terminated by either of the signatories. Under its provisions, beginning with the fiscal year 1954, Spain would receive $226 million in economic aid—$141 million for military and $85 million for nonmilitary purposes. The bases to be built would fly the Spanish flag and would be under Spanish command that would provide their external security. The bases would revert to Spain, with certain removals provided for, at the termination of the agreements. The agreement was not a mutual defense pact, however. Article 1 was carefully worded to exclude this provision. In the first article, the United States promised to aid both Spanish military and defense-oriented industrial efforts but concluded with the following reservations:

Such support will be conditioned, as in the case of other friendly nations, by the priorities and limitations due to the international commitments by the United States and to the exigencies of the international situation and will be subject to Congressional appropriations.[49]

It is said by critics, both in Spain and abroad, that the agreement revitalized a precarious regime and that the United States indirectly contributed to the entrenchment of the dictatorship. Economic assistance came at the crucial time when Franco's policy of autarchy was moribund. Moreover, since Spain had no external enemies, military assistance would be used to equip and train Spanish fighting forces that functioned almost exclusively to keep order at home.[50]

The reestablishment of diplomatic relations, the pacts with the Vatican and the United States, and the entry into the United Nations began an era that was to have a profound impact on the social, economic, and political life of Spain. After almost seventeen years of isolation (if one counts the years from the outbreak of the Civil War), Spain opened herself to the world—to its money, primarily, and to its ideas, unavoidably, with the accompaniment of both their beneficial and pernicious influences. Spain was virgin territory for the foreign investment that came pouring into the country after America's initial seeding. Within a few years, the nation began to suffer from all of the ills of sudden and unplanned industrialization and modernization: depopulation of the countryside and overpopulation of the cities; urban sprawl, slums, and pollution; the exploitation of natural resources and the destruction of natural beauty in the pursuit of quick profit; an imbalance in supply and demand that led to unrest within the class most adversely affected by the constantly rising cost of living, the untrained or poorly trained, semiliterate proletariat. Under the policy of autarchy, which had supported most of the society just above the subsistence level, the plight of the worker had been comparatively little worse than that of the rest of his countrymen, and dissent was minimized through mutual misfortune. When capitalism made its reentry into Spain with the stimulus of foreign investment in the 1950s, the plight of the laborer became desperate as inflation reduced him almost to penury. Legally he could no nothing about it. Under existing law conceived for an earlier time and for a different economic philosophy (the national-syndicalist inspiration of the Labor Charter), the worker could not demonstrate, organize, bargain collectively, or strike, yet the law said little about the regulation of the entrepreneur except that "the management of the firm shall be responsible for its contribution to the common good of the national economy."[51] Under the new capitalism, this vague restriction failed to prevent the economic elite from amassing enormous profits at the expense of the worker.

The proletariat's discontent was echoed by the university students. The young men and women who made up the first generation beyond the immediate experience of the Civil War responded not to the past but to the present and to the future. Moreover, the presence of the foreigners who were coming into Spain by the millions each year had an exhilarating effect on the young, who had been isolated from outside influences since the end of the Civil War. The regime had not forbidden Spaniards to travel abroad, but poverty kept the average man or woman at home. Until the world started to come to Spain in the 1950s, Spaniards were innocent of the postwar period. In February, 1956, the regime suffered its first bloody confrontations with the restless students of the University of Madrid, and for the first time since the Charter of the Spanish People had been promulgated in 1945, Franco suspended its guarantees for three months by decreeing a state of exception throughout Spain.[52]

As the regime resisted the first of its major postwar challenges, the old guard of the F.E.T. y de las J.O.N.S. saw, in the mid-1950s, what it considered to be the opportune moment to achieve finally what Franco had prevented it from accomplishing since the mid-1930s—the creation and control of a truly national-syndicalist state that would discipline the system and destroy in the bud the neocapitalism attractive to the economic elites and to the emerging urban middle class and the socialism attractive not only to the workers but also to a growing number of intellectuals and a large percentage of students. At this juncture, Franco made one of his most momentous political decisions. He rejected the party's nationalist-syndicalist solution for Spain's economic problems and opted instead for the continuation, support, and encouragement of neocapitalism—to be led and directed by modern technocrats who came primarily from the Opus Dei.[53] Franco dealt a staggering blow to the economic aspirations of those in the F.E.T y de las J.O.N.S. who looked to the syndicalist ideas of the 1930s to solve Spain's economic problems of the 1950s and beyond.

Had the F.E.T. y de las J.O.N.S. been eliminated from the arena of power because of Franco's procapitalist decision? Yes and no. It was exalted to become the symbol of national unity while it was simultaneously shorn of a great part of its political power. On May 17, 1958, Franco, personally and without permitting prior debate in the Cortes, promulgated the fifth Fundamental Law of the Spanish constitution, the Ley de Principios del Movimiento Nacional (Law on the Principles of the National Movement).[54] By this decree Franco institutionalized through the F.E.T. y de las J.O.N.S., now called the *Movimiento* (Movement),[55] a value system that would act as the anchor for the full sail of the inevitable but yet unknown changes that would come about as the result of the new direction in Spanish society. In language reminiscent of that used during the "crusade" of the Civil War, Franco in the new law recalled falangist principles, not the economic principles that he had rejected but those that spoke of God and Eternal Spain, destiny, unity, faith, brotherhood, and the tonic triad of family, municipality, and syndicate. He proclaimed three short articles. The first made the principles of the Movement "by their very nature permanent and unalterable." In other words, they became immutable articles of faith unable to be changed even by constitutional amendment. The second article declared that all public office holders "shall be bound to the strictest observance of these principles." They were required to swear an oath of loyalty to the principles at their investiture. The third article made null and void all laws and dispositions "that injured or defamed the Principles." In other words, no political ideology contrary to the principles would be tolerated. The Movement became constitutionally the only road to political participation. It had been the only road since the decree of unification of 1937, but until 1958 its place within the political system had not been recognized and institutionalized in a Fundamental Law.

The Fourth Phase: 1959-1975

The beginning of this period overlaps the one preceding it. Chronologically it starts in 1957 when members of the Opus Dei made their first appearances in the cabinet, but the impact of these men was not made manifest until 1959 when the fruit of their efforts, the Stabilization Plan, was introduced. Thus, effectively, the period dates from 1959 with the implementation of the plan and ends in 1975 with the death of Franco.

This period witnessed (1) the emergence of the Opus Dei as a major force within Spanish society and politics;[56] (2) the adoption of neocapitalism, engineered by the members of the Opus Dei in the government, as the new economic philosophy of the Franco regime; (3) the decline in the power and prestige of the traditional Falangists; (4) the final institutionalization of Franco's political system in the Ley Orgánica del Estado (Organic Law of the State), the last of the Fundamental Laws, proclaimed on January 10, 1967; (5) the constitutional separation of the roles of head of state and head of government provided for in Title III of the Organic Law; (6) Franco's designation on July 22, 1969, of Prince Juan Carlos to be his successor; (7) the appointment on June 9, 1973, of Luis Carrero Blanco as prime minister; (8) the assassination of Carrero Blanco on December 20, 1973; (9) the death of Franco on November 20, 1975; and (10) the accession of Juan Carlos as king of Spain.

Most of the above phenomena can be listed as discrete and chronological events, but in reality they are intimately related and form the almost seamless fabric of the last half of the Franco era. The emergence of the Opus Dei, the retrocession of the Falangists, and the adoption of neocapitalism make up the initial threads of the skein. In 1957, for the first time, men identified as members of the Opus Dei were appointed to the cabinet—Alberto Ullastres as minister of commerce and Mariano Navarro as minister of the treasury (*Hacienda*).[57] These men were instrumental in the adoption of the Stabilization Plan in effect from 1959 until 1962—the austerity program devised to pull Spain out of the inflationist spiral into which she had been swept since the first heady influx of money and investments following the international reemergence of the country in the early 1950s. Spain had been unprepared for the economic repercussions of these windfalls; moreover, she was still using economic devices that had been adopted during the now moribund policy of autarchy—among others, trade restrictions, multiple exchange rates, subsidization of inefficient producers in the name of self-sufficiency. The Stabilization Plan was designed to regularize and rationalize the chaotic economic conditions of Spain in the mid-1950s, to bring the economic policies of the abandoned autarchic past and those of the emerging neocapitalist present into focus, and to prepare for the future and pave the way for the first Development Plan put into operation in 1963.

The Stabilization Plan called for either the extension or initiation of the following programs: (1) a freeze on wages in the public sector; (2) the reduction of governmental spending; (3) the tightening of commercial credit; (4) the reform of tax laws to increase revenue and reduce demand; (5) the gradual elimination of subsidies to marginal producers; (6) the abandonment of multiple exchange rates and the adoption of a single exchange rate. This amounted indirectly to a devaluation of the peseta making it more attractive to buy from Spain than to sell to her, thereby improving the balance of payments. In July, 1959, the government increased taxes on tobacco, matches, telephones, and gasoline. Of particular importance to foreign investors was the cabinet's decision in the same month to raise from 25 to 50 percent the level of foreign investment and control allowable in Spanish enterprises and to ease the rigid restrictions that would impede the quick repatriation of profits to the countries supplying investment capital. Already in 1958 Spain had joined the Organization for European Economic Cooperation (later renamed the Organization for Economic Cooperation and Development), the International Monetary Fund, and the World Bank— memberships which facilitated Spain's international economic intercourse and symbolized her continued emergence from isolation.

For the country as a whole the Stabilization Plan was a success.

> The immediate results were very good and won the applause of the participating international agencies. The credit limits, public austerity, and devaluation seemed to meet effectively the critical problems of inflation and balance of payments. Imports fell from $612 million to $477 million for the first nine months of the program while exports rose from $305 to $405 million. More important, reserves, virtually exhausted at the beginning, had grown to $463 million after one year. During the same period, prices rose by 2 percent. The stability of the price index probably had something to do with selling off inventories built up in earlier inflationary periods. While this affected the production decline of 1959-60, it also led to restrained import demand. [58]

For the working class, however, the plan caused great hardship. Ironically the class that earlier had suffered from inflation was now suffering from the Stabilization Plan adopted to bring inflation under control. Besides having a ceiling put on their wages, many workingmen lost the opportunity to earn either overtime pay or supplementary income from the second job many of them held in an effort to improve their lot. As marginal producers, who had been subsidized during autarchy, were forced to shut down when their subventions stopped, their employees glutted the labor market. No longer did the surviving employers have to pay overtime in order to maintain production. There was now more than enough manpower that would work for regular pay. Moreover, the excess working force, in looking for primary employment, filled those jobs which had been secondary sources of income before austerity. While there was not massive unemployment as such, real wages declined as much as 50 percent in some cases, producing much the same effect as unemployment itself.

In the beginning of the period of neocapitalism, however, the regime, for reasons that had nothing to do with Spain, was exposed to much less violence that could have been anticipated given the plight of the working class. During the late 1950s and early 1960s, thousands of Spanish workers left Spain to find jobs in those Western European countries whose booming economies were demanding more laborers than their own domestic manpower resources could supply.[59] The

Franco regime profited in two ways. Not only was internal pressure from discontented workers released through emigration, but those same workers sent back to their families in Spain the major portion of their earnings thereby helping to build up foreign exchange badly needed for the developing Spanish economy. When the great demand for foreign labor slackened in Northern Europe, however, Spanish workers returned to Spain and joined the growing chorus of opposition.

In February, 1962, during the final phases of the Stabilization Plan, Franco created the post of *comisario del plan de desarrollo* (commissioner for developmental planning). The position was awarded to López Rodó, and he and his fellow technocrats from the Opus Dei conceived the long range, multistaged development plans for which the Stabilization Plan had laid the foundation. In July, 1962, Franco appointed his seventh cabinet, and its makeup reflected the growing political importance of the Opus Deists. In addition to the two holdovers from the previous cabinet, Ullastres and Navarro, the Opus Dei members on the new cabinet were Manuel Lora Tamayo, minister of education; Gregorio López Bravo, minister of industry; and Jesús Romeo Gorría, minister of labor. (The commissioner for developmental planning became a cabinet minister without portfolio in 1965.)

The Spanish development plans conceived and implemented by the technocrats of the Opus Dei were borrowed and duplicated almost point for point from the French plans that had been greatly responsible for the postwar economic recovery of France. The details of these plans are beyond the scope of this study, but their general scheme called for cooperation between the state and private enterprise combining elements of capitalism and socialism. The scheme, in Spain as in France, called for indicative planning in which the state conceived the overall design binding on the public sector but optional for the private. Those private businessmen who chose to take part in the plan derived such benefit, however—in the forms of tax advantages, depreciation allowances, availability of credit, preferential allocation of raw materials, incentives for relocation of industry to underdeveloped regions of Spain—that acceptance of the plans was widespread and enthusiastic on the part of most entrepreneurs once they overcame their initial reluctance. The kind of aggressive economic action the plan encouraged from private enterprise was not part of the experience of most Spanish businessmen, who for almost two decades had lived under the policy of autarchy when nearly all initiative had come from the state. Under indicative planning, initiative would be shared. Goals would be established by the state, but the implementation of those goals would depend largely upon the creativity of private entrepreneurs. With some modification made necessary because of the legal impediments to labor's role in economic policy-making in Spain, the following statement about French planning could apply with almost equal validity to the Spanish:

> The key to French planning was its indicative character. In the language of the period, this represented a middle way between nonplanning, or simple economic projection for informational purposes, and the centralized, control economies of the communist world. This long-range plan projected investment growth rates and related macro-economic objectives with optimal policy mixes called for by the targets. The policy projections were mandatory for the public sector but only indicative or suggestive for the private sector. The plan developed through an elaborate series of meetings in which various groups in the economy were represented, including business leaders, public officials, experts, and representatives of labor organizations. The committees of the plan, taking cognizance of official growth targets and macroeconomic projections along with public expectations, then developed plans for their economic sectors.[60]

Major opposition to the development plans came primarily from the Falangists, who controlled the syndicates and not only saw their hopes for a national-syndicalist economic order dashed by neocapitalist programs but also saw their heretofore powerful influence in economic policy-making dangerously eroded. Pitched battle resulted between the traditional Falangists, who represented the old order, and the Opus Deists, who represented the new.

> The syndicalist leaders saw themselves squeezed out of their preeminent position in policy-making, virtually ignored by the new economic team. The Opus Dei ministers and the syndicalist leaders frequently were simply different human types. The technocrats often saw the syndicalist leaders as petty politicians, given to demagogic appeals for mass support, crude, a carry-over from an earlier phase of Spain's development, much perhaps as a successful executive sees a political boss in the United States. The syndicalist leaders, in turn, saw the new economic leaders as cold, mechanical, ruthless, and autocratic. The antagonism between the two elites had smoldered from the beginning, and it broke into flames on several occasions in the 1960s. The feud between Navarro Rubio and the Falangist housing minister José Luis Arrese became so acute that Franco replaced Arrese in March, 1960.[61]

It is significant that the man replaced was not the Opus Deist but the Falangist who had been secretary-general of the Movement in Franco's third cabinet formed in May, 1941, and who had served in various capacities throughout the following two decades.

The success of the Opus Deists was symbolized and secured by an event that was deeply political, far removed from the the realms of economics and indicative planning. Here we find another of the threads in the skein referred to earlier. On July 22, 1969, Franco declared Juan Carlos to be his successor, bypassing the prince's father, Don Juan de Borbón, and rejecting the constitutional option allowing the designation of a regent to rule following Franco's death. Article 6 of the Law of Succession in the Headship of State reads:

> At any moment the Head of State [Franco] may propose to the Cortes the person who he thinks should succeed him either as King or as Regent, under the conditions laid down by this law, and similarly, he may submit for the approval of the Cortes the revocation of the person proposed by him even though this person might have been accepted by the Cortes.[62]

The designation of Juan Carlos as his successor assured for Franco the continued legitimacy of the political system he had created. Had Franco chosen Don Juan—the son of Alfonso XIII, the last reigning king of Spain, who had gone voluntarily into exile in 1931 but *who did not abdicate*—the entire legitimacy of the Franco era could have been challenged after Franco's death. The Civil War had brought an end to the Second Republic; there were no remaining rational-legal elements of Republican legitimacy. But the monarchy preceding the Republic had never given up its claim to sovereignty. Don Juan was the direct link to that sovereignty, and his selection by Franco would have carried not only the new rational-legal legitimacy which emerged from the Fundamental Laws created by Franco but also would have carried the direct traditional legitimacy of the Bourbon dynasty. In fact, many of the supporters of Don Juan claimed that he would be head of state not by the workings of Franco's constitution but by the heredity that predated the Franco regime and that in reality made his regime, like the Republic before it, an interlude and not a recommencement.

By choosing Juan Carlos, Franco accomplished an intricate feat. Although Juan Carlos was the grandson of Alfonso XIII, he was not his immediate heir and thus was not within the direct hereditary lineage. Juan Carlos on becoming king would reach that position not by inheritance from his father, the immediate heir to Alfonso XIII, but solely by the act of Franco following the procedures set forth in the Fundamental Laws and, on two essential occasions, sanctioned by the Spanish people. The first approval came in 1947 when by referendum the people accepted the Law of Succession in the Headship of State, which declared Spain to be a kingdom; the second approval came in 1966 when, again by referendum, the people accepted the Organic Law of the State, the last of the Fundamental Laws and the keystone of the Spanish Constitution. Juan Carlos would carry the *direct* rational-legal legitimacy of the Franco political system, but because he is the grandson of a king and would have eventually become king by royal succession had there been no interruption in 1931, he also would carry the *indirect* traditional legitimacy that he inherited through his father. Thus, by designating Juan Carlos, Franco accomplished the seemingly impossible feat of simultaneously breaking with and maintaining links with the past. When Franco died on November 20, 1975, and Juan Carlos became king of Spain, the legitimacy of the Franco regime was secured and perpetuated. Unless the Spanish people decide otherwise and create a totally new political system, all future Spanish governments will have their legitimacy in Franco, who in effect established a new branch of the Bourbon house, no longer Alfonsine but Juancarlist.

Let us now pick up the thread connecting these events with the Opus Deists and the Falangists. The Opus Deists had supported the cause of Juan Carlos while the Falangists had supported not Don Juan but a regent. Following the death of Franco, a regent would have been beholden to his Falangist supporters who were the enemies of the Opus Dei. According to this strategy, the power and influence of the Opus Deists would thereby have been undermined or destroyed, and the new economic direction into which they had moved Spain could then have been reoriented. Had the Falangists been more prescient, however, they would not have picked the impossible option and would not have allowed themselves to have been outmaneuvered by the Opus Deists. No regent could have possessed those qualifications that made Juan Carlos the only choice possible in Franco's strategy for the final legitimization of his political system. The Opus Deists understood the scheme and championed it. The Falangists, having identified themselves with the regency, were left vulnerable and weakened when Franco chose Juan Carlos.

The ascendant power of the Opus Deists reached its zenith in Franco's ninth cabinet, appointed on October 29, 1969, and popularly referred to as *monocolor* (monochromatic) because of its almost total dominance by Opus Deists. For the first time since 1936, Franco appeared to have abandoned the balance of forces he had scrupulously maintained in all of his cabinets. Falangists, military men, and traditionalists were present in the new government, but they were so heavily outnumbered that their voices were effectively muted. Of the eighteen cabinet posts four were occupied by men identified exclusively with the Opus Dei and seven by men who were identified partly with the Opus Dei and partly with older pillars of the regime like the military and the traditionalists. The Opus Deists maintained their hegemony throughout the life of the ninth cabinet and throughout the following two cabinets. It was only after the assassination of Prime Minister Carrero Blanco, himself intimately linked with the Opus Dei, that the political strength of the society waned. When Carlos Arias Navarro succeeded Carrero as prime minister in Franco's twelfth cabinet (his last), appointed on January 4, 1974, no vestiges of the Opus Deists remained. They were certainly not out of politics; they were present everywhere in the government. But they were in temporary eclipse at the ministerial level due in part to the reemergence of the classic forces of order—the military and the Falange—in reaction to the assassination of Carrero and in part to the overexposure of the men of the Opus Dei whose purity and selfless dedication had come under deep suspicion. Their absence from the twelfth cabinet was partial vindication for their enemies whose efforts to dislodge them had hitherto been unsuccessful.

The Opus Dei had been unable to rid itself of the deep stain of scandal it had acquired in the Matesa affair, which broke into the open in August, 1969. The fact that only two months later in October the Opus Deists dominated the monochromatic ninth cabinet in some way brought vindication to the society and showed that Franco would remain at least publicly unmoved by the accusations. Moreover, his repudiation of the group in which he had placed almost total confidence would have been tantamount to an admission of his monumental misjudgment. But the issue was not allowed to die by the enemies of the Opus Dei, the military and particularly the Falangists, who had hoped that that scandal would destroy the credibility of the Opus Dei and reestablish for the Falangists the influence they had lost in the maneuverings over the designation of Franco's successor in July, 1969. Perhaps the assassination of Carrero and Franco's subsequent political remobilization of the forces of order offered the regime its first opportunity to circumscribe the power of the Opus Deists without the regime's losing face.

The byzantine intricacies of the Matesa affair are not pertinent to this study. It is sufficient to show in what way the Opus Dei became involved and thus exposed to public vilification. Matesa is an acronym for Maquinaria Textil del Norte de España, S.A. (Textile Machinery of Northern Spain, Inc.). The company was incorporated in 1956 in Pamplona by the Catalan industrialist Juan Vilá Reyes and members of his family. Matesa grew quickly and became very rich. By 1969 it employed over 2,000 people in Spain and had branches in at least a dozen countries, in the United States operating as American Iwer. The scandal broke when it was discovered that over an eight-year period governmental loans from the Banco de Crédito Industrial (Bank of Industrial Credit), totaling in pesetas the equivalent of approximately $83 million, had been fraudulently diverted from their original purposes. The loans had been made to facilitate the production of textile machinery for export, yet of the 20,381 machines for whose manufacture the company had negotiated the loans with the government, only 13,450 had actually been produced. Of these only 10,636 had been exported, out of which only 2,321 had actually been sold. Remaining unsold in warehouses outside Spain were 8,315 machines. In addition, the money diverted from the 7,381 machines that had not even been manufactured had been used by Matesa to acquire subsidiary companies in Spain and other textile companies in foreign countries, to pay personal expenses of the company directors, and to make loans to companies not affiliated with Matesa. Thus, not only had money been fraudulently used but also the money legitimately used had gone into the manufacture of equipment no one seemed to want. Since Opus Deists had made almost all the economic decisions in the regime since the late 1950s, it was impossible for them to escape blame even if their direct involvement could not be proved. Few believed that a scandal of such dimension and of such longevity could have occurred without the collusion of men in the highest decision-making positions. The Opus Dei disavowed any wrongdoing, but its enemies used the affair in an attempt not only to expose the immediate culpability of Opus Deists but also to undermine and destroy the credibility of their entire economic program, which had been in operation since 1959.

It was not until the appointment of the twelfth cabinet in 1974 that the enemies could feel some satisfaction, however. Among the opponents to the Opus Deists were the following men, all of whom occupied cabinet posts at the time the scandal became public in August, 1969: Manuel Fraga Iribarne, minister of information and tourism, associated with the Falange; José Solís Ruiz, secretary-general of the Movement (the Falange); Admiral Pedro Nieto Antuñez, minister of the navy; and Fernando María Castiella, foreign minister identified with Acción Católica (Catholic Action). These men went into temporary eclipse after 1969 but, as will be seen in Chapter 11, they are among the most powerful men in post-Franco Spain.

Constitutionally, the most important event of the period under discussion was the promulgation of the Ley Orgánica del Estado (Organic Law of the State), the seventh and final Fundamental Law.[63] In effect, the Organic Law closed the door on the past and symbolized and actualized the completed political system whose structure Franco had begun to build in the midst of the Civil War. The law reconciled the inconsistencies that existed among the six earlier Fundamental Laws, reworded the few vestiges of terminology that could be called fascist, and continued political liberalization (or if liberalization is too optimistic a term, then what this author earlier called "the retreat from authoritarianism"). It provided for directly elected family representatives to the Cortes, and it separated the role of head of state from the role of head of government. As of January 10, 1967, the day the Organic Law went into operation, Franco's system was ready for posterity in the form Franco considered to be essentially fixed. Irrespective of the language, which seems to welcome necessary, future constitutional modifications, it is permanence that is revealed in the final paragraphs of the speech delivered by Franco on November 22, 1966, at a special session of the Cortes to which he presented the draft of the Organic Law. The address was a kind of constitutional valedictory.

> With this reference to the necessary changes in the old laws, the field is clear for the purpose of disclosing the contents of the new Organic Law of the State, which completes our new institutional cycle, although it is still open to subsequent and possible improvements or adjustments, if they should become necessary, because we do not believe that the Constitution is a pure and simple legacy of the past, the determining product of history, the result of events or doctrines accepted by our forbears, although we may keep tradition alive in so far as it is related to the historical achievements of living principles. Neither do we accept a rationalist view which attempts to offer us a universal and abstract model of institutions, valid for all countries, irrespective of their social structure and their cultural way of life, as I have already indicated to you. In the face of both attitudes, which confronted each other tragically in Spain from 1808 to 1936, we must continue cautiously with our new open order and fundamental laws based on the knowledge of the past and bearing in mind the future which we can only partly foresee. For this very reason we have not attempted improvised joint decisions, neither have we abstained from building, little by little, an institutional edifice which will not spend itself at the same time as man. *We have followed a prudent evolution without forgetting that the life of countries is measured by centuries. On giving this decisive step, which, to a certain point, puts an end to a period, we do not close the door to subsequent modifications and complements, but these will have to be made along the established course and with the necessary guarantees so as to avoid dangerous improvisations.*
>
> *In it you will see an organic regulation of all our institutions, capable of functioning like an organic system under any of the situations which it is possible to foresee.* You will observe that besides bringing up to date all

these institutions which have been created during the period of twenty years, from 1938 to 1958, new mechanisms and guarantees are outlined. In accord with our Catholic sense, special consideration has been given to the improvements of the doctrine of the Church; an ample democratization of the political process is taking place in the reformed composition of the Cortes, of the National Council and of the Council of the Realm and of their renovated faculties; improvements are being made to the already very advanced legal order of the provisions connected with the exercise of high advisory and control bodies and of a most ample means of appeal of "contrafuero."

The National Movement can very well be defined both as mother of our principles and stimulator of political expansion within an ordered concurrence of criteria. A balanced system is established for the primary organs of the State and their reciprocal relations; the successory provisions are perfected and clarified. A just executive power is established headed by the President of the Government, who is entrusted with the political and administrative direction of the country.

The Cortes fully assume the legislative and controlling function and through a Council of the Realm, in which the Cortes are integrated to a great extent, intervene in the most important nominations. *The Armed Forces take on the task of guaranteeing security and order, as well as the unity and independence of the Nation.* Adequate measures are provided for as protection against serious emergencies. Local Administration is given adequate consideration as befits the natural realities and basical [sic] structures of the community.[64]

In order to gain testimony to this permanence, on December 14, 1966, Franco presented the Organic Law to the people for approval through referendum. The total number of eligible voters was 21,803,397. Of that number 19,446,709 citizens voted. Yes votes numbered 18,643,161; no votes, 372,692. There were 440,687 ballots either blank or invalid.[65]

In the major political events following the promulgation of the Organic Law, we find, once again, the threads of the skein referred to at the beginning of this section. The designation of Juan Carlos as Franco's successor and the appointment of Carrero Blanco as prime minister were decisions that emerged from the workings of the Organic Law and of the other Fundamental Laws and began the preparation of Spain for the future as conceived and executed by Franco. The significance of the designation of Juan Carlos has already been analyzed. The appointment of Carrero made operative the provision of Title III of the Organic Law, which separated the role head of state from that of head of government. Until the Organic Law came into effect there was only *one* role, that of caudillo, which combined the roles of head of state and head of government. The caudillo was also chief legislator and chief of party. All of the roles were to be performed by Franco as long as he should will it. The Organic Law established the fact that there were *two* roles, but from January 10, 1967, until June 9, 1973, Franco continued to play both parts. On the latter date Franco gave up the position of head of government (but under the law could have taken it back at any time) and made Carrero Blanco his first prime minister. From the point of view of stability and continuity, Carrero's assassination on December 20, 1973, was more significant than his nomination six months earlier. During that strange Christmas holiday from the assassination until the nomination of Carlos Arias Navarro on January 4, 1974, the Spaniards remained incredibly calm. The country did not panic. The people displayed a political maturity that appeared to have surprised even themselves. The army and the police did not have to be called out to keep order, nor was a state of emergency ever declared. Neither of these alternatives would have been unexpected in an authoritarian political system that since the outbreak of the Civil War had witnessed almost no personal, physical violence against its governing elites. The post-Franco system passed its first test, and in that sense, the system appeared to be working. A second, but less severe, test of the stability of the polity took place a few months later. On July 19,1974, under the terms of a decree issued by Franco three days earlier, Juan Carlos temporarily assumed the role of head of state when Franco became incapacitated following the first of the illnesses that would eventually take his life. After his partial recovery, Franco resumed his role but was compelled to relinquish it again on October 30, 1975. Franco died three weeks later on November 20, 1975.

Notes

1. For the documents in Spanish, see María Carmen García-Nieto and Javier M. Donézar, *La Guerra de España, 1936-1939* (Madrid: Guadiana de Publicaciones, 1974). For English-language translations of the Statutes and the Twenty-six Point Program and of the Decree of Unification of April 19, 1937, see Charles F. Delzell, *Mediterranean Fascism, 1919-1945* (New York: Harper & Row, 1970), pp. 273-77 and 296-303.

2. Franco's creation of the F.E.T. y de las J.O.N.S. has been discussed on pp. 101-103 of this study.

3. Law of January 30, 1938.

4. Ibid., Article 17. Following the war Franco was further empowered to make laws without even *consulting* the cabinet: Law of August 8, 1939, Article 7.

5. Not everyone is in agreement about the total number of Franco's cabinets.

There are political observers who believe that changes made by Franco in key personnel in an existing cabinet established a new cabinet and did not merely alter the existing one. Since the cabinet was responsible to Franco alone and did not emerge from the Cortes, it cannot be known with certainty what went on in Franco's mind, whether he did or did not consider certain changes to have constituted the creation of an entirely new government.

6. Fernández Cuesta had been made secretary-general in 1937.

7. For an informative analysis of Franco's balancing act and the makeup of his cabinets, see Paul H. Lewis, "The Spanish Ministerial Elite, 1938-1967 [the Council of Ministers under General Francisco Franco]," *Comparative Politics* 5 (October 1972): 83-106. See also the article by Juan Linz in *Cleavages, Ideologies, and Party Systems*, E. A. Allardt and Y. Littunen, eds., Westermarck Society Transactions, vol. 10, Helsinki, 1964.

8. *Fundamental Laws of the State: The Spanish Constitution*, Labor Charter. In the official English-language translation of the Fundamental Laws, the word *fuero* is translated in two different ways. The Fuero de Trabajo is called the Labor Law, and the Fuero de los Españoles is called the Statute Law of the Spanish People. This author will use the more traditional translation and refer to a *fuero* as a charter, a more appropriate term which carries strong historical connotations.

9. For a discussion of the syndicates, see Appendix A.

10. Jorge Solé-Tura, *Introducción al Régimen Político Español* (Barcelona: Ediciones Ariel, Esplugues de Llobregat, 1971), pp. 23-24.

11. See pp. 72-73 in this study.

12. Solé-Tura, *Régimen Político Español*, p. 23.

13. García-Nieto and Donézar, *La Guerra de España*, p. 261.

14. *Palabras de Franco* (Bilbao: Editora Nacional, 1937), p. 15.

15. Decree of Unification, April 19, 1937, in García-Nieto and Donézar, *La Guerra de España*, p. 287.

16. *Palabras del Caudillo*, p. 315.

17. Ibid., pp. 324-25.

18. Ibid., p. 406.

19. Ibid., p. 407.

20. Ibid.

21. Ibid., pp. 451-52. Emphasis added. Burgos and Salamanca were in Nationalist territory; Barcelona and Valencia were in Republican territory.

22. In his second cabinet Franco had appointed a soldier, General Agustín Muñoz Grandes, to replace Fernández Cuesta as secretary-general of the Movement. In March, 1940, Muñoz resigned (and in 1941 became commander of the Blue Division). After his resignation the party headship was left vacant until November, 1941. Serrano, who was already head of the Junta Política, the permanent executive organ of the party, was by default left in virtual control of the F.E.T. y de las J.O.N.S.

23. *Fundamental Laws of the State: The Spanish Constitution*, Constitutive Law of the Cortes.

24. Ibid.

25. *Fundamental Laws of the State: The Spanish Constitution*, Charter of the Spanish People.

26. Ibid.

27. Ibid.

28. Ibid.

29. Ibid.

30. Ibid.

31. *Fundamental Law of the State: The Spanish Constitution*, Law of the National Referendum.

32. See p. 122 of this study.

33. *Fundamental Laws of the State: The Spanish Constitution*, Law of Succession in the Headship of State.

34. Ibid., Article 2.

35. Ibid., Article 10.

36. Ibid.

37. *Cuadernos para el Diálogo*, November 1963, pp. 21-22.

38. The monument built by Franco to honor those who were killed during the Civil War. Franco is buried there.

39. *Palabras del Caudillo*, p. 331.

40. Ibid., p. 334.

41. Ibid., p. 450.

42. Donald S. Detwiler, "Spain and the Axis During World War II," *Review of Politics* 33, no. 1 (January 1971): p. 37.

43. Gabriel Jackson, *The Spanish Republic and the Civil War, 1931-1939* (Princeton, N.J.: Princeton University Press, 1965), pp. 526-40.

44. *The Spanish Civil War*, pp. 631-33.

45. *La República, la Era de Franco*, pp. 349-58.

46. Ibid., p. 356.

47. Spain did not enter in proud vindication, however. She was admitted as the result of a package deal between the USA and the USSR, each of the superpowers agreeing to accept the other's candidates.

48. *New York Times*, September 27, 1953, p. 16.

49. Ibid.

50. In the first ten years, the United States poured into Spain more than $1.5 billion in economic assistance and more than $500 million in military aid. The pact was renewed in 1963 and 1970. The agreement between the United States and Spain is still in force. In fact, it has been raised in status. For the first time the two countries signed a Treaty of Friendship and Cooperation on January 24, 1976, which was approved by the Senate on June 21. The previous accords had been executive agreements. The treaty does not commit the United States to come to the defense of Spain. Thus the treaty falls short of the defense relations existing in the North Atlantic Treaty Organization (NATO) in which an attack on one is considered to be an attack on all, but there is a moral obligation implied on the part of the United States. The treaty extends the use of the naval and the air bases and seeks to coordinate defense policy with NATO. In return, Spain is to receive $1.22 billion in credits and grants for military, technical, and

cultural assistance.

51. *Fundamental Laws of the State: The Spanish Constitution,* Labor Charter, Article 8, Sec. 2.

52. *Fundamental Laws of the State: The Spanish Constitution,* Charter of the Spanish People, Articles 14, 15, and 18.

53. For a description and analysis of the Opus Dei, see Appendix B.

54. *Fundamental Laws of the State: The Spanish Constitution,* Law on the Principles of the National Movement.

55. The F.E.T. y de las J.O.N.S. had always been referred to as a movement and not as a political party, but after its national-syndicalism had been almost totally excised, it was no longer referred to as *"la Falange"* (with its national-syndicalist connotations from the 1930s) but as *"el Movimiento"* (with its more contemporary significance).

56. See Appendix B.

57. The first public political appearance of the men of the Opus Dei was made in 1956 when Laureano López Rodó, an important member of the society, was named technical secretary-general to Admiral Luis Carrero Blanco, the subsecretary of the prime minister *(subsecretario de la presidencia).* The *presidencia* is the office of the prime minister who was, of course, Franco. Carrero Blanco as Franco's first secretary for all practical purposes ran the government on a day-to-day basis. The position was extremely powerful but until 1951 remained relatively obscure because it was not represented in the cabinet. In 1951 Franco made the secretaryship a cabinet post and thus publicly revealed the importance of Carrero Blanco. Anyone whom Carrero should sponsor or assist would be in a position to exert strong influence on both the making and implementation of policy. López Rodó was placed in such a position in 1956 and was influential in bringing other members of the Opus Dei into the government.

From the point of view of the balance of forces Franco always maintained in his cabinet, Carrero Blanco, at the beginning of his political life, had been identified exclusively with the military, but as the years passed his affiliation and sympathies with the semisecret Opus Dei became common speculation among the power elite. By the 1960s Carrero became openly identified with the society.

58. Charles W. Anderson, *The Political Economy of Modern Spain: Policy Making in an Authoritarian System* (Madison: University of Wisconsin Press, 1970), pp. 147-49.

59. Tamames in *La República, la Era de Franco,* p. 414, includes the following table:

	Migrations within Europe		
Year	*Departures*	*Returns*	*Emigratory Balance*
1959	20,580	22,209	- 1,629
1960	40,189	12,194	27,995
1961	116,524	8,315	108,209
1962	147,692	46,314	101,348
1963	145,859	52,730	93,129

1964	192,299	98,993	93,306
1965	181,278	120,678	60,600
1966	130,700	131,700	-1,000
1967	60,000	85,000	-25,000
1968	66,217	51,653	14,564
1969	92,160	29,600	62,560

During this same period, there were 283,486 departures to places other than Europe and 240,799 returns, with an emigratory balance of 42,687.

60. Charles W. Anderson, *The Political Economy of Modern Spain*, p. 166.
61. Ibid., p. 168.
62. Fundamental Laws of the State: The Spanish Constitution, Law of Succession in the Headship of State.
63. Ibid., Organic Law of the State.
64. Ibid., Speech of His Excellency the Head of the State at the Extraordinary Session of the Spanish Cortes on the 22nd of November, 1966, pp. 35-37.
65. Keesing's Contemporary Archives, vol. 16, 1967-1968, p. 21832.

7
The Political Structure of
the Franco Regime

The Head of State and the Council of the Realm

Franco's power was absolute. The authority which was granted to him by the decrees of September 30, 1936, January 30, 1938, and August 8, 1939, continued in force until the moment of his death. He was head of state, head of government, head of party, and chief legislator. Whatever powers he decided to share during the latter years of his regime were not irrevocably given away. The cautious liberalization of the political system—beginning with the Constitutive Law of the Cortes (1942), continuing with the Charter of the Spanish People (1945), the Law of the National Referendum (1945), the Law of Succession in the Headship of State (1947), and the Law of the Principles of the National Movement (1958), and ending with the Organic Law of the State (1967)—did not apply to Franco. None of the restrictions on the power of the head of state to be discussed in this and the following sections of this chapter applied to Franco. The Organic Law of the State contained the following Transitory Dispositions, which were integral to it:

I. When the provisions of the Law of Succession have been fulfilled, the person called to exercise the Headship of State, as King or Regent, shall assume the functions and duties assigned to the Head of State in the present law.

II. The attributions granted to the Head of State by the laws of January 30, 1938, and August 8, 1939, as well as the prerogatives bestowed upon him by Articles 6 and 13 of the Law of Succession, shall subsist and remain in force until the eventuality referred to in the preceding paragraph.

III. The National Leadership of the Movement is vested for life in the person of Francisco Franco, Caudillo of Spain. Upon the fulfillment of the provisions of the succession, it shall pass to the Head of State and by his delegation, to the President of the Government.[1]

The head of state is now King Juan Carlos, who under the Organic

Law of the State enjoys the following power:

> The Head of State is the supreme representative of the nation; personifies national sovereignty; exercises supreme political and administrative power; is vested with the national leadership of the Movement and ensures the strictest observance of its principles and other Fundamental Laws of the Kingdom as well as the continuity of the state and of the National Movement; guarantees and ensures the regular functioning of the high organs of state and the proper coordination between such organs; sanctions and promulgates laws and provides for their execution; exercises the supreme command of the Army, Navy and Air Force; safeguards the maintenance of public order at home and the security of the state abroad; lends his name to the administration of justice; exercises the prerogative of pardon; confers, in accordance with the law, appointments, public office and honors; accredits and receives diplomatic representatives; and performs whatever acts are required of him by the Fundamental Laws of the kingdom.[2]

The most important powers of the head of state, however, are shared with the Council of the Realm composed of the following members:

1. The prelate of the highest rank and seniority among those who are *procuradores* in the Cortes.
2. The captain-general, or in his absence, the lieutenant-general, in active service, with the most seniority of the army, navy, or air force, in that order.
3. The chairman of the Joint Chiefs of Staff or, in his absence, the most senior of the three chiefs of staff of the army, navy, and air force.
4. The chief justice of the Supreme Court of Justice.
5. The chairman of the Council of State.
6. The president of the Spanish Institute.
7. Two councillors elected by vote of each of the following groups of *procuradores* in the Cortes:
   a. Party
   b. Syndicates
   c. Municipalities
   d. Family
8. One councillor elected by vote by each of the following groups of *procuradores*:
   a. University rectors
   b. Professional associations[3]

The council is a kind of miniature Cortes and represents, in keeping with organic concepts, the basic Spanish institutions: the Church, the military, the courts, the family, the municipalities, the syndicates, the universities, and the professions. It is most probable that all of the members of the Council of the Realm will be *procuradores* in the Cortes, but the military men may not be unless they happen to have a seat as one of the twenty-five *procuradores* appointed directly by the head of state.[4] The chairman of the council is the president of the Cortes.

The head of state has the following powers, which theoretically he may exercise only with the assistance of the Council of the Realm:

1. He may prorogue a legislative term for grave reason for a specified period of time.[5]
2. He may take exceptional measures when external security, the independence of the nation, the integrity of the territory, or the national institutions are in imminent danger.[6]
3. He may submit to a national referendum a bill which he considers to be of extraordinary importance but which otherwise would not require a referendum as would the creation of a new Fundamental Law or the revision of an existing one.[7]
4. He appoints the prime minister from among three candidates (proposed by the Council of the Realm).[8]
5. He may remove the prime minister.[9]
6. He appoints the president of the Cortes from among three *procuradores* (proposed by the Council of the Realm).[10]
7. He may refuse to sanction laws passed by the Cortes.[11]
8. He may declare ordinary laws unconstitutional (an action in *contrafuero*).[12]

The power of the head of state would appear to be relatively contained if one is willing to accept the Council of the Realm as a legitimate organ of restraint. There are those, however, who believe that, apart from the power to legislate by his own fiat—a power belonging to Franco alone and not transferred to his successor—the present head of state has power almost commensurate with that of the caudillo. These opinions are based on a careful reading of the seven Fundamental Laws, whose terminology could either maximize or minimize the power of the king depending upon the interpretation of the wording and upon the attitude of the sovereign. Articles 15 and 18 of the Organic Law of the State[13] use unambiguous language when the former states that the head of state may demand the resignation of the prime minister *"de acuerdo con el Consejo del Reino"* ("in agreement with the Council of the Realm") and when the latter states that the prime minister may call for the resignation of the members of his cabinet *"aceptada por el Jefe del Estado"* ("with the approval of the head of state"). Yet, in Article 10 of the Organic Law, which lists formidable powers of the head of state, the words used to qualify that power are *"asistido por el Consejo del Reino"* ("assisted by the Council of the Realm"). There are those who claim that the word *"asistido"* is too imprecise and could be interpreted to have less than binding significance particularly when other articles and other laws use language that is not susceptible to misinterpretation. Article 16 of the Constitutive Law of the Cortes states that "the president of the Cortes shall submit to the Head of State, for his sanction, the laws approved by the Cortes which should be promulgated within a month of their receipt by the Head of State."[14] Article 17 of the same law states that "the Head of State, through an explanatory message and with the prior favorable ruling by the Council of the Realm, may return a law to the Cortes for renewed deliberation."[15]

The articles make it obligatory that a bill passed by the Cortes receive the sanction of the head of state before it may become a law. Moreover, sanction is to be followed by promulgation within a month. There is a clear distinction drawn between "sanction" and "promulgation." It is unclear, however, if the head of state has the absolute right to veto legislation by refusing his sanction since there is no specific provision in the Fundamental Laws for a bill automatically to become a law in the event it is rejected by the head of state and subsequently repassed in the Cortes by a majority greater than that needed for its initial approval. May the head of state refuse to sanction and not return a bill to the Cortes or is the bill automatically sent back to the Cortes if the Council of the Realm approves? In the official English translation of Article 17, the operative verb is "may return," which would appear to allow discretion. Must the head of state ask the Council of the Realm for its approval thereby giving the initiative to return a bill to the Cortes to the head of state? May the Council of the Realm initiate the action thereby forcing the hand of the head of state? If the bill is returned to the Cortes, its reconsideration could be blocked by the operation of Article 8 of the Constitutive Law of the Cortes, which specifies that the legislative order of the day is determined by the president of the Cortes (an appointee of the head of state) in agreement with the government.[16] If a bill reemerges from the Cortes in the same form in which it first was passed, does the bill automatically become law or must it once again obtain the sanction of the head of state? Could the head of state thereby indefinitely delay the enactment of legislation to which he was opposed? Or if he alone could not, could he together with the Council of the Realm do so? Since promulgation is distinct from sanction, may the head of state sanction but refuse to promulgate? In Article 16 of the Constitutive Law of the Cortes, the conditional tense of the verb is used. The laws "should be promulgated within a month of their receipt by the head of state" (*"debarán ser promulgadas"*), phraseology which, as in Article 17, would appear to allow discretion.[17]

Article 10 of the Organic Law of the State declares that the head of state shall be assisted by the Council of the Realm "to take exceptional measures when external security, the independence of the nation, the integrity of its territory or the institutional system of the kingdom are exposed to serious and imminent threat, giving a documented account to the Cortes."[18]

The ambiguity of the terminology "assisted" has already been discussed; the ambiguity of the entire provision potentially opens the door for constitutional dictatorship. The exceptional measures are not spelled out, nor is the nature of a "threat" clarified. Moreover, except for being bound to give "a documented account to the Cortes," the head of state appears to be otherwise unrestrained. There are no additional institutional requirements, nor are there any limitations on the period of time during which the exceptional measures may be in force. A head of state committed to democratization and willing to see his powers enfeebled by disuse through a narrow interpretation of royal prerogatives could establish a tradition which over time might come to bind his successors. But a head of state determined to exert his power to the fullest could find adequate constitutional justification through a broad interpretation of the Fundamental Laws.

The Council of Ministers

The Council of Ministers (called the cabinet or the government, all synonomous terms) is made up of the prime minister, fifteen ministers who head departments, and three ministers without portfolio. Those who head departments are the ministers of : (1) foreign affairs, (2) justice, (3) army, (4) navy, (5) air, (6) treasury (*Hacienda*), (7) interior (*Gobernación*), (8) public works, (9) education and science, (10) labor (11) industry, (12) agriculture, (13) commerce, (14) housing, and (15) information and tourism. Those ministers without portfolio are: (1) the secretary-general of the party (the second-in-command who runs the party on a day-to-day basis in the name of his chief, the National Leader—the prime minister by delegation of the head of state); (2) the commissioner of planning; and (3) the minister of syndicalist relations.

Until the positions were separated by the 1967 Organic Law of the

State, Franco was *constitutionally* both head of state and head of
government (i.e. prime minister). Since the separation, there exists a
curious constitutional relationship among the Cortes, the prime
minister and his cabinet, the Council of the Realm, and the head of state
that makes the locus of power difficult to discover unless we accept the
primacy of royal authority. The prime minister and the cabinet are not
responsible to the Cortes nor do they emerge from it. The government is
responsible solely to the head of state. The prime minister is appointed
by the head of state from among three candidates proposed by the
Council of the Realm. He holds his office for five years constitutionally
limited by the Organic Law of the State, [19] but he may be reappointed at
the end of that time. He retires: (1) upon the expiration of his term; (2) at
his own request subject to the approval of the head of state with
notification given to the Council of the Realm; (3) at the request of the
head of state in agreement with the Council of the Realm; or (4) at the
proposal of two-thirds of the Council of the Realm because of prime
ministerial incapacity.[20] The other members of the cabinet are
appointed by the head of state on the proposal of the prime minister.
Each retires: (1) on the retirement of the prime minister; (2) at the
request of the prime minister with the approval of the head of state; or (3)
at his own request with the approval of the head of state at the proposal
of the prime minister. [21] The prime minister and the other members of
the cabinet sit in the Cortes as ex officio members. As such they are
agents of the head of state within the Cortes. They are neither the
spokesmen for the Cortes before the head of state, nor are they the
expression of majority opinion within the Cortes. Theoretically, since
there are no constitutional provisions for political parties in Spain but
only for a National Movement that itself is the expression or
embodiment of the general will, there is neither a government nor an
opposition in the usual parliamentary sense, nor can there be
constitutionally until and unless radical revision of the Fundamental
Laws takes place. A discussion of systemic changes will make up the
larger part of the final chapter of this study.

   The Council of Ministers is brought into session and presided over by
the head of state. It is the cabinet's function theoretically to do no more
than to *assist* the head of state in determining policy, initiating
legislation, executing the laws, and administering the great departments
of state.[22] In this latter capacity, the cabinet has rule-making authority,
and it may exercise delegated legislation through the head of state upon
the authorization of the Cortes.[23] The prime minister and his fellow
ministers are collectively responsible for decisions made by the cabinet,
and each minister is individually responsible for acts carried out by him

or authorized by him to be carried out by others. Either the prime minister or the individual minister concerned is responsible for the actions of the head of state who remains constitutionally inviolable.[24] It is the opinion of some Spanish observers that inviolability in reality means not political but civil and criminal inviolability. These critics reason that since the prime minister and his cabinet are the agents of the head of state they are ipso facto responsible for him politically because they are his alter ego. Thus, according to their reasoning, inviolability has to apply to other than political activity and must, by logical deduction, apply to all other royal behavior. In short, these critics believe that the king has been placed by the constitution above the civil and criminal law.

Given the complexity of modern government and the inability of a single man like the head of state to be able personally to oversee more than the general direction of politics, each minister enjoys a large degree of autonomy and power provided he continues to have the confidence of the prime minister and ultimately of the head of state. Moreover, the prime minister, who is not even theoretically first among equals but is first followed by the rest of his ministers who are equal among themselves, occupies a particularly powerful position as head of government answerable only to the head of state. Of course, the observations made about the inability of the head of state to do more than oversee the general direction of policy would also apply with equal vigor to the prime minister. The latter, however, mines a unique source of political power as the active head of the party,[25] the chief purveyor of patronage throughout the entire political system, at the national, the provincial, and the local levels.

The Cortes

Composition

There are eight groups which make up the unicameral Spanish legislature—some elected directly by the people (defined to include only heads of family and married women), some directly appointed by the head of state, some who occupy their legislative posts automatically because of positions held in other parts of the sociopolitical structure (in other words, ex officio), and some, the largest number, indirectly elected by various corporate bodies often at four or five electoral steps removed from those who cast the first ballot.[26] The eight groups are: the political group, the syndicalist group, the local group, the family group, the cultural group, the professional group, the group of high office holders, and the group directly appointed by the head of state.

The political group includes the entire membership of the National Council of the Movement. The membership of the National Council includes the following men:

1. the prime minister appointed by the head of state
2. the secretary-general of the party appointed by the national leader of the party, (i.e., the prime minister)[27]
3. six directly appointed by the national leader of the party
4. forty national councillors directly appointed by the head of state[28]
5. one councillor elected by each of the fifty Spanish provinces plus one each for Ceuta and Melilla (the Spanish enclaves in Morocco) from among members of the provincial councils of the party[29]
6. twelve councillors representing the three basic organic pillars of the regime, the family, the community, and the syndicate (four from among the *procuradores* in the Cortes representing the family; four from among the *procuradores* in the Cortes representing the community; and four from among the *procuradores* in the Cortes representing the syndicates)[30]

The syndicalist group.[31] There are 150 *procuradores* who represent the twenty-nine individual, nationwide syndicates and the national Syndicalist Organization, which controls all the syndicates together as a body. From the individual syndicates come:

1. four *procuradores* (one each representing the employers, the workers, and the technicians, plus the national president) chosen by each of the twenty-nine syndicates with the exception of the Farm Workers and Herders
2. twelve *procuradores* chosen by the Farm Workers and Herders
3. three *procuradores* chosen by the Syndicalist Federation of Commerce[32]
4. two *procuradores* chosen by the Cooperative Societies[33]
5. one *procurador* each elected by the Brotherhood of Fishermen, the Association of Artesans and Small and Medium Businessmen, and the National Press Association

From the national Syndicalist Organization come:

1. the secretary-general and the deputy secretary-general
2. the presidents and secretaries of the National Council of Employers and the National Council of Employees
3. the directors of the administrative and financial and of the aid

and promotional sections of the national Syndicalist Organization[34]

The remaining *procuradores* needed to complete the constitutionally required 150 syndicalist *procuradores* are chosen by the Permanent Committee of the Syndicalist Congress. The number 150 is fixed and permanent.

The local group represents the municipalities and the provinces.

1. There is one *procurador* in the Cortes from each province representing the municipalities within that province. He is chosen in the following manner. Each council of each municipality within each province chooses a delegate from among its councillors and the mayor to assist at a provincial electoral meeting. At this meeting each delegate casts a vote weighted according to the size of the municipality he represents (the weights being 10,000; 1,000; 100; 10; and 1 vote). Balloting continues until a single candidate from all the delegates present at the meeting receives an absolute majority. There is, in addition, a *procurador* for each of the municipalities over 300,000 population and Ceuta and Melilla.

2. There is one *procurador* in the Cortes representing each of the provinces chosen from the councillors elected to the ·provincial council.[35] The complex election process begins at the level of the municipal council. Municipal councillors are elected in the following manner. One-third of the councillors are directly elected by heads of families and (since October, 1970) by married women, and one-third are elected by the syndicates organized at the local level. These elected councillors as a body co-opt the last one-third from among distinguished local residents representing professional, economic, and cultural interests who have been listed by the governor of the province. The municipal councils in turn elect from their members and the mayor the representatives to the provincial councils.[36]

The family group is the only group directly elected to the Cortes. This group came into existence with the Organic Law of the State promulgated in 1967. Until that time there were no *procuradores* directly elected to the Cortes even though the Fundamental Laws from the beginning had declared the family to be one of the three major organic pillars of the state. Each province sends two *procuradores* to the Cortes elected by those heads of families and married women over twenty-one years of age.[37]

The cultural group is composed of the following representatives:

1. the rectors of the eighteen national universities, appointed by the government

2. the president of the *Instituto de España* (Spanish Institute, which unites and heads the eight Royal Academies appointed by the government)[38]
3. two *procuradores* elected by the Royal Academies from their members
4. the president of the Consejo Superior de Investigaciones (Council for Advanced Scientific Research), appointed by the government
5. two *procuradores* elected from among the members of the Council for Advanced Scientific Research

The professional group is composed of the following representatives:[39]

1. the president of the Instituto de Ingenieros Civiles (Institute of Civil Engineers)
2. one representative elected from the Association of Engineers that forms the institute
3. two representatives from the Colegios de Abogados (Colleges of Lawyers)[40]
4. two representatives of the Colegios de Médicos (Medical Colleges)[41]
5. one representative from each of the following colleges:[42]
   a. *Agentes de Cambio y Bolsa* (Stock Exchange Agents)
   b. *Arquitectos* (Architects)
   c. *Economistas* (Economists)
   d. *Farmacistas* (Pharmacists)
   e. *Licenciados y Doctores en Ciencias Políticas* (Bachelors and Doctors of Political Science)
   f. *Licenciados y Doctores en Ciencias y Letras* (Bachelors and Doctors of Science and Letters)
   g. *Licenciados y Doctores en Ciencias Químicas y Físico-Químicas* (Bachelors and Doctors in Chemical and Physico-chemical Sciences)
   h. *Notarios* (Notaries)
   i. *Procuradores de los Tribunales* (Court Attorneys)
   j. *Registradores de la Propriedad* (Property Recorders)
   k. *Veterinarios* (Veterinarians)
6. three representatives from the Cámaras Oficiales de Comercio (Official Chambers of Commerce)
7. one representative of the Asociaciones de Inquilinos (Tenant Associations)

8. one representative of the Cámaras de Propriedad Urbana (Chamber of Urban Property Owners)

The *group of high office holders* (all appointed by the head of state) includes:

1. all the members of the cabinet
2. the president of the Consejo de Estado (Council of State)[43]
3. the president of the Tribunal Supremo de Justicia (Supreme Court of Justice)
4. the president of the Consejo Supremo de Justicia Militar (Supreme Council of Military Justice)
5. the president of the Tribunal de Cuentas del Reino (Court of Exchequer of the Kingdom)
6. the president of the Consejo de Economía Nacional (National Economic Council)

The group directly appointed by the head of state. The head of state directly appoints twenty-five *procuradores* to the Cortes. Under the terms of Article 2, j, of the Constitutive Law of the Cortes the appointments must be approved by the Council of the Realm. Those appointed are men who have distinguished themselves in military, ecclesiastical, or administrative duties, or who have in some way been of outstanding service to the nation.[44]

Function

The Cortes is not a political body if by political is meant the power to hold the government responsible for its actions. The government is not the agent of the Cortes nor does the government emerge from the Cortes. The government is responsible solely to the head of state, who appoints and dismisses the cabinet. All ministers automatically sit in the Cortes ex officio as members of the government. The legislature is linked functionally to the executive by the president of the Cortes[45] who, although a member of the legislature, is not the agent of the Cortes but of the government and of the head of state. The president of the Cortes is appointed for six years by the head of state from three *procuradores* proposed to him by the Council of the Realm.[46] He retires: (1) at his own request with the approval of the head of state assisted by the Council of the Realm; (2) at the decision of the head of state in agreement with the Council of the Realm; or (3) because of incapacity recognized by two-thirds of the *procuradores*.[47] The president has almost total control over the Cortes and has among his powers those: (1) to swear in all *procuradores* and assign to them their duties, titles, and credentials; (2) to make all committee assignments on the proposal of the Standing Committee of the Cortes[48] with the approval of the government; (3) to appoint all committee chairmen; (4) to convoke the full Cortes; (5) to decide if plenary sessions shall be open or closed to the public; (6) to preside at plenary sessions; (7) to apply the rules of procedure at all plenary sessions; (8) to arrange the order of the day for the plenary sessions of the Cortes with the approval of the government; and (9) to arrange the order of the day for the committees of the Cortes with the approval of the government.[49]

The Cortes has a number of nonpolitical, legislative functions if by legislative one means deliberative and not representative. Its principal task is to elaborate and approve all laws,[50] but there are exceptions to this power. First, the government, at its initiative, may, for reasons of urgency, request that the head of state legislate by decree. The head of state may or may not accede to the request.[51] Second, the head of state, at his initiative, assisted by the Council of the Realm, may take "exceptional measures when external security, the independence of the nation, the integrity of its territory, or the institutional system of the kingdom are exposed to serious and imminent threat, giving a documented account to the Cortes."[52] Third, the government, at its initiative and with the authorization of the Cortes, may submit for the sanction of the head of state dispositions with the force of law—a form of delegated legislation.[53] With these exceptions, all bills must pass through the Cortes, first through the permanent committees and then through the plenary of the Cortes.[54] Constitutionally, certain bills have to pass successfully only through committee in order to become law, but in practice almost all bills are approved by the full Cortes, which in reality merely rubber-stamps the decisions of the committees. The committees do most of the legislative work, but this statement should not be interpreted to mean that committees are powerful. Spanish legislative committees have approximately the same amount of discretion as do British parliamentary committees once Second Reading in the House of Commons has determined a bill's fate. Spanish committees may amend, change, and clarify but may not alter the basic shape and content of a governmental bill if the government does not approve.

Not all bills are of governmental origin, however. Bills may also begin in the Cortes, but the process is difficult and has been rarely employed. Only twice since 1943 have proposals of legislative origin been turned into law. In fact, all procedure for action of legislative origin is arduous. Bills originating with an individual *procurador* not only must be submitted for the consideration and approval of the president of the Cortes but also must carry the signatures of at least fifty *procuradores*. An individual *procurador* may introduce amendments to governmental bills; may, with permission of the president of the Cortes, orally question ministers in plenary sessions of the Cortes; and may submit written questions and prayers to the government. The government is required to respond under the rules established by the Cortes, but because the cabinet is not responsible to the Cortes the answers are usually general, and little detail is proffered. Amendments for an entire bill must carry at least five signatures. The amendments must be submitted to a subcommittee of the pertinent permanent committee, but in the event an amendment is rejected by the subcommittee, only the first signatory is allowed to defend the amendment orally before the full committee. The decision of the full committee is submitted to the plenary of the Cortes, which may by majority vote accept or reject the work of the committee. If an amendment has been rejected at the committee stage but has received the favorable vote of at least one-fifth of the committee membership, its sponsors may be allowed to present their case to the plenary, but once again only the first signatory is allowed to speak. From the above explanation, it is clear that all procedure is designed to deter legislative initiative.

The Cortes plays several constitutional roles. The government is empowered to recognize by a two-thirds majority the incapacity of the head of state. This decision must be communicated to the Council of the Realm. If, by the same majority, the council should agree with the government, the president of the Council of the Realm (who is president of the Cortes) notifies the Cortes, which within eight days shall vote a resolution declaring the incapacity of the head of state. The resolution must be passed by two-thirds of the *procuradores* present who must number at least the absolute majority of all members.[55] The Cortes, along with the Council of the Realm, must approve royal abdications or renouncements of any nature and the marriages of the sovereign or of his immediate successors.[56] The Cortes must approve all treaties or agreements that affect the sovereignty or the territorial integrity of the nation.[57] The Cortes must vote by a two-thirds majority any modification or derogation of a Fundamental Law, which action must then be approved by national referendum.[58]

The Ambiguous Relationship among the Head of State, the Council of the Realm, the Government, and the Cortes

Article 2, Section 2 of the Organic Law of the State reads: "The institutional system of the Spanish state is based on the principles of unity of power and coordination of functions."[59] While Franco was alive unity was absolute; coordination was honored in theory but was practiced only within the limits tolerated by the caudillo. Now that the succession has taken place and the machinery of coordination has come into operation, the lines of political authority form a convoluted pattern that, critics say, traces power circuitously but unremittingly back to an absolute head of state—once again, as it was during the Franco era, sacrificing coordination to unity. The defenders of the system claim that, on the contrary, the lines of authority interact in such a way that power has no single locus but moves in constant flux among a number of bodies or positions, none of which has ultimate ascendancy over the rest. According to this logic, the system achieves the results of checks and balances without the institutional devices of the separation of power that, according to organic theory, divides sovereignty and undermines unity and coordination.

It is possible to support with equal weight both the critics and the apologists of the present Spanish system. The Spanish constitution is not a precisely conceived, single document but rather a collection of seven Fundamental Laws, written at different times over a thirty-year period, all of whose inconsistencies have not been reconciled. Moreover, the imprecise language used in writing these laws makes their meaning ambiguous. It may be that those who wrote the laws were "careless" rather than "imprecise," but "careless" connotes nondeliberate action, and it is impossible to know if they were or were not aware of how they were using language. Nor is it possible to know if they were or were not studiously providing for the possibility of disparate interpretation that would enable the system to evolve, after the passing of Franco, in the direction indicated by the major political forces in post-Franco Spain, but within the limits of the constitution, thereby obviating the necessity for potentially traumatic, fundamental systemic change. No one can know with certainty. Until the system evolves, however, and through evolution takes a different shape, it might be worthwhile to consider the following observations.

Neither the prime minister nor the other members of the cabinet emerge from the Cortes. The head of state appoints the prime minister who in turn presents the members of his cabinet for the approval of the head of state. The prime minister and his cabinet are responsible not to the Cortes but to the king. The appointment of the prime minister must be made from among three nominees proposed by the Council of the Realm which itself emerges almost in its entirety from the Cortes many of whose members have been directly or indirectly appointed by the head of state, who may remove them. Could the Council of the Realm deliberately nominate three men who would be unacceptable to the head of state? Would the head of state be forced to choose one of those three or might he refuse to nominate? Could an impasse result between the council and the king? Who would break it? The constitution is silent. Could the king call for the resignation of those members of the Council of the Realm who are his appointees? There would be nothing to prevent the king from doing so, but his appointees do not make up the majority of the council. He appoints seven of the councillors. The remaining ten are elected within the Cortes.

Either the prime minister or an appropriate minister must countersign all official actions of the king. Could either refuse? Could the situation arise in which no member of the cabinet would take responsibility for an action of the king? The king may, of course, remove the prime minister (and with him automatically the rest of the ministers), but he may do so only with the agreement of (*de acuerdo con*) the Council of the Realm.[60] Could not the Council refuse its approval thereby forcing the head of state to keep an unwanted government? On the other hand, an obstinate but irremovable government could accomplish nothing because it would be unable to have its decisions carried out without the approval of the king.

The Cortes cannot hold the cabinet or the king responsible for their behavior. All laws, however, must be passed by the Cortes, which may not be dissolved. Under the constitution it may be prorogued by the king assisted (*asistido*, that imprecise word) by the Council of the Realm, but there are no constitutional provisions for dissolution and the calling of new elections.[61] Could the Cortes refuse to pass legislation proposed by the king and the Council of Ministers? Could an impasse emerge between the Cortes on the one hand and the king and cabinet on the other? The king, however, could be empowered by the government to rule by decree "giving notice to the Cortes" of his intended action.[62] Moreover, in the event of national emergency the king may take "exceptional measures," assisted (*asistido*) by the Council of the Realm.[63] Could the king overcome the refusal of the Cortes to pass his legislation by ruling by decree? If the Council of the Realm took exception to this action, could it call for the resignation of the prime minister thus making it impossible for the government and the king to cooperate? But the council may call for the resignation of the prime minister by two-thirds majority and only then for prime ministerial incapacity.[64] May the prime minister be declared incapacitated for carrying out a constitutionally sanctioned function, i.e., the assumption of responsibility for the actions of the head of state? Viewed from a different perspective, could the prolonged refusal of the Cortes to pass legislation be interpreted as a national emergency thereby bringing into operation Article 10 of the Organic Law of the State, which allows the king to take "exceptional measures"? To use this power, however, he must be assisted (*asistido*—once again that ambiguous term) by the Council of the Realm.[65] Since the Council of the Realm emerges from the Cortes, could not the council refuse its assistance if its members felt that their parent body was correct in refusing to pass legislation?

If the king were to decide to use his power in a manner both the government and the Council of the Realm considered to be illegitimate, could the king be removed, i.e., forced to abdicate, because of incapacity?[66] May incapacity be interpreted to mean political incapacity? The term usually connotes physical or mental not political inability, but the constitution is silent on this point. If, on the other hand, the government were supportive of the political behavior of the king and took responsibility for him, could the Council of the Realm demand the resignation of the prime minister and then propose to the king for the premier's replacement three nominees sympathetic to the views of the Council of the Realm? If the Council of the Realm, the government, and the king were of one mind, however, would any action to discipline the king thereby be stopped? There is no provision in the constitution that allows the Cortes to take the initiative in calling for ministerial resignation or royal abdication.

The Lesser Councils

The Council of Regency (Consejo de Regencia)

The Council of Regency is much less important now that Franco is dead and Spain has a king; in fact, the council's role was reduced from the day (July 22, 1969) that Franco designated Juan Carlos to be his successor, though under the Law of Succession in the Headship of State Franco could have changed his mind irrespective of the approval the Cortes had given to the man selected to follow him.[67]

The council is composed of the following three men: the president of the Cortes; the highest-ranking prelate serving as councillor of the realm with the most seniority; and the captain-general (or in his absence the lieutenant-general) with the most seniority in the active service of the army, navy, or air force, in that order. The council's task is to act as head of state in the event the head of state were to die without a direct heir or be declared incapacitated (or in the case of Franco, were he to have died without having named a successor). If the king should die without a direct heir, the council, within a period of three days, convokes the

Council of the Realm and the Council of Ministers, which together choose the appropriate person of royal blood to be king, or in the event such person is not available, a Spanish male who "by his prestige, capacity, and possible service to the nation"[68] should act as regent. The terms and conditions for the duration of the regency are determined by the Council of the Realm and Council of Ministers. Either the proposed king or the regent must then be approved by the Cortes before which the successor swears his oath of allegiance to the principles of the National Movement and of the other Fundamental Laws.[69]

If the king has a direct heir, which under the terms of the Law of Succession must be a male at least thirty years of age, then upon the monarch's death the Council of Regency, acting as temporary head of state, convokes the Cortes and the Council of the Realm to receive from the new king the oath of allegiance. Until the death or incapacity of the sovereign, the Council of Regency has no further duties.

The Council of State (Consejo del Estado)

The Council of State is the highest consultative body in Spain, outranked only by the cabinet and the Council of the Realm.[70] The council is constitutionally established and organically reflects, as do all other councils, the basic national institutions: the Church, the party, the armed forces, the syndicates, the courts, and the universities. It is made up of a president appointed by the head of state, eight ex officio members who sit on the council because of their positions in other bodies (to which bodies most have been directly appointed by the head of state), and seven members directly appointed by the head of state for three-year terms. The ex officio members include the Cardinal Primate of Spain, the vice secretary-general of the party, the chief of the Joint Chiefs of Staff, the attorney-general of the Supreme Court of Justice, the rector of the University of Madrid, the Minister of Syndical Relations, the director-general of the *Contencioso del Estado*, [71] and the director of the *Instituto de Estudios Políticos* (Institute of Political Study), a research and publishing foundation affiliated with the party. The seven councillors directly appointed come from among ex-cabinet ministers, archbishops and bishops, national councillors of the party, generals from the army and air force and admirals from the navy, and diplomatic personnel with the rank of ambassador.

The power of the Council of State is not commensurate with its prestige. In fact, it has little power but acts in an advisory capacity aiding the government in drafting bills, applying the law through administrative regulations, interpreting agreements and contracts entered into by the governmental departments and agencies, settling jurisdictional disputes among the ministries, and interpreting treaties. It also advises the Council of the Realm on appeals of *contrafuero*. Most of the work is done not by the councillors, whose appointments are largely honorific, but by members of one of the superelite bureaucratic *cuerpos* (corps), the Letrados del Consejo del Estado (Attorneys of the Council of State). These attorneys and the councillors to whom they report work in sections more or less parallel to the ministers.

The Appeal of *Contrafuero*

The appeal of *contrafuero* is the Spanish equivalent to the American judicial review that tests laws for constitutionality. In Spain the appeal is not taken by an aggrieved or injured individual, nor is it initiated by a judicial action. The test must come before the Council of the Realm within two months of the publication of a law or of a governmental resolution in the *Boletín Oficial del Estado* (*Official Bulletin of State*). After that date, an action in *contrafuero* is precluded.

The appeal may originate in two places. By a resolution of two-thirds of its members, the National Council of the party may challenge the constitutionality of any law, decree-law, or governmental resolution. In the case of laws to be submitted for referendum, the National Council must give its opinion regarding the possible existence of grounds for an appeal to *contrafuero*.[72] This requirement applies not only to a law derogating or amending a Fundamental Law that must be submitted to referendum [73] but also to any law the head of state may decide to submit for referendum.[74] The Cortes, through the two-thirds vote of its Standing Committee,[75] may challenge the constitutionality of decree laws (which by their very nature bypass the legislature)[76] and governmental regulations (which originate with the bureaucracy). The Cortes may not challenge the constitutionality of laws because it would be questioning the legality of its own actions. Until a bill becomes a law, however, the Standing Committee of the Cortes may question a bill's constitutionality and make its opinion known to the president of the Cortes, who then requires the substantive committee from which the bill emerged to reconsider it.

If a law, decree-law, or regulation is challenged, it goes before the Council of the Realm, which notifies the head of state. The Standing Committee or the president of the Cortes are also notified so that either may appoint a representative to defend the law's constitutionality before the council, which, during appeals of *contrafuero*, is chaired by its ranking judicial member, the chief justice of the Supreme Court of Justice. The council sets up a Committee of Inquiry presided by the head justice (*presidente*) of a division of the Supreme Court of Justice and composed of one member of the National Council of the party, one permanent councillor of state, and one *procurador* from the Cortes. The committee studies the case and makes its recommendation to the council, which votes a resolution. If the council considers the law, decree-law, or regulation to be unconstitutional, its resolution is submitted to the head of state. It is not clear from the language of Title 10 of the Organic Law of the State, which is devoted to the appeal of *contrafuero*, if the head of state is required to promulgate the proposal of the Council of the Realm or if the decision is left to his discretion. Article 59 reads: "As a guarantee of the principles and norms infringed by *contrafuero* the right of appeal before the Head of State has been established."[77] Article 62 reads: "The Council of the Realm . . . shall propose to the head of state the resolution taken."[78] There are no words that carry the weight of obligation on the part of the head of state.

Again one sees how much power is wielded by the post-Franco head of state. The head of state and the cabinet are the initiators of legislation, and the head of state must also sanction and promulgate the laws passed by the Cortes. Unless the Fundamental Laws have been designed to give to the successors of Franco power equal to his, is there not the potential for abuse of power in granting to the initiator of law the discretion to decide upon its constitutionality? If the head of state is allowed to govern by decree on the initiative of the cabinet (all of whose members are appointed by him and are responsible solely to him and not to the Cortes), once again is there not the potential for abuse of power in allowing the head of state discretion in promulgating the unconstitutionality of his own decrees? Finally, under Article 10, d, of the Organic Law of the State, the head of state, assisted by the Council of the Realm, may take exceptional measures in times of emergency.[79] Are these measures constitutionally testable? The Organic Law appears to be silent on this point. If they are not testable, then may not a head of state uncommitted to the democratization of the system use this provision to rationalize personal, arbitrary government? If the measures are testable, is it not anomalous that the same council that assists the head of state in taking exceptional measures is also the council that must make the resolution of unconstitutionality submitted to the head of state for promulgation?

Notes

1. *Fundamental Laws of the State: The Spanish Constitution*, The Organic

Law of the State, First Transitory Disposition.
   2. Ibid., Article 6.
   3. Ibid., The Law of Succession in the Headship of State, Article 4.
   4. See p. 169 in this study.
   5. *Fundamental Laws of the State: The Spanish Constitution*, Organic Law
of the State, Article 10.
   6. Ibid.
   7. Ibid.
   8. Ibid., Article 14.
   9. Ibid., Article 15.
   10. Ibid., Constitutive Law of the Cortes, Article 7.
   11. Ibid., Organic Law of the State, Article 10.
   12. Ibid., Articles 59, 60, 61, 62.
   13. Ibid., Articles 15, 18.
   14. Ibid., Constitutive Law of the Cortes.
   15. Ibid.
   16. Ibid.
   17. *Deberán* is the future tense, but its meaning idiomatically in this usage is
conditional.
   18. Ibid., The Organic Law of the State.
   19. Ibid., Article 14, II.
   20. Ibid., Article 15.
   21. Ibid., Articles 17 and 18.
   22. Ibid., Article 13.
   23. Ibid., Article 51.
   24. Ibid., Article 8.
   25. Ibid., Article 25.
   26. The appointed members of the Cortes sit at the discretion of the head of
state; the ex officio members sit while they occupy the post that automatically
allows them their seats in the Cortes. The rest of the *procuradores* sit for four
years.
   27. Until his death Franco was the national leader of the party. With his death
the terms of Article 25 of the Organic Law of the State, by which the prime
minister becomes national leader of the party and head of its Standing
Committee, came into operation.
   The prime minister and the secretary-general are examples of those cases in
which a man sits in the Cortes in more than one capacity. The prime minister
and the secretary-general (who sits in the cabinet because of his party position)
would automatically be members of the Cortes because they were a part of the
government. As the reader recalls, the government does not emerge from the
Cortes, but sits in the Cortes ex officio because it is the government.
   28. Now that Franco is dead, this is a self-perpetuating group. Franco could
have removed any of these men at will, but at his death, the forty sitting
appointed councillors became a permanent body whose members must retire at
seventy-five years of age. Vacancies will be filled by vote of the Plenary Council
of the party choosing from among three candidates proposed by this permanent

group (Article 22, Organic Law of the State).

29. For electoral purposes within the party, each province is considered equal irrespetive of its population, giving to the provincial councillors as a group a rural and conservative bias and seriously underrepresenting those provinces in which Madrid and Barcelona are located.

30. This is another example of dual and circular representation. All of the members of the National Council of the party sit in the Cortes, but twelve of those members are *procuradores* already sitting there.

31. For a description and explanation of the syndicates, see Appendix A.

32. The Syndicalist Federation of Commerce functions in a manner very similar to the other syndicates but has a separate legal classification. See *Ley Syndical* (Syndical Law) Article 31 and *Disposiciones Adicionales, Segunda* in *Leyes Fundamentales y normas complementarias* (Madrid: Boletín Oficial del Estado, 1973), pp. 303-47.

33. Cooperative Societies have always been an important part of the Spanish working-class society, and for that reason they have been awarded representation in the Cortes.

34. These are appointive positions within the bureaucracy of the Syndicalist Organization.

35. Because each province is considered equal irrespective of population, as in the case of the provincial representatives of the party discussed in note 29, the *procuradores* representing the provincial councils have a rural and conservative bias and seriously underrepresent the provinces in which Madrid and Barcelona are located.

36. In the vast majority of cases it will be the mayor who is chosen to sit on the provincial council. Each province is administered by a governor appointed by the head of state, and each municipality is administered by a mayor. In municipalities over 10,000 population, he is appointed by the minister of the interior and in municipalities under 10,000 by the governor. The governor is also the provincial head of the party, and the mayors under his control are the local chiefs.

37. An unmarried man or woman of any age cannot vote. It is unclear if an unmarried man who came to head a family because of the incapacity or death of a mother or father would have the vote. By contrast, in the referenda all men and women over eighteen may vote.

Again, because the provinces are considered equal irrespective of population, the comments made in notes 29 and 35 are applicable here. Moreover, because all political organizations—both parties and pressure groups—were prohibited in Spain until 1976, each candidate for the family group in the past ran on his or her own resources. No fund-raising of any kind was allowed. Consequently, the representatives of the family group have come overwhelmingly from the economically comfortable strata of society. The implications of the new law allowing political associations will be discussed in the last chapter of this book.

38. The Royal Academies are (1) *Bellas Artes* (Fine Arts); (2) *Ciencias Exactas, Físicas y Naturales* (Exact, Physical, and Natural Sciences); (3) *Ciencias Morales y Políticas* (Moral and Political Sciences); (4) *Española* (Spanish

Language); (5) *Farmacia* (Pharmacy); (6) *Historia* (History); (7) *Jurisprudencia y Legislación* (Jurisprudence and Legislation); (8) *Medicina* (Medicine).

39. The glaring omission among the professional groups is those associations representing teachers either at the university, secondary, or elementary levels.

40. Similar to the American Bar Association.

41. Similar to the American Medical Association.

42. The colleges are professional associations. The law is open ended; if new professional associations come into being they shall receive representation in the Cortes under the provisions of Article 1, i, of the Constitutive Law of the Cortes.

43. For a description of the structure and function of the Council of State see pp. 175-176.

44. Franco was exempt constitutionally from requiring approval of the Council of the Realm. His successors are not exempt.

45. In the official English-language translation of the Spanish Constitution, the *presidente de las Cortes* is called the speaker of the Cortes. I believe it would be less misleading to refer to him as the president of the Cortes to avoid possible confusion in the mind of the reader with the speaker of the American House of Representatives or of the British House of Commons, neither of whom he resembles.

46. The reader will recall that these restrictions or limitations on the appointive and dismissive powers of the head of state apply only to the successors of Franco. Franco's power was without bounds.

47. *Fundamental Laws of the State: The Spanish Constitution*, Constitutive Law of the Cortes, Article 7.

48. Each of the eight groups represented in the Cortes is represented on the Standing Committee, a kind of Cortes in miniature, which acts in the name of the Cortes between sessions and in addition has the authority: (1) to initiate action to declare the incapacity of the president of the Cortes and (2) to initiate the appeals of *contrafuero*.

49. Carlos Iglesias Selgas, *Las Cortes Españolas* (Madrid: Cabal Editor, 1973), pp. 189-95.

50. *Fundamental Laws of the State: The Spanish Constitution*, Constitutive Law of the Cortes, Article 1.

51. Ibid., Article 13.

52. Ibid., Organic Law of the State, Article 10.

53. Ibid., Article 51.

54. The permanent committees of the Cortes more or less parallel the ministries in their areas of competence.

55. *Fundamental Laws of the State: The Spanish Constitution*, Law of Succession in the Headship of State, Article 14.

56. Ibid., Article 12.

57. Ibid., Constitutive Law of the Cortes, Article 14.

58. Ibid., Law of Succession in the Headship of State, Article 10.

59. Ibid., Organic Law of the State.

60. Ibid., Article 15.

61. Ibid., Article 10.

62. Ibid., Constitutive Law of the Cortes, Article 15.

63. Ibid., Organic Law of the State, Article 10.

64. Ibid., Article 15.

65. Ibid., Article 10.

66. Ibid., Law of Succession in the Headship of State, Article 14.

67. Ibid., Article 6.

68. Ibid., Article 8, I, II.

69. Ibid., Constitutive Law of the Cortes, Article 9, and Organic Law of the State, Article 50, a.

70. Ibid., Organic Law of the State, Article 40, IV.

71. The *Contencioso del Estado* has the function of an administrative court.

72. *Fundamental Laws of the State: The Spanish Constitution*, Organic Law of the State, Article 65.

73. Ibid., Law of Succession in the Headship of State, Article 10.

74. Ibid., Law of the National Referendum, Article 1.

75. See note 48 for the composition of the Standing Committee.

76. *Fundamental Laws of the State: The Spanish Constitution*, Organic Law of the State, Article 60.

77. Ibid.

78. Ibid.

79. Ibid.

8
The National Movement

On May 17, 1958, near the beginning of the period of the most profound socioeconomic change to occur within Spain since the end of the Civil War, Franco personally promulgated the Ley de Principios del Movimiento Nacional (Law on the Principles of the National Movement). The law was the sixth of the seven Fundamental Laws that make up the Spanish constitution, but hierarchically it outranks all the others. It is the only Fundamental Law declared to be eternal.

> The principles contained in the present decree, the synthesis of those inspiring the Fundamental Laws legalized by the nation on the sixth day of July, nineteen hundred and forty-seven, are by their very nature, permanent and unalterable.[1]

The law inscribed the creed of the state as it had evolved since its creation by Franco in 1936 and placed its canons within the ark of the National Movement, the transmutation of the F.E.T. y de las J.O.N.S.

The F.E.T. y de las J.O.N.S. had been the only party in Spain since Franco's call for unification on April 19, 1937, when all other political organizations and parties were dissolved and declared illegal.[2] At that time, the F.E.T. y de las J.O.N.S. had the characteristics of a fascist party. Its aggressive statutes were set forth on July 31, 1939. Article 1 reads:

> The *F.E.T. y de las J.O.N.S.* serves as the militant inspirational Movement and basis of the Spanish state. . . . The *F.E.T. y de las J.O.N.S.* provides the disciplined means whereby the people, united and orderly, are linked to the state, and the state inculcates in the people the virtues of service, fraternity and hierarchy. . . . The *F.E.T. y de las J.O.N.S.* constitutes a permanent guardian of the eternal values of the fatherland.[3]

Article 5 declared that there were two classifications of members, militants and adherents. Militants were: (1) those who had been members either of the Falange Española de las J.O.N.S. or of the Comunión Tradicionalista before their merger creating the F.E.T. y de las J.O.N.S. on April 20, 1937, or those who had been admitted directly by the political junta prior to the publication of the Statutes of the F.E.T. y de las J.O.N.S. decreed on August 4, 1937; (2) those who were members of the Nationalist armed forces; or (3) those who had been admitted by the personal decision of the caudillo or who had been recommended by the provincial headquarters for outstanding service to the Rebel cause before or during the war.[4] Adherents were those later admitted by the secretary-general of the F.E.T. y de las J.O.N.S. or by the provincial or local chief. Article 7 of the party statutes reads:

> Adherents shall serve in the *F.E.T. y de las J.O.N.S.* without any of the rights or status of members thereof. Prior to the expiration of five years the appropriate provincial chief must decide clearly the status of the adherent, either raising him to the category of militant or excluding him from the organizaiton.[5]

It would appear that the F.E.T. y de las J.O.N.S. was an elitist state party that exalted its members over their fellow citizens and made membership an overt act of choice excluding all those unwilling to stand and be counted. It would also appear that party militancy would be essential for those who aspired to high political posts.

These two observations are correct if one looks at the Franco regime superficially, but the simple truth obscures the accurate appraisal of the place that the F.E.T. y de las J.O.N.S. came to occupy in the Spanish political system. In a sense, everyone had to be a Falangist in Franco's Spain. One could not fail to go through the rituals of the party because they were the rites of the victors, but the degrees of devotion varied greatly. One's identification with other organizations—the military, the monarchists (Alfonsine), the traditionalists (Carlist), the Church, *Acción Católica* (Catholic Action), and later on, Opus Dei—came to categorize a man much more precisely than membership in the F.E.T. y de las J.O.N.S. Only those who identified themselves exclusively with the party, who regarded themselves as party men above all else, came to be considered Falangists for the purposes of the political balance that Franco assiduously maintained from the beginning of his rule.[6] Franco did not permit the party to be the sole organ of recruitment for national political office. It was never necessary to work oneself up through the party in order to occupy positions of leadership in the state. Consequently, the apparatus of the party did not parallel the structure of the state, nor did it absorb, and by absorption, dominate the state. Never was the F.E.T. y de las J.O.N.S. more than one of the several organizations considered by Franco to be the pillars of his political system.

Even in Franco's first cabinet created on February 1, 1938, at the height of Falangist fervor, only three out of the thirteen ministers were identified with the party, and two of those three had dual affiliations, Ramón Serrano Súñer with the C.E.D.A.[7] and the Count of Rodezno with the traditionalists. Only Raimundo Fernández Cuesta was an orthodox Falangist. Perhaps even more indicative of the party's position as only one among several contending groups within Franco's uniquely pluralist system was the inability of its militants to capture the most important ministries relating to the direct control of the people: interior,[8] education, and the armed forces. True enough, from February 1, 1938, until May 20, 1941, a Falangist was in charge of the Ministry of the Interior, but that Falangist was Serrano Súñer, Franco's brother-in-law, who was never beyond the caudillo's grip. From May 20, 1941, until the present, no one whose primary identification has been with the party has been in control of the Ministry of the Interior. The Ministry of Education, with its vast potential for socialization, has been in the hands of men closely linked to the Chruch—traditionalists, monarchists, Catholic Action, and Opus Dei. The men who have headed the ministries overseeing national defense (the Ministry of National Defense in the first cabinet, and the separate ministries of the army, navy, and air force in all succeeding governments) have been identified intimately and exclusively with the military. The first men to administer the Ministry of Information and Tourism, which was established in July, 1951, and to which were transferred the regulation and censorship of publishing and the media, were Falangists—Gabriel Arias Salgado and later, José Solís Ruiz. But by 1951, the party's joint-tenancy in political power had been firmly established by Franco, and its claim to hegemony was no longer a serious threat.

Yet, irrespective of the nature of its role in the political system, the F.E.T. y de las J.O.N.S. was the only political party in Spain. It was not the only avenue to political power, but no other avenue that labeled itself a party was able to exist legally. In fact, no political associations of any kind (parties or pressure groups) were able to function within the law. One was a Falangist or one was nothing. Spain may have been different from the conventional model of the nondemocratic, single party state, but for those who opposed the regime, the party remained narrowly based, exclusionist, and irrevocably linked to its fascist origins. As the political system evolved, however, and as more and more allegiant citizens were needed to take part in Spain's socioeconomic reawakening, Franco sought to change the image of the Falange. He stressed the differences between what he disparagingly called a party and what he considered to be his own political movement. In the official anthology of his public utterances called *Pensamiento Político de Franco* (*The Political Thought of Franco*), there is a section dedicated to the Movement containing a subsection entitled: "The Difference between Movement and Party."[9] It is not clear how Franco differentiated between the detested "political party" and the exalted "movement"; he defined neither of them. It is clear, however, how he attempted to expand the appeal of his regime and to bring into its folds more and more Spaniards until ideally it would include everyone in Spain, victor and vanquished alike.

> They err who maliciously consider us to be a party when we constitute an authentic national movement which is constantly on the move toward perfection and which does not become still with the rigor mortis of parties.
>
> .   .   .
>
> You know that the Falange is a movement in the service of the father-land. It aspires to the unity of all peoples and lands of Spain. We are not a hermetic organization; we are a community in the spirit of service with doors open to the collaboration of all Spaniards, with hearts ready to embrace all the anxiety of the country, all the anguish of our brothers, all the longings of those who suffer, of those who hunger and thirst for justice. We are the projection in time of a revolution—not a revolution that passes on but one that endures and is on the march.[11]
>
> .   .   .
>
> There is room for all Spaniards in this great task, and the fatherland needs everyone. The ranks of the Movement continue to be open to who-ever comes to it with honesty and in the spirit of service.[12]
>
> .   .   .
>
> Because the Movement did not represent the privilege of the conquerors nor the submission of the defeated but the opportunity offered to all Span-iards to satisfy their longings for social revolution, it is possible today for us to face the problems of growth united in the certainty that we have found the system of open democracy and of authentic representation suit-able to the national aspirations of peace and social justice.[13]
>
> .   .   .
>
> The Movement is an enterprise common to all Spaniards without distinctions of origins or affiliations.[14]

In May, 1958, Franco decreed the unity of the Spanish people to be an accomplished fact in the Law on the Principles of the National Movement. The role of the National Movement was not made clear, however, nor was it yet revealed how the Movement differed from a political party or how it differed from the F.E.T. y de las J.O.N.S. Moreover, irrespective of the alleged breadth of the embrace of the Movement, there were no allowances in the 1958 law for any political organizations outside of the representative system enshrined in the law and based upon the family, the municipality, and the syndicate. It would appear from the wording of the law that declared illegal any "political organization" outside the Movement that, by implication, the Movement itself was an organization or party, in fact, if not in name little different from its predecessor, the F.E.T. y de las J.O.N.S. Once again the ambiguity of the language used in writing the Fundamental Laws contributed to confusion within the Spanish society. In fact, "confusion" is too temperate a word; "precariousness" would be more accurate. If the Movement were an organization, i.e., a party, then those Spaniards who were not adherents and who desired to change the political system legally from within would be forced into opposition outside the law because allegiance to the principles of the Movement would be synonymous with allegiance to the single party. If, on the other hand, the Movement were not a party but only the expression of what might be called the new sense of community among Spaniards, then those who made up that community (in other words, all Spaniards with the exception of those on the far left) would be free to organize associations with programs based on varying interpretations of what the nature of that community should be and of what institutional form it might assume in the future. Yet, if there could be varying interpretations regarding the political community, how would that plurality of opinion (and the potential for conflict the word plurality connotes) square with the immutability of the principles of the Movement?

The ambiguity was compounded in the Organic Law of the State, promulgated on January 10, 1967. This was the seventh and last of the Fundamental Laws and the one created in part to reconcile contradictions in the preceding six and to bring the entire "constitution" into focus. Article 4 of the Organic Law reads:

> The National Movement, the communion of the Spanish people in the principles cited in the preceding article, informs the political system, open to all Spaniards, and for the better service of the country, promotes political life on the basis of an orderly concurrence of criteria.[15]

The National Movement is referred to as a community; no mention is made of the Movement as an organization. But it is still not certain if the community is open to all Spaniards. In other words, is the Movement open to all Spaniards just because they are Spaniards, in the same way that citizenship belongs to all Spaniards, or is it open only to those Spaniards who adhere to its principles? If the Movement is open only to adherents, does membership in the Movement necessitate an overt act of allegiance by which act those who swear are included in the political system and those who do not are excluded from it—once again setting Spaniard against Spaniard and thereby destroying the community?

On June 28, 1967, the Cortes passed the Ley Orgánica del Movimiento y de Su Consejo Nacional (Organic Law of the Movement and of Its National Council).[16] The legislation institutionalized the National Movement and set up its hierarchy and national leadership. Article 1 of the law repeated verbatim Article 4 of the Organic Law of the State, which referred to the Movement as a community. It did not, however, clarify what was meant by "community." On December 20, 1968, the leadership of the Movement decreed the Estatuto Orgánico del Movimiento (Organic Statute of the Movement), which referred to the Movement as a community.[17] But Article 2 of the statute referred to the Movement as a "political institution," thereby further confusing an already complex situation. Did "political institution" mean that the Movement was an organization with the characteristics of a party?

> The Movement as a political institution realizes its ends through the organs and entities mentioned in Article 2 of the Organic Law of the Movement and of its National Council whose regulations are developed in the present statute and assures the manifestation of opinion and the responsible participation of Spaniards in public life.[18]

But it was Title III of the Organic Statute, entitled "Associative Bodies of the Movement," which caused the greatest furor. For the first time since 1936, the regime appeared to be sanctioning differences of political opinion among the citizenry and allowing these differences to be institutionalized in associations. The precise definition of what would be considered an association was not given, however. The controversy over what is meant by "associations" remained unsettled until after Franco's death and until Spain began to move in a democratic direction. The resolution of this controversy will be analyzed in the last chapters of this study, but a discussion of the implications of the articles in Title III is essential to the present exposition. Article 11 reads:

> All Spaniards over eighteen years of age may promote the creation of associative bodies for the development of their goals subject to the legal regulations of the Movement.[19]

Article 15 reads:

> Associations in the Movement may be established with the purpose of contributing to the formulation of opinion on the common base of the principles of the Movement, in the service of national unity and the common good, for the concurrence of criteria, in conformity with Article 4 of the Organic Law and the State and Article 2 of the Organic Law of the Movement and its National Council.
>
> These associations shall contribute to the legitimate contrast of opinions with full guarantee of personal liberty in order to make possible the critical analysis of concrete solutions [to the problems] of government and the ordered formulation of programs which are oriented to the service of the community.[20]

The articles were masterpieces of circumlocution and led to disparate interpretations. For those who believed that the regime was beginning to relax its hold, the articles, in allowing associations, seemed to be laying the foundation for what could eventually become political parties. Seen from this perspective, the Movement was a communion including all Spaniards who would be able to organize within the Movement a wide range of political opinion. For those who were not so sanguine, the articles were constitutionally unnecessary and were designed to underscore the reality that all *political* expression would take place exclusively within the Movement, considered by these observers to be an organization (that is, a party) and not a communion. According to their argument the articles were unnecessary because all Spaniards theoretically were already guaranteed the freedom of association in the Charter of the Spanish People promulgated in 1945. Consequently, the only reason for the inclusion of the articles regarding associations in the Organic Statute of the Movement was to make clear that political associations were distinct from other kinds of associations. Groups could be organized within the Movement for the purposes of the expression and exchange of opinions, but these opinions could never take the form of programs presented to the people. In short, political parties (other than the Movement) and independent political pressure groups were and would remain illegal.

In addition, the associations which might come into existence have to receive the approval of the leadership of the Movement. Thus, it is the Movement itself which allows or disallows the exchange of opinion within its organization. Article 18 of the Organic Statute of the Movement reads:

> The creation of associations and federations requires the approval of the

Standing Committee of the National Council when it concerns national
or regional entities and in other cases approval of the Standing Committee
of the Provincial Council.

The approval of associations or federations will take place when in the
judgment of the competent organ the following conditions are fulfilled:

First. The prior determination of goals.

Second. The persons who seek recognition must fulfill the requirements
set forth by the legal associative rules of the Movement and must not be
under penal incapacity or incapacity set forth in Article 10 of the present
statutes.

Third. The statutes [of the entities seeking recognition] must not
contain clauses contrary to the fundamental principles, the laws, or the
associative rules of the Movement, or be contrary to public morals or order.

Fourth. All formal requirements of the associative rules of the
Movement must be fulfilled.[21]

Furthermore, organized associations once approved by the appropriate
committees of the Movement could later have their approval revoked for
reasons set forth in Article 22 of the Organic Statute of the Movement.

The approval of associations or federations shall be revoked when:

a. their activity is contrary to the principles of the National
Movement or the other Fundamental Laws;

b. they contravene the terms of the laws or infringe the norms of the
present statute;

c. they alter their goals or seriously contravene the terms of their own
statutes;

d. a member commits an act contrary to the National Movement and
the corresponding association does not take the necessary steps to prevent
these acts or discipline the wrongdoer;

e. it utilizes disciplinary measures within the association or federation
which restrict personal liberty.[22]

The last provision is particularly significant. "Disciplinary measures . . .
which restrict personal liberty" is interpreted by some to mean the
internal discipline imposed by groups like the Communists. In other
words, should an association originally approved change its nature or
goals and impose what would be considered internal discipline
(irrespective of the decision of the members of the group to accept that
discipline), that association by those acts alone would automatically
become illegitimate.

The Organization of the National Movement

The National Movement is organized along dual lines. At all levels the directive organs are appointed from the top. At the provincial and local levels the collegial, representative organs—the councils—are elected (directly or indirectly) from the bottom; at the national level, the collegial representative organ, the National Council, is in part elected from the bottom and in part appointed from the top. In addition to the representative and directive organs, there are associations and brotherhoods *(hermandades)* at the local level and their counterparts federated at the provincial level and confederated at the national level. These groups have various goals and are organized either for the purpose of defending and promoting the family or some aspect of family life or are organized around social, cultural, charitable, professional, or educational interests. Educational interests may take the form of study groups supportive of a particular doctrinal interpretation of the principles of the Movement. For the most part, these associations and brotherhoods are innocuous. Their political potential, which could be explosive, and the controversy that swirls about that activity have been discussed in the preceding parts of this section.

The local council has exclusively deliberative and advisory functions. It is made up of representatives from: (1) the local syndicates; (2) the local governmental body (the *ayuntamiento,* city hall); and (3) the local associations and brotherhoods affiliated with the Movement. All the representatives are elected from within the membership of these three groups. In addition, a certain number of local councillors (the number depending upon the size of the community) is elected directly by the municipal citizens over the age of eighteen. It is interesting to note that voting for the family representatives in the Cortes is limited to the heads of household and married women, but in party elections, as well as in the referenda, all citizens over eighteen may take part. Finally, three councillors are appointed: the chairman, who is always the local party chief, and two other members appointed by him.

The local party chief is appointed by the provincial party chief. At these levels there is direct linkage between the governmental system and the party apparatus because the provincial party chief is the governor of the province, appointed by the prime minister, and the local party chief is the mayor, appointed by the governor.[23] The mayors of major cities, like the governors, are appointed by the prime minister. The local party leader is at once the agent of his provincial and national superiors and the chief executive of the local party whose spokesman he is and over whose council he presides. Since the local council's function is primarily deliberative and advisory, however, there is little occasion for conflict between the two roles of the local party chief.

The provincial council has functions almost identical to those of the local council. Its size is fixed at fifty-one members irrespective of the population of the province. Its make-up is much like that of the local

Organization of the National Movement

Representative and Directive Organs

Representative Organs	Directive Organs	Associative Bodies
Local Council	Local Chief	Associations, Brotherhoods
Provincial Council	Provincial Chief	Associations, Brotherhoods, Federations
National Council	Secretary General	Associations, Brotherhoods, Federations, Confederations
	Chairman of the National Council (Prime Minister)	
	Titular Head of the Movement (King Juan Carlos)	

council with two exceptions. No member of the provincial governmental body (Diputación Provincial) sits on the provisional council of the party, nor are there any councillors directly elected by the people of the province. Instead, the local councils choose from among their members representatives who sit on the provincial councils.

The provincial party chief is appointed by the chairman of the National Council at the proposal of the secretary-general of the party. His functions vis-à-vis the provincial council parallel those of the local chiefs vis-à-vis the local councils. Once again, the likelihood of conflict between the provincial party chief and the provincial council is remote. In reality the party is governed completely from above. At the provincial and local levels no decisions of the councils are binding on the party executives, and the executives are directly responsible to their superiors.

The National Council is different from the provincial and local councils. Its composition has already been described in the section dealing with the Cortes. The entire council sits ex officio as members of the Cortes, but twelve members of the Cortes sit on the National Council, which arrangement produces the bizarre circularity of representation explained in Chapter 7.

The functions of the National Council are unusual. The council has the privilege of drafting legislation for consideration by the Cortes. In addition, as mentioned earlier, the council has the right to begin actions in *contrafuero*. In fact, it is the only body having the right to challenge the constitutionality of any act of executive or legislative origin that it considers may contravene the Fundamental Laws. The Cortes may constitutionally question only those acts of executive origin; it would be illogical for the Cortes to question its own behavior. Yet a paradox lies in the fact that the National Council is itself a part of the Cortes; thus one part of the national legislative body has the privilege to challenge the behavior of the whole. This gives the council the unique power of being possibly able to bring an action in *contrafuero* against a bill that successfully became a law but to which the council *in its capacity as National Council of the Movement* was opposed. Within the Cortes the council members number approximately 115 out of a total membership of approximately 560 *procuradores.* Therefore, even if all the councillors were to bloc vote within the Cortes, they could easily be outvoted. Bloc voting would be highly unlikely, however, because 12 members of the National Council come from the Cortes, and these individuals would probably be more oriented toward the Cortes from which they emerge than toward the National Council on which they sit ex officio. But when the council sits as the National Council of the Movement, its 12 members from the Cortes could be overwhelmingly outvoted by the remaining national councillors. On the National Council there are 40 members who were appointed by Franco and who now, since his death, have become a group that will perpetuate itself through co-option. Most likely these councillors would be much more oriented toward the council to which they were directly appointed or co-opted than toward the Cortes in which they sit ex officio. Their dominant position within the council could force a vote that could challenge the constitutionality of a legislative act to which they were opposed but against which their party voices had been overwhelmed in the Cortes.

It is for these reasons that the critics of the existing system say that the National Council functions as an upper house. The Council is not an upper house, of course, but it undeniably occupies a position difficult to assess according to the conventional criteria of governmental organization.

The National Executive is made up of: (1) the titular head of the National Movement, King Juan Carlos; (2) the working head of the Movement, the prime minister, who is chairman (*presidente*) of the National Council; and (3) the secretary-general of the Movement who is vice-chairman (*vicepresidente*) of the council. The secretary-general runs the party on a day-to-day basis and is a member of the cabinet. He is appointed and dismissed in the same manner as are all other cabinet ministers. Until his death, Franco was both titular and working head of the Movement. With the succession, the roles have been separated in accordance with the provisions of Article 25 of the Organic Law of the State.

Notes

1. *Fundamental Laws of the State: The Spanish Constitution*, Law on the Principles of the National Movement, Article 1.

2. See p. 102 in this study.

3. García-Nieto and Donézar, *La Guerra de España*, pp. 260-61.

4. Ibid.

5. Ibid.

6. See pp. 122-125 in this study.

7. See p. 70 in this study.

8. The Ministry of the Interior (called *Gobernación* in Spain) is in charge of the police and all internal security.

9. *Pensamiento Político de Franco* (Madrid: Servicio Informativo Español, 1964), pp. 67-114.

10. Ibid., p. 83.

11. Ibid., p. 84.

12. Ibid., p. 92.

13. Ibid., p. 112.

14. Ibid., p. 113.

15. *Fundamental Laws of the State: The Spanish Constitution*, Organic Law of the State.

16. Ley 43/167, de 28 de junio, Orgánica del Movimiento y de Su Consejo Nacional, in *Leyes Fundamentales y Normas Complementarias* (Madrid: *Boletín Oficial del Estado*, 1973), pp. 99-117.

17. Decreto 3170/1966, de 20 de diciembre (Jefatura Nacional del Movimiento), por el que se aprueba el Estatuto Orgánico del Movimiento, in *Leyes Fundamentales y Normas Complementarias*, pp. 119-142.

18. Ibid., p. 121.

19. Ibid., p. 124.

20. Ibid., pp. 124-25.

21. Ibid., p. 126.

22. Ibid., p. 127.

23. It is at this linkage between the government and the party where one part of the impact of the National Movement has been so enormous throughout Spain. Because of this connection, the purveyors of all governmental patronage at every political level—local, provincial, and national—were active party men. Thus, almost all non-civil service appointees in Spain, men and women numbering in the hundreds of thousands, owed their livelihoods to the Movement. Many of these people were unskilled, from the most humble classes: doormen, attendants (little more than runners who abound in every official building), janitors, cleaning men and women, night watchmen, nonmilitary or nonpolice guards, building superintendents, public gardeners, street cleaners, and the like. The allegiance of these people and their dependents to the Franco regime was, to a large degree, bought. Or if their allegiance was not bought then at least their silent acceptance.

The other part of the powerful impact of the National Movement throughout Spain has been its intimate connection with the syndicates that organize all producers and workers in the country (see Appendix A). From 1957 to 1969 the head of the syndicalist organization and the secretary-general of the movement were centered in one man, José Solís Ruiz, who controlled all major appointments in the vast bureaucracy of the syndicalist apparatus.

9
The Civil Service

The Franco regime had very little effect on the bureaucracy that has administered Spain since the nineteenth century. Even today parts of the civil service remain basically unchanged in spite of reforms that were made in 1918 and in the 1960s. The bureaucracy in its present form finds its origins in the 1870s when the spoils system finally replaced the practice of selling public office, a practice already beginning to disappear at the time but still existing to a degree in some ministries. Already in 1852, Juan Bravo Murillo, the first prime minister with modern bureaucratic ideas, had enacted reformative legislation that in theory provided for recruitment by merit, regularization of pay, and rationalization of job classification. These changes, which formed the foundation of the modern Spanish civil service and which remained fundamentally untouched until the major reforms in 1918, were not honored in practice, however. The worst features of the ancien régime finally disappeared after the second restoration of the Bourbons in 1875 when offices could no longer be sold, but Spain adopted the spoils system at the very time when many progressive nations were abandoning it.[1]

The spoils system was particularly corruptive in Spain. In a polity of ruling elites where access to power was limited, *caudrillas* of bureaucratic officeholders grew up around the major political personalities who were followed into and out of office by their bands of hirelings. A man could make a career of being the protégé of his sponsor, and the patronage system became so stylized in Spanish life that the word *cesante* (literally, a dismissed public servant) became the descriptive term, often pejoratively used, for those temporarily out of a job. The Spanish system differed from that in the United States, for example, even during the worst years of American spoilage. In the United States, society was relatively open, and competition for political office was widespread and keen. At the national level there were no closed groups of men who were in perennial rivalry for the same political positions and who with regularity followed one another into and out of office. The successful American national politicians who were able to grant patronage in the form of jobs occupied elective posts in constant contention, and the recipients of the spoils of office were as temporary and as heterogeneous as were the men who parceled them out. It was almost impossible for a coterie of bureaucratic hangers-on to attach itself to a politician, for neither the civil servant for hire nor the politician who sponsored him could count on a dependable, if sporadic, lifelong public career.

This was not the situation in Spain, however, where society was almost closed and where high political office was available only to a few. Those who competed for executive decision-making positions surrounded themselves with sycophants who made a career of serving their host. This situation seriously corrupted the public service. Those who became a part of the bureaucracy were involved in incessant intrigue. Since public office was only a sometime thing, it was practical to build security for those lean years when one's sponsor was out of power and for old age when there would be no income at all. Graft, as a consequence, was rampant. Moreover, those who were out of office—both politician and civil servant—had a vested interest in governmental instability, for the only hope of reentering the service of the state lay either in the collapse of an existing government or in the resignation or ouster of a particular minister. During the last two decades of the nineteenth century, the two major parties shared political leadership by prearrangement and maintained a kind of stability. Alternation of parliamentary control between the conservatives and the liberals was achieved by electoral fraud orchestrated through the Ministry of the Interior.[2] Thus it was rarely possible for a government to fall in the usual manner, yet each civil servant knew that at the next election he would be out of a job because his sponsor would no longer be in power. After the deaths of Sagasta and Cánovas, the alternating of liberals and conservatives came to an end, and the coalition cabinets which subsequently governed Spain were by nature unstable. Consequently, competition among political parties grew acute, and within each political party rivals to high office with their entourages of dependents were in perpetual maneuver to occupy coveted ministries. Thus politician and civil servant alike sought the quick turnover of governments. Perhaps this would be the time to comment that the term civil servant is hardly an accurate one. These bureaucrats were not servants of the state in the Prussian sense nor were they servants of the public in the British sense. For the most part, the bureaucrats were in the service of their patrons, and the state or government was abused for personal advantage.

There were men who were exceptions to this mentality, however, and it was they who developed the *cuerpo,* or corps, which after the 1870s eventually became the basic unit of the Spanish bureaucracy. Unfortunately, the *cuerpo,* which started out as a corrective for the abuse and corruption of spoils, became in turn the source of a new kind of bureaucratic dysfunction. Starting in the last two decades of the nineteenth century, men with expertise and training who were indispensable to the running of the state and whose work could not be performed by the untrained, poorly educated "professional amateurs" who made up the bulk of the Spanish bureaucracy, began to resist the spoils process. Their indispensability became their weapon, and they obtained through its usage exemptions from the general laws applying to the rest of the civil service. Engineers and lawyers created the first *cuerpos,* and they acquired the status of "special corps" created by special laws recognizing their existence separate from the spoils system. The corps came into being in order to achieve permanence of employment, and the success of the earliest corps led to the creation of more special corps until larger and larger numbers of civil servants found protection from dismissal within the security of their particular *cuerpo.* The pressure applied by these corps on succeeding Spanish governments finally achieved what all the bureaucrats sought, both the regular civil servants and those organized into *cuerpos*—permanence of employment.

The Ley de Bases (Basic Law) of 1918 finally put an end to the spoils system. In addition, it raised salaries and provided for improvement in the techniques of recruitment by merit. More importantly for the future of the Spanish bureaucracy, the law sanctioned the presence of the special corps, not only those already in existence but also those that might be created in the future. The civil service was then reorganized in the following manner. *Within each ministry* there would be created two general corps recruited and administered by that ministry separately and independently—a technical-administrative corps open to university graduates (the equivalent of the administrative and executive classes in Great Britain, for example) and an auxiliary corps, with clerical functions, open to high school graduates. It was the intention of the reformative law that within each ministry the technical-administrative general corps would be the major bureaucratic body advising the government and carrying out its will, but the existence of the special corps made rivalry the inevitable result. Within most ministries the special corps had the advantage. The most prestigious *cuerpos* had always recruited from the same educational levels the newly established general corps were only now beginning to mine. Even if it were possible, it would take years for the general corps to recruit men of the quality that the special corps had always attracted. Moreover, the older special corps already possessed bureaucratic skills that the new general corps would have to develop. Within some ministries the general corps emerged the dominant voice; within others (usually the most important ones) the special corps pushed the general corps into subservience, and in many instances men belonging to the technical-administrative corps were acting in clerical capacities because the major positions had been captured by the special corps.

Each special corps is organized within a particular ministry and is attached permanently to it. Within a single ministry may be a dozen or more special corps each organized around a particular function or set of functions.[3] There are no interdepartmental corps comparable to those in the French bureaucratic system, for example. Even a *cuerpo* like the highly prestigious Abogados del Estado (State Lawyers), which may function interdepartmentally, remains attached to its parent ministry through which its members are recruited, paid, and promoted. As a result of the noninterdepartmental nature of the *cuerpos*, great proliferation and duplication have arisen over the years. For example, there are eight corps of doctors, seven corps of architects, two corps of interpreters, four corps of judges, three corps of architects, two corps of mining engineers, two corps of industrial engineers, two corps of veterinarians, two corps of chaplains, two corps of chauffeurs, two corps of postmen, two corps of professors of advanced education, twenty-eight corps of professors of high school and vocational education, and four corps of elementary school teachers. The list could go on and on. Each corps is separate and independent from the other. Since there are no servicewide classifications guaranteeing the same pay and benefits to each bureaucrat performing the same function at the same level of competence and seniority, a doctor in one corps in one ministry, for example, may make considerably more money than a doctor in another corps in the same ministry or in another corps in another ministry, and depending upon the size and prestige of his corps may be promoted more quickly than his professional colleagues of similar training, expertise, and seniority in other corps.

Each special *cuerpo* has sought to build an empire within its ministry, and the elite corps have been particularly successful in their endeavors. Major bureaucratic positions within a ministry are not assigned to a functionary who fulfills criteria linked to rationalized job classification but to members of *cuerpos* that have secured control over specific functions. It is one's position and seniority in one's *cuerpo* which determines the acquisition of administrative posts. A bureaucratic position is filled *automatically* by a particular corpsman irrespective of the presence of another man within the ministry who might be better equipped or who might have seniority but who is not a member of the corps to which a particular function has been assigned. Moreover, the more powerful *cuerpos* have been successful in bringing more and more functions under their control so that oftentimes a *cuerpo* will absorb functions lying outside the expertise around which the corps had been originally created. Thus, any distinction in a practical, operative sense between a special corps and a general one completely disappears so that many originally specialized corps now carry on generalized functions, and once absorbed, the new functions remain the patrimony of the corps.[4]

Over the years certain special *cuerpos* have become the superelites and as a consequence have amassed great power and prestige. Among the superelites are: (1) the Cuerpo Diplomático (Diplomatic Corps); (2) the Abogados del Estado (Lawyers of the State); (3) the Letrados del Consejo de Estado (Attorneys of the Council of State); (4) the Catedráticos de Universidad (University Full Professors); (5) Catedráticos de Escuela Técnica (Full Professors of the Advanced Technical Schools); (6) the Carrera Judicial (Judges); (7) the Carrera Fiscal (Attorneys General); (8) the Inspectores Técnicos (Technical Inspectors); and (9) the Ingenieros de Caminos, Canales, y Puertos (Civil Engineers). Because the nature of their professional activity requires years of higher education, these corps attract superior university graduates, and since university education is still almost exclusively the preserve of the middle, upper-middle, and upper classes, the members of the elite *cuerpos* represent overwhelmingly the top strata of Spanish society. Moreover, working for the government within an elite *cuerpo* is one of the most prestigious occupations in Spain.[5] There is, consequently, a circular effect: the intellectual elites enter these corps, and in turn because of the corps' celebrity they attract more elites so that socioeconomic status and high bureaucratic position go hand in hand, perpetuating in each corps not only a unique weltanschauung but also veritable dynasties that have been built within certain *cuerpos*.[6]

Perpetuation is secured through control of recruitment. A member of a special *cuerpo* is recruited not into the civil service per se but into the *cuerpo* itself, access to which is accomplished by the successful passage of examinations given by the corpsmen who sit on the selection boards. Examinations may be of two sorts, written and oral, the latter called *oposiciones,* which are carried out publicly among contenders for the limited number of positions open within a particular corps. In other words, *oposiciones* are a kind of gladitorial feat whose victors are determined by the decisions of the judges. A person's style, bearing, presence, breeding—a host of highly subjective qualities—enter into the criteria by which he is judged. This recruitment system resembles the British "country-house technique" (officially called Method II) for selecting upper-level British civil servants in which a person's social graces count perhaps as much as his intellectual qualifications in securing access to a prestigious bureaucratic future.[7] In Spain a person may have to go through several examinations. In the event one is not successful in the acquisition of a place within the *cuerpo* he prefers, he must go through the same process all over again either in the same corps or in other corps until finally he is accepted by one of them. Many elite corps almost predetermine recruitment through influence in the educational system. Certain engineering *cuerpos,* for example, are intimately associated with certain *escuelas técnicas* (technical schools) and thus help to shape the curriculum on which the graduates will later be tested for admittance into the corps.

The patrimony of a *cuerpo* goes far beyond job control, however. The special *cuerpos* have legal status and may own property, organize cooperative and mutual societies, and manage their own investment portfolios. If rich enough, they may offer to their members retirement, sickness, and unemployment benefits supplemental to those provided by the state. They may lend money to their members to finance personal needs—the purchase of a house or the education of a child, for example. Some offer bonus payments to a member when he marries or has a child, or to his widow when he dies. Many provide a variety of insurance coverages.[8] Everything depends upon the wealth of a particular *cuerpo.* It is, in part, for this reason that membership in an elite corps is so coveted. An individual who is accepted into a *cuerpo* is in reality joining a family company whose assets he automatically shares, and many of those companies are extraordinarily rich.[9] Money to fund their projects comes from assessments on members and in the old, rich, and powerful *cuerpos* from the dividends on past investments. Moreover, until the reforms of 1964, many *cuerpos* received *tasas,* or fees charged for official services rendered. For example, the finance inspectors (who were Abogados del Estado) received a percentage of the taxes whose collection they oversaw. Customs inspectors received a percentage of the duty they levied. In reality, the *tasa* was a form of official graft, or to put it another way, a kind of tip much like an automatic gratuity included on a customer's bill at a restaurant. Since the reform of 1964, the *tasa* no longer goes automatically to the *cuerpo.* All *tasas* go to the Ministry of the Treasury, which in turn allocates shares of them to the individual ministries, which in most cases are controlled by *cuerpos.* For all practical purposes, little has been changed. Moreover, as it was before the reform, the amount of money collected in *tasas* still remains confidential information and has never been made known to the public. This is not the only information unavailable to the public. No one knows even in close approximation how many members of *cuerpos* there are in the nation's service or how much money each member earns from the government. There are 206 *cuerpos* organized within the Administración Civil del Estado (Civil Administration of the State).[10] The number of members within each *cuerpo* differs according to the method used to classify membership. Since few official statistics are kept and since there is no civil service–wide method of recording statistics, no precise figure exists. The size of a *cuerpo* may be judged by the number of positions officially consigned to it within a ministry. All the positions assigned may not be filled, however. The size could thus be judged by the number of positions actually filled. Finally, the size of a *cuerpo* may be judged by the total number of living people who have been brought into its ranks but who may not be presently working within the bureaucracy because they are either on temporary leave of absence, or occupy a political position (either in the Cortes or in a ministry), or have found permanent employment outside the civil service, or are retired. Julio Feo and Luis Romero give estimates gathered from 6 reliable statistical sources. Depending upon the source used, the total number of members of all of the *cuerpos* within the 15 ministries in the national government varies between 159,933 and 245,908.[11]

Nor is it possible to know how much money a particular civil servant makes. An elaborate system of remuneration has been devised over time. Each civil servant at a particular level earns the same basic annual salary. If he is the member of a *cuerpo,* this base pay is multiplied by a coefficient scaled from 1.3 to 5.5. Each *cuerpo* has its official coefficient. Thus the salary of each member of a *cuerpo* is multiplied by the official coefficient in order to arrive at his basic *cuerpo* pay. In addition, a civil servant can earn what is called discretional pay for such functions as being "head of a unit," having "greater responsibility," working a "double day," putting in "extraordinary hours," performing "extra-ordinary work," or any combination of the above supplements.[12] The classifications are limited only by the ingenuity and imagination of those who seek to expand them. It is impossible to know what the total sum of money earned may be because discretional pay appears in the budget in a lump sum and is not itemized in the appropriation. On top of all this, the overwhelming majority of civil servants holds more than one job, the second many times in the private sector. This practice is against the law, but the more powerful *cuerpos* have been able to secure exemptions from its enforcement, and the rest have simply been able by collusion to ignore the law's existence. It is estimated that the highest paid civil servants in Spain earn forty times the incomes of the lowest paid—the highest differential in Europe.

In 1964 the state initiated reforms that it hoped would bring order to the labyrinthine civil service and bring under control the fiefs of the special *cuerpos*. Andrés de Oliva de Castro and Alberto Gutiérrez Reñón have written: "The lack of structuring of the *cuerpos* gives to the civil service a decidedly cantonalist character which makes the Spanish administration appear to be a great confederation of *cuerpos*."[13] The reform has so far been relatively ineffectual. Not only have the entrenched interests in the elite *cuerpos* resisted it, but according to Juan Linz and Amando de Miguel, they are fully aware neither of the need nor of the nature of such reform.[14] While this element within the civil service remains unconvinced, it is unlikely that fundamental change will be forthcoming.

The Ley de Funcionarios Civiles del Estado (Law of the Civil Servants of the State), passed in February, 1964, did away with the classifications established in the reform of 1918. The technical-administrative corps in each ministry were abolished, and in their places were created a single interdepartmental administrative corps meant to resemble the British executive class and a single interdepartmental technical corps to resemble the British administrative class, the highest level of the British bureaucracy. The separate auxiliary corps in each ministry were replaced by a single interdepartmental auxiliary corps resembling the British clerical class. From within the technical corps, the reform envisaged the emergence of a superelite from those especially gifted civil servants who had taken postentry training in the newly established Escuela Nacional de Administración Pública—E.N.A.P. (National School of Public Administration). The three interdepartmental corps and the E.N.A.P. were placed under the direction of the prime minister's office. The law also gave to the government the authority to reduce the number of existing special corps and to impede the creation of new ones. There have been some changes. Some of the less important special corps have been done away with or have been consolidated with others for better efficiency and less duplication, but the powerful special corps still maintain their identity. Mario Trinidad Sánchez has written: "It is interesting to point out that on top of any other factor, the present structure of the *cuerpos* is the most important obstacle to the plans to modernize the Spanish civil service and the cause of the major part of the irrationalities and breakdowns of its functions."[15]

In all probability nothing will begin to be altered fundamentally until Spain makes changes similar to those made in France following World War II. Before the war the superprestigious nontechnical *grands corps* recruited their members directly and exclusively from the private École Libre des Sciences Politiques (Free School of Political Science) in Paris. After the war the school was nationalized and placed within the University of Paris. Other schools like it were created in certain provincial universities so that a person not living in Paris (or able to afford to go to school there) would not be disadvantaged. The postgraduate École Nationale d'Administration—E.N.A. (National School of Administration)—was created and accepted only those college graduates able to meet its rigid entrance requirements. At the end of the second year (in a course of study lasting three years), the students at the E.N.A. take examinations. Depending upon their choice of corps, the successful bureaucratic postulants are accepted into the *grands corps.* Those who are not successful in their reach to the top become by default members of the regular civil service. A similar reform would benefit Spain. The elite special *cuerpos* would be restructured interdepartmentally and access to them would be through the E.N.A.P. The new superelite in the interdepartmental technical corps would be manned by members of the special *cuerpos.* Those who sought entry into these *cuerpos* but were unsuccessful would enter the interdepartmental administrative corps. All this is pure speculation, however. There is no indication that more profound change is presently being given serious consideration.

In the modern, complex, positive state the distinction between the political and bureaucratic functions becomes increasingly blurred. Advisory opinions made by highly trained civil servants using knowledge unavailable to the politician have gained such importance that bureaucratic decisons are in reality political, if by political one means the performance of an indispensable role in policy formation. Yet irrespective of the melding of the two functions, most developed polities attempt to maintain the distinction as much as possible. For example, a person is forbidden to be simultaneously a civil servant and a politician. In most systems the bureaucrat may take no part in any overt partisan activity other than voting. In some systems, like the British, a civil servant may not enter certain types of private enterprise directly from the public service until the passage of a prescribed period of time.

In Spain many of these prohibitions exist in law, but in practice they are dishonored. In theory a civil servant may not sit in the Cortes nor may he hold a ministerial post, yet many of the most influential positions in the cabinet are and have been held by bureaucrats, and they have always made up a major percentage of the *procuradores* directly appointed by Franco. Over the years the highest political positions in certain ministries traditionally have gone almost exclusively to members of certain elite *cuerpos,* the Ministry of Finance and the Ministry of Public Works, for example. A man may sit in the Cortes or occupy a ministerial post while a member of a *cuerpo.* He, of course, will be on leave of absence, but because of the nature of the corps— simultaneously a professional, a social, and a financial organization— members never sever their ties. This is particularly true of the most prestigious *cuerpos* from which come the corpsmen appointed to political posts. Moreover, since members of the elite *cuerpos* very often hold important positions in the private sector, primarily in business and the professions, there exists an intimate linkage between the political, the bureaucratic, and the economic elite structure. In addition, since members of the most prestigious *cuerpos* come almost exclusively from the highest strata of Spanish society,[16] there is a symbiotic relationship between the political, economic, bureaucratic, and social elites so that for the most part they are not competitive plural elites but are rather manifestations of a single ruling elite.

These corpsmen have been given a considerable amount of discretion in the political decision-making process. In Franco's technique of governing, the various pillars of his regime were balanced within the cabinet. The spokesmen for these conciliated interests were often the corpsmen appointed to political posts. Ultimate decision making always lay with Franco, of course, but until unresolvable conflict had to be reconciled by him, competitive inputs from these balanced groups determined policy to a great extent. At the same time that bureaucratic appointees held political office, they still maintained their allegiance to the *cuerpos* and to the ministries from which they emerged and to which they would return. Thus bureaucratic interests always intruded into the political process. The full-time administrators turned part-time politicians became, for the civil service, internal pressure groups (or torsion groups, as J.A. Yarza has so perceptively called them[17]), which perpetuated and expanded the bureaucracy's role in political policy-making.[18]

In the Cortes the civil service makes its vote heard primarily through the *procuradores* directly appointed by Franco and the *procuradores* who represent the cultural groups, many of whose members are in governmental service and thus are bureaucrats.[19] These representatives find their way to the committees of the Cortes, which do most of the legislative work.[20] As Kenneth Medhurst writes:

Thus groups represented in the Chamber seek access to commissions [committees] in whose proceedings they have an interest. They also manoeuvre to obtain amendments to official proposals. Amendments are usually technical in nature and have an apparently marginal significance, but they are frequently a means of moderating attacks upon special interests. . . . Indeed, a close examination reveals that much of the conflict within the Cortes is between spokesmen for competing bureaucratic interests.[21]

Notes

1. In the United States the Pendleton Act was passed in 1883. See Paul P. Van Riper: *History of the United States Civil Service* (Evanston, Ill.: Row, Peterson and Co., 1958). In Great Britain the Civil Service Commission was established in 1855, and since 1870 open competition has been the normal means of entry into the bureaucracy. See G. A. Campbell, *The Civil Service in Britain*, 2nd ed. (London: Duckworth, 1968) and R. A. Chapman, *The Higher Civil Service in Britain* (London: Constable, 1970).

2. See p. 31 in this study.

3. For an excellent essay on the formation of the *cuerpos*, see Andrés de la Oliva de Castro and Alberto Gutiérrez Reñón, "Los Cuerpos de Funcionarios" in *Sociología de la Administración Pública Española*, vol. 17 of the *Anales de Moral Social y Económica* (Madrid: Centro de Estudios Sociales de la Santa Cruz del Valle de los Caídos, 1968).

4. Ibid., pp. 123-32.

5. For an analysis of the social stratification within the Spanish bureaucracy, see José Cazorla Pérez, "Funcionarios y Estratificación Social" in *Sociología de la Administración Pública Española*, vol. 17 of the *Anales de Moral y Económica*.

6. Mario Trinidad Sánchez, "La estructura de Cuerpos y la posibilidad de un planteamiento unitario de los problemas profesionales de los funcionarios," paper presented in Madrid in April, 1971, to a conference of the Asociación Española de Administración Pública concerning the Spanish bureaucracy.

7. See Hugh Thomas, ed., *Crisis in the Civil Service* (London: Blond, 1968). See also Frank Stacey, *British Government, 1966 to 1975, Years of Reform* (London: Oxford University Press, 1975), chap. 7.

8. Andrés de la Oliva de Castro and Alberto Gutiérrez Reñón, "Los Cuerpos de Funcionarios," pp. 138-41.

9. A *cuerpo* is like a family in many ways. In a poll cited by Juan J. Linz and Amando de Miguel, 80 percent of those interviewed said that their three closest friends were members of a corps, and 43 percent said that their most intimate friend was in the same corps with the person interviewed. "La Elite Funcionarial ante le Reforma Administrativa," in *Sociología de la Administración Pública Española*, vol. 17 of the *Anales de Moral Social y Económica*, pp. 216-18.

Ministry	Number of Cuerpos
1. Prime Minister's Office	22
2. Foreign Ministry	4
3. Justice	29
4. Treasury	24
5. Interior	34
6. Public Works	9
7. Education and Science	41
8. Labor	3
9. Industry	8
10. Agriculture	10
11. Commerce	6
12. Information and Tourism	12
13. Housing	4

11. Julio Feo and José Luis Romero, "La Administración Pública Comparada en Tres Paises Continentales: España, Francia, y Alemania," in *Sociología de la Administración Pública Española*, vol. 17 of the *Anales de Moral Social y Económica*, pp. 330-31.

12. Andrés Nieto, "Estructura de las Rentas Funcionariales," in *Sociología de la Administración Pública Española*, vol. 17 of the *Anales de Moral Social y Económica*, pp. 193-98.

13. "Los Cuerpos de Funcionarios," p. 146.

14. "La Elite Funcionarial ante la Reforma Administrativa," pp. 220-49.

15. "La estructura de Cuerpos y la posibilidad de un planteamiento unitario de los problemas profesionales de los funcionarios," p. 1.

16. See José Cazorla Pérez, "Funcionarios y Estratificación Social," pp. 69-86, and Juan J. Linz and Amando de Miguel, "La Elite Funcionarial Española ante la Reforma Administrativa," pp. 199-200.

17. J. A. Yarza, "Clasificación de puestos de trabajo y reglamentaciones orgánicas," in *Documentación Administrativa*, no. 81 (September 1964), quoted in Andrés de la Oliva de Castro and Albert Gutiérrez Reñón, "Los Cuerpos de Funcionarios," p. 94.

18. For an informative analysis of the political function of the Spanish bureaucracy, see Kenneth Medhurst, "The Political Presence of the Spanish Bureaucracy," *Government and Opposition* 4, no. 2 (Spring 1969):235-49.

19. See pp. 167-69 in this study.

20. See pp. 169-71 in this study.

21. Medhurst, "The Political Presence of the Spanish Bureaucracy," p. 243.

10
The Opposition

The Background

Franco brought thirty-nine years of peace to Spain. This author was in Spain in 1964 and vividly recalls the celebration of the twenty-fifth anniversary of the end of the Civil War. The jubilee paid homage to *"Veinticinco Años de Paz"* ("Twenty-five years of peace")—the slogan which embroidered every public speech and emblazoned every public place throughout the peninsula during the year of commemoration. To most of those remaining members of the generation that had lived through the war and had seen and suffered its abominations—*"los que hicieron la guerra,"* "those who made war," as they are called in Spain— that accomplishment alone would have been enough to justify Franco's rule. Moreover, many of the children of that generation share the sentiments of their parents. One has only to travel in Spain and speak to men and women who are today middle-aged to appreciate the pervasiveness of this feeling.

But Franco brought more than peace; he also brought prosperity. Again, one has only to travel in Spain at the present time and compare the country now to what it was at the beginning of the period of the economic take-off in the 1950s. The mind boggles at the visible transformation. Part of this change is revealed in statistics. Per capita income grew at the rate of 3.3 percent a year between 1951 and 1960, and between 1951 and 1958 the gross national product per capita increased at an annual rate of 4.45 percent—a figure higher than that in any other European country except Italy and West Germany.[1] The national income (measured in thousands of millions of pesetas) grew from 258 in 1954 to 793 in 1964.[2] The gross national product (measured in thousands of millions of pesetas calculated at the value of pesetas in 1969) rose from 785.4 in 1953 to 2,011.7 in 1969.[3] Based on the period 1953-54 as 100, agricultural production went from 92.96 in 1953 to 139.40 in 1963; fishing increased from 99.0 in 1953 to 172.3 in 1963; and industrial production went from 94.9 in 1953 to 215.6 in 1963.[4] The per capita consumption of steel measured in kilograms rose from 42 in 1953 to 100 in 1963.[5] The per capita consumption of cement measured in kilograms went from 99.7 in 1953 to 279.8 in 1963.[6] From 1955 to 1963 the consumption of electrical power measured in kilowatt hours per capita rose from 416 to 764.[7] In 1960 4 percent of Spanish homes had a refrigerator, and 1 percent had a television set.[8] In 1969, the percentage of Spanish homes with a refrigerator was 85, with a television set 79, with a washing machine 66, and with an automobile 34.[9] The number of telephones per 1,000 inhabitants went from 19 in 1948 to 80 in 1965.[10] In the 1960s, people spoke of the Spanish economic miracle as they had spoken earlier of the German and of the Italian.

Yet opposition to the political system developed concomitantly with the prolongation of peace and the expansion of prosperity. In fact, economic growth was the catalyst for the opposition that began to germinate in the 1950s because socioeconomic change did not lead to meaningful political change, and opposition to the regime intensified as economic mobility and liberalization made political immobility increasingly intolerable.[11] At the beginning the anomaly was suffered primarily by the working class, which bore the brunt of the disparity, and it was in this stratum of Spanish society where the new opposition began to brew. But opposition soon spread to university students and intellectuals, and their cause and that of the proletariat began to be defended by progressive members of the clergy within the Spanish Church who took courage and inspiration from the liberalization that came out of the Vatican Council.

In the early 1950s, Franco made the decision that was to alter Spanish society permanently. What prompted this decision will probably never be fully understood, nor can it be known if Franco fully realized what the repercussions of it would be. But the manner in which he handled the changes made inevitable the internal conflict that ensued and that continues to this day, and he unwittingly destroyed even the facade of the unity that had been his constant goal since he became caudillo in 1936. Had he allowed the political system to evolve at the same pace as the economic system, in other words, had he supported the kind of change in politics he had initiated and encouraged in economics, he perhaps could have brought Spain to the threshold of political maturity and could have prepared the Spanish people for participation in the inevitably difficult years to follow his death.

Franco chose to do otherwise, however, and the Spanish polity after the 1950s became increasingly dysfunctional in spite of the massive economic growth of the country and the increased personal prosperity of the people, for the political institutions were out of synchronization with socioeconomic reality. Had the decade of the 1950s been a political watershed, it is probable that the earlier years of the Franco regime would have been reappraised—not excused but placed within the context of their decades, the 1930s and 1940s, periods that elsewhere in Europe had thankfully started to become a part of history and whose horrors had began to be mitigated by time. But by maintaining the political continuity while altering the socioeconomic continuity, Franco welded his links to the past and made the past impossible to forget. Moreover, Franco made it impossible for Spain to move forward politically while he lived and made it problematical how successfully she would move forward after he died.

Perhaps he could not have done otherwise. To have broken politically with the past would have been to destroy his carefully constructed personal legitimacy. It was Franco's greatest dilemma, but it was of his own making. Perhaps his failure was psychological—the inability to judge what the Spanish people would and would not tolerate. So long as Franco remained within his own familiar period of time—the Civil War, the dark noon of his life, and the future as the projection of the consequences of the war—he assessed the Spanish polity with great accuracy. But when he entered the "unknown"—the modern world he embraced in the 1950s—he lost his perspective. Moreover, he was ignorant of the systemic nature of change, the impossibility of altering one aspect of society without that alteration causing change or the demand for change in every other aspect. Perhaps he could have learned from the people, but he basically distrusted them. Even the little political participation he allowed—the referendum and later, but more significantly, the direct election of family representatives to the Cortes—was not given the chance to realize its potential. The Cortes remained an echo chamber for the voice of Franco; it did not become the forum for the voice of the people.

In the early 1950s, Franco chose to abandon the policy of autarchy—the strategem for economic and military self-sufficiency adopted after the end of World War II—and move the country toward internationalism and neocapitalism under the direction of technocrats and experts identified with the Opus Dei.[12] The decision to abandon was inevitable. Spain had exhausted whatever good could come from autarchy. There simply were insufficient natural resources and inadequate domestic capital to allow the country to continue to go it alone and survive. Economic pressures were building within the system—privation and stagnation coupled with inflation[13]—that could either be contained by massive repression or be released by some form of liberalization, i.e., a relaxation of the rigid governmental controls over the economy that autarchy demanded. Moreover, the polarization taking place in the world as a result of the cold war and of the war in Korea made Spain's isolation anachronistic. The West, in the form of American defense needs, came to Franco, and he made the decision to welcome the overture. Spain's needs—from Franco's point of view the urgency to move beyond autarchy—and the needs of the West from the American point of view—the only Western point of view that mattered in the early 1950s—coincided. Franco's profound anticommunism made the coincidence congenial, but embracing the West, or more accurately embracing the United States with its vigorous and aggressive capitalism, made the American economic philosophy almost impossible to resist once American aid was accepted. Since the 1930s, Franco's antiliberalism and anticapitalism, at least in his public utterances, had been as deep-seated as his anticommunism, but by the early 1950s both domestic and foreign events made the former less odious than the latter, and Franco moved Spain toward liberal neocapitalism.

For the oligarchy, which had been one of the pillars of the Franco regime from the beginning, the decision was extraordinarily favorable. That class had already profited enormously during the period of autarchy. Franco's earlier decision to make Spain self-sufficient had given the advantage to those who controlled the economic structure, and, in the name of Spain's security and independence from the detested world that had turned its back, the oligarchy was protected from the demands of labor and from foreign competition. Tariffs and exchange controls kept out cheaper foreign goods or allowed in only those goods considered essential to Spain's maintenance and defense but that Spain herself could not produce. These devices benefited the oligarchy but disadvantaged the masses, who paid dearly for overly priced products. Moreover, defense contracts let by the state to build Spain's independent armament capacity also profited the established entrepreneurs. Labor was kept totally disciplined through the state-controlled syndicates, which organized every economic enterprise, and through the Ministry of Labor, which set the wage scale for every workingman in the country. Any unauthorized action by labor was prohibited by law. Labor was forbidden to organize, and Article 222 of the Penal Code made the strike seditious. The workingman did have job security during this period because the state restricted the employers' right to discharge an employee, but the fate of the workingman was determined directly by the state and indirectly by the oligarchy, which controlled the economy and was part of the governing coalition. Moreover, the entrepreneur, although compelled to be organized with labor in the syndicates, was able to circumvent the syndicates' control and to influence the political elites directly through a wide variety of business-oriented associations, many of which predated the Franco regime and continued to flourish under it.[14] The laborer, on the other hand, had virtually no voice in either economic or political policy formation.

Once the decision was made to embrace neocapitalism, the Spanish oligarchy grew even more rich and powerful. True enough many of the smaller entrepreneurs were driven out of business when the system's protective hand was removed and marginal and inefficient producers could no longer keep pace, but those who survived grew and flourished. They came to have an even greater stake in the Franco regime than they had had in the beginning.

Labor, however, was not so fortunate, and it is here where Franco's handling led inevitably to the emergence of the new opposition to his regime and, by extension, to the neocapitalism with which the regime came to be identified. The political system maintained over labor most of the controls that were enforced during the period of autarchy. While the oligarchy was comparatively free to play the capitalist game, labor was disallowed those rights already won in all other capitalist countries, most importantly the right to organize in independent unions and to strike. The Spanish political system under neocapitalism continued to operate to the benefit of the oligarchy at the expense of the workingman without the possibility of resurrecting those rationalizations for the same relationship used during the period of autarchy, i.e., the defense and security of the nation against a hostile world. The world was no longer hostile, or rather, the Western world could no longer indulge its full hostility once Spain became a friend of the United States.

Given the reality that Spain was still overwhelmingly a working-class nation, how did the regime expect to continue to keep the proletariat controlled if massive repression were not to be employed? Did it expect the worker to remain submissive under the new economic order? It must be stated that for the employed the state set up as extensive a compulsory system of social benefits as did any comparable Western European country. Much of the coverage predated the Franco regime, but existing benefits were extended and new benefits were added. Benefits included accident insurance for workers in both industry and agriculture providing medical care plus monetary compensation depending upon the degree and permanence of injury; old age and invalidism insurance; health insurance, including economic assistance for maternity cases and funeral expenses; supplements for dependent children; subsidies paid to widows and orphans; scholarships available to orphans between the ages of fourteen and eighteen who choose to continue education;

marriage bonuses; bonuses paid at the birth of children and, in keeping with the Catholic spirit, special bonuses for those who produce many children; and salary supplements to help meet family responsibilities. After the abandonment of autarchy with its almost guaranteed employment, unemployment insurance was provided. In addition, the Franco regime promoted compulsory participation in Mutualidades Laborales (Workers' Mutual Societies), whose coverage in many instances overlaps and supplements that provided by the state. A part of the *mutualidades* is the Crédito Laboral (Workers' Credit Union), which lends money to workers who wish to set themselves up in business. Financing is also made available at minimum interest rates to enable the workingman to buy housing. Since the funding for most of the social benefits comes in large part from contributing employers, the state has sought to give the worker a vested, if indirect, interest in the stability of the existing political and economic system that would be jeopardized by extremist demands.

But demands were made, and despite his relative protection against personal and family adversity, the worker grew increasingly restive and used the strike as his major weapon irrespective of its illegality. In turn the regime made concessions in an attempt to forestall or foreclose dissension. In 1953, a system of *jurados de empresa* (literally, factory juries) was established in every firm employing more than fifty workers.[15] (In the event a particular firm had more than one factory, each factory had to have its own *jurado*.) The *jurados* were made up of from four to twelve delegates (*vocales*), depending upon the size of the factory or firm, elected by the workers themselves. The *jurados* had been provided for in the decree of August 18, 1947, but enabling legislation was not forthcoming until labor unrest began to foment after the first widespread strikes in post–Civil War Spain that broke out in Barcelona in March, 1951, and quickly spread to Madrid, Vizcaya, and Guipúz-coa.[16] Article 2 of the decree empowered the *jurados* to:

1. submit proposals of methods to increase or improve production and achieve greater working efficiency,
2. verify that applicable social legislation is carried out within that factory,
3. study and propose methods of accident prevention . . . ,
4. report on and make proposals concerning the physical, moral, cultural, and social welfare of producers as well as for their technical education,
5. be informed regularly by the President of the *jurado* [who is appointed by and represents management] as to the progress of

production, prospects for orders, deliveries, and the like,

6. examine the plant's work rules and submit a report on them to the Ministry of Labor,

7. give opinions on production bonuses and piece rates in cases wherein the undertaking is not entitled to fix them, or on appeals against rates set by the undertaking in other cases,

8. give opinions on proposals made by the undertaking for plus payments for difficult or dangerous jobs where the law calls for such extra payments,

9. supervise the granting of family allowances in accordance with the legislation in force.

10. appoint representatives of the employees to oversee the operations of the company store,

11. give opinions in cases wherein the undertaking wishes to lay off men or modify the conditions of labor, before the undertaking sends its requests to the government,

12. supervise the application of funds dedicated to government-run welfare programmes and to represent the enterprise before any of the government fund agencies,

13. supervise the application of funds dedicated to social programmes by the undertaking,

14. act as a channel of communication of the aspirations and desires of the producers to the management and in turn to production or the rights and duties of the producers,

15. conciliate in cases wherein producers are not satisfied with their assigned category, and, when accord is not reached, a hearing will be held and a copy of the proceedings forwarded to the Syndical Organization and the Labour authority for use in further proceedings,

16. carry out whatever duties may be asked them by the President of the *Jurado*.[17]

In brief, the *jurado* was little more than a vehicle for communication and consultation. Neither the state nor the firm was bound by its decisions.

In 1958 the role of labor was expanded when the Ley de Convenios Colectivos (Law of Collective Contracts) allowed for binding collective bargaining between labor and management.[18] After April 24, 1958, the wage rates of workers were no longer set by the Ministry of Labor (which would later establish minimum wage rates, however) but would be the result of mutual agreement between labor and management. The law

was passed primarily not to benefit labor but to facilitate the operation
of the policy of economic liberalization introduced by the technocrats of
the Opus Dei who entered the cabinet in 1957. But labor profited because
for the first time the workingman was brought into the economic
decision-making process. The law was designed to stimulate produc-
tivity by linking wages to the prosperity of the firm, the two variables
brought into relative balance not by governmental fiat but through
agreement between the workers and the entrepreneurs. The state was not
excluded from the process, however. In the event a deadlock should
occur between the negotiators, the Ministry of Labor was empowered to
provide compulsory arbitration. For agreements reached at the level of
the individual plant, the *jurado de empresa* became the spokesman for
labor thereby giving to the *jurado* more than the consultative or
communicative role it had had since 1953.

> Both institutions—the *jurados de empresa*, as a form of workers
> committee, and the system of collective bargaining—could then be
> interpreted as linked with the changes in the economy. They were
> instances of controlled institutional changes which were intended to be an
> answer to the new requirements of economic development and to the
> resulting institutional inconsistencies. Both attempted to absorb the
> informal but increasingly important role of shop-floor workers'
> representatives and informal worker-manager negotiations, and they were
> stimulated by the management. Both tried to bridge the gap between
> official and obsolete institutions on the one hand, and non-official
> institutional alternatives.[19]

Labor unrest grew, however, and strikes continued to spread;
moreover, strikes became increasingly antisystemic. Bread-and-butter
issues remained of primary importance, but political issues loomed
larger and larger, particularly the demand to be able to form
independent unions unassociated with the official syndicates and the
demand to have the right to strike. Once again, the state made
concessions when by decree it allowed professional strikes for increased
pay or for changes in working conditions. In December, 1965, Article 222
of the Penal Code was amended to decriminalize professional strikes, but
the state was adamant in its refusal to permit political strikes, which
remained illegal and subversive. Moreover, it was the state that
categorized the strikes.

There are some observers of Spanish politics who speculate (and
lament because they fear their speculation is an accurate appraisal)
that the regime awaited the mellowing of the opposition from the
laboring masses, meanwhile treating militants with great severity. By

the process of *embourgeoisement* the worker would come to enjoy the fruits of the consumer society and come to accept the regime, strategically modified over the years, as the source of the good life. As a result labor's antisystemic and antipolitical posture would relax. According to those who speculate in this manner, the regime had already successfully courted the newly emergent urban middle class, whose unrest had been assuaged by the benefits of the economic miracle and whose political demands had been muted by concessions in the form of limited political participation and partial liberalization of certain civil rights, particularly freedom of expression and freedom of religion. The family representatives who came into the Cortes under the provisions of the Organic Law of the State passed on January 10, 1967, spoke primarily for this new class. On March 18, 1966, the Cortes had passed the new Ley de Prensa e Imprenta (Press and Publishing Law), which did away with the prior censorship to which all printed material had been rigorously subject since the decree of April 29, 1938, proclaimed in the midst of the Civil War. On June 28, 1967, the Cortes approved the Ley de Libertad Religiosa (Law on Religious Freedom), whose third article declared that religious beliefs could no longer disqualify Spaniards before the law. Under the terms of the law, civil marriage would be allowed for non-Catholics, participation in religious ceremonies in the army and in the schools would no longer be obligatory, and non-Catholic religious associations could organize and publicly practice their faith.

In spite of the foregoing improvements in Spanish society, serious flaws remained that might account for the opposition that continued to flourish during the later Franco years and that continues now in the post-Franco period irrespective of increasing well-being and in spite of limited concessions to demands for civil liberties and political participation. First, economic well-being, which dampens political demands, is enjoyed primarily in the first flush of prosperity. Once the good life can be taken more or less for granted, demands other than those strictly material grow in importance. The new urban middle class has started to arrive at that point; the economic miracle began almost twenty years ago, and even though the standard of living in Spain is below that of the other Western European countries, for a large number of Spaniards the standard has already reached the Western European level, and for an even larger number it soon will. This increasingly better educated and articulate group is now demanding complete political freedom and full participation in the political process. Second, the worker is finding the wait too long between his present status (undeniably better than it was but not yet equal to that of his fellow laborers in the rest of Western Europe) and that of the middle class to which he is expected to aspire. Moreover, once he achieves middle-class status he will then find himself in the same politically frustrated position as those who are already there. Third, the state, while granting concessions to demands for participation and increased civil rights, managed to husband adequate sanctions, making the so-called liberalization little more than a lure for anyone except those who choose to ignore the cynical deception. For example, the Law on Religious Freedom allows public, non-Catholic worship, but non-Catholic groups must be inscribed in a specially created register in the Ministry of Justice, and prior approval has to be obtained from the civil governor in each province before public worship may take place. Thus what might be allowable in one province could be disallowed in another. The very size of the entire non-Catholic community in Spain—Protestant, Jewish, Orthodox, and Muslim, totaling approximately 37,000[20] in 1967— makes the restrictions even more indicative of the arbitrary nature of liberalization. Under no circumstances could this small group be a threat to the security of the state; in fact the Law on Religious Freedom has weakened non-Catholic identification, a large part of which was merely a means of showing one's opposition to the regime. Now that religious freedom has been recognized, non-Catholic participation has fallen off because conversion was more political than confessional. There appears to be almost no interest in Protestantism among present-day Spaniards. In Spain even atheists are Catholic.

The press law of 1966 did away with prior censorship but did not free the writer or publisher from responsibility. In fact, under the new law a writer or a publisher is more vulnerable than he was under the decree of 1938.[21] Under the old law the state decided beforehand what was permissible and what was not. A writer or publisher could fall under the suspicion of the authorities for what he dared to say, but he could not be accused of breaking the law by publication because the state decided what could or could not appear in print. Under the new press law, a writer is free to write and a publisher to publish, but each is subject to subsequent sanction if what is written or published is later considered to be against the law. Moreover, the offensive publication—newspaper, magazine, journal, or book—can be confiscated after it has appeared on the newsstands or in the bookshops. Even if a writer or publisher was not found criminally liable, he could still be administratively culpable, fined and suspended from practicing his trade and thus from earning his living. Article 2 of the law grants the state enormous discretion in determining guilt:

Freedom of expression and the right to publish information have no other limits than those imposed by law.

The following are limitations: respect for truth and morals; respect for the Law on the Principles of the National Movement and the other Fundamental Laws; the demands of national security, the security of the state and the maintenance of internal public order and external peace; due respect for the institutions and the people in the criticism of political and administrative behavior; the independence of the courts and the safeguarding of privacy and of personal and family honor.[22]

In order to restrict freedom of expression even more, the Cortes passed the Ley Sobre Secretos Oficiales (Law on Official Secrets) on April 5, 1968. Under its provisions the state theoretically recognizes the right of the public to be informed of the government's activities with the exception of classified information defined as those "affairs, acts, documents, notices, data, or objects whose knowledge by unauthorized persons could harm or threaten the security of the state or compromise the fundamental interests of the nation in regard to national defense, external peace, or constitutional order." The classification may be determined either by the cabinet or by any of its members, by the heads of diplomatic missions abroad, or by the head of the Joint Chiefs of Staff. In emergencies the classification may be made (subject to review within seventy-two hours by any of the individuals enumerated in the preceding sentence) by the director-general of security, the director-general of the Civil Guard, the chiefs of staff of each of the three branches of the armed services, the chief of air defense, the captain-general of each army, navy, or air force region into which Spain is divided, and the civil governor of each province.

Three Periods of Opposition

Opposition to the Franco regime can be divided into three periods: the first took place during the Civil War; the second occurred after the Civil War until the 1950s; and the third dates from the 1950s to the present and is called in Spain the new opposition.

In the first period, opposition came mainly from among those Nationalists who attempted to block the creation of the kind of regime being set up by Franco. These antagonists included José María Gil Robles, the leader of the discredited C.E.D.A.[23] who eventually went into voluntary exile; Manuel Hedilla, the heir to the leadership of the original Falange who believed that Franco was perverting the philosophy and ideals of José Antonio and using the cult of the dead and martyred chief to further the caudillo's own cause; and Manuel Fal Conde, the Carlist leader who resisted the forced unification of his own

Comunión Tradicionalista with the Falange Española y de las J.O.N.S. In April, 1937, Franco jailed Hedilla and exiled Fal Conde.[24]

In the second period, opposition, none of it successful, came from many sources. The Alphonsine monarchists sought to restore the monarchy. Until the end of the Civil War most monarchists had supported Franco because realistically they had no other choice; Franco was the champion of the forces on the Right, which included the monarchists. After the Rebel victory in 1939, however, and particularly after it became evident, following the Russian campaign, that the Axis would lose the World War, the monarchists became more vocal, encouraged by what appeared to be the anti-Franco, pro-democratic posture of the Alfonsine heir to the throne, Don Juan de Borbón, the son of Alfonso XIII. In March, 1945, Don Juan issued the Manifesto of Lausanne, a mildly liberal document setting forth his political views designed to appeal to Allied opinion. Heartened by his statement and hopeful of Allied intervention that would liberate Spain, monarchist opposition intensified during the next two years but was defused after 1947 when Franco, in the Law of Succession, shrewdly declared Spain to be a kingdom, albeit for an indeterminate future without a king. In the following year, Franco met for the first time with Don Juan to discuss the future of the monarchy. Following their audience, which took place on board Franco's yacht in the Bay of Biscay and not on Spanish territory,[25] monarchist opposition to Franco's regime grew even quieter. At the meeting, Don Juan agreed that his son, Juan Carlos, would be educated in Spain. There was no agreement about the restoration, however, but in effect the decision to allow Juan Carlos to be schooled in Spain was a tacit acceptance by Don Juan of the legitimacy of the Franco regime.[26]

After the end of the Civil War and until the Allied victory appeared certain, opposition within the regime also came from pro-nazi Falangists who wanted an authentic national-syndicalist state to be created in Spain. They openly supported the Axis cause hoping that a German victory would force Franco into unconditional fascism. After the war began to go against the Axis, this group withered with the exception of the clandestine Ofensiva de Recobro Nacional-Sindicalista (Offensive for National-Syndicalist Recovery) founded by the obdurate Falangist Eduardo Ezquer, whom Franco finally jailed in 1942. During this same period opposition came from the defeated Loyalists who both from within Spain and from exile in France organized forces to topple the Franco regime. Those who went underground in Spain immediately following the end of the Civil War, particularly the anarchists, were ruthlessly hunted down and destroyed. Following the end of World War II, guerrilla fighters, primarily Communists, came across the Pyrenees from France and waged warfare in the mountains of northern Spain. By the end of the 1940s, however, these bands had been crushed by Franco's army.

It is noteworthy that the Communists learned a valuable lesson from their ill-fated campaign. They found out that resistance to the Franco regime would have to come from within the system—a discovery they put into operation years later during the third period of opposition. The guerrilla campaign gained for them, however, a legitimacy that later was to work to their great advantage. By contrast, it was during this same second period of opposition when the socialists lost most of their credibility, a loss which among the Spanish masses has not been recouped to this day. The socialists were convinced that the victorious Allies would never allow the Franco regime to continue. In order to make themselves acceptable to those who they thought would liberate Spain, i.e., the non-Communist Allies, the socialists in exile disassociated themselves from the Communists. When the Western Allies failed even to attempt to oust Franco, the socialists were left with no strategy. It is ironic that the socialists, who had been the most militant force on the Left during the Second Republic, should find themselves replaced in popular sentiment by the Communists, who had been virtually powerless until the outbreak of the Civil War and who, during that war, had acted as the conservative instrument of the Soviet Union.[27]

In the third period, beginning in the 1950s, opposition grew because of the policies and attitudes of the Franco regime already analyzed in the first pages of this chapter. Opposition emerged out of the failure of the regime to respond to demands for whose origins the regime itself was responsible. Even though some elements of the opposition had links to the past, to the Second Republic, and to the Civil War and its aftermath, the opposition was essentially new, devoid of nostalgia.

Labor

Opposition from labor had both Communist and Catholic origins, but these origins lay in the reality of the 1950s, not in the memory of the 1930s. Other important labor forces from pre–Civil War Spain began to make comebacks during the 1950s, but their success was limited. The old socialist union, the Unión General de Trabajadores, and the old anarchist union, the Confederación Nacional del Trabajo, promoted a new clandestine labor organization, the Alianza Sindical (Syndical Alliance), but within two years it split between those seeking to lead the movement from inside Spain and those seeking to lead it from exile in France. Militants inside Spain broke away to form the Alianza Sindical Obrera (Syndicalist Workers' Alliance), but neither it nor its parent organization survived. In part, its prewar aura weakened its postwar pertinence. Moreover, both organizations had international linkages to the International Confederation of Free Trade Unions. As so often has been the case in Spanish history, international connections seem to have a deadly effect on Spanish institutions. Only Catholic and Communist organizations appear to be immune to this persistent guilt by foreign association.

The Catholic labor groups were manifestations of the growing anti-Franco sentiments within the Spanish Church. The larger significance of these sentiments will be analyzed in another section of this chapter. The first Catholic groups were organized as legitimate spiritual associations and thus were able to avoid a head-on conflict with the regime. Gradually their activities became less spiritual and more political, and many of their members landed in jail. In the meantime, however, they had penetrated the official, state-controlled labor organizations and had gained for Catholicism some of the legitimacy the working masses usually reserved for Marxist groups. For the first time in recent history, not all Catholic institutions were supportive of the Right nor defensive of the regime. The first and most important of the Catholic working-class associations was the Hermanos Obreros de Acción Católica (Catholic Action Workers' Brotherhood) created in 1945. It was soon followed in 1947 by the more activist Juventudes Obreros Católicos (Young Catholic Workers) and in 1949 by the even more militant Vanguardias Obreras Católicas (Vanguard of Catholic Workers). Militancy was measured primarily by the willingness of the groups to absorb Marxist ideas and cooperate with Marxist groups.[28] The most recent Catholic labor groups are the Federación Sindical de Trabajadores (Syndicalist Federation of Workers) and the more militant Acción Social de Trabajadores (Workers' Social Action). Many of their founders came from the three older organizations, and both groups have been active in the Comisiones Obreras (Workers' Commissions), which will be discussed shortly.

The Communists had a more difficult organizational task. They could not operate under a confessional cover like that used by the Catholic brotherhoods. Their tactics, as a result, had to be adapted to their illegality. Their early efforts to mobilize the working force on a grand, national scale proved ineffectual. In May, 1958, they prepared the *Jornada de Reconciliación Nacional* (Day of National Reconciliation) as a massive demonstration against the regime. The party called for work stoppages and boycotts of public transportation, but their plans were not successful. In June, 1958, they called for a national general strike, but this, too, met with little success. The Communists then changed their tactics, abandoned the grandiose for the workaday, and began a slow, methodical boring from within, their efforts, as Jon Amsden describes them, characterized by "hard work, risk-taking and the maintenance of their political views in the background."[29] They operated primarily within the Workers' Commissions at the level of the individual place of employment, and through example rather than harangue and rhetoric converted more and more of the laboring force.

The Catholics and the Communists found themselves working competitively within the Workers' Commissions, which began to spring up in places of employment throughout Spain beginning in 1962. The commissions were clandestine organizations of labor militants, both Catholic and Communist, which came into being because of what many workers considered to be the inadequacy of their official representatives (*vocales*) on the *jurados de empresa*, the bargaining agents for labor in the contractual agreements made with management.[30] The official representatives, even though chosen by the workers from among themselves, more often than not were the compliant tools of the syndicates rather than the aggressive spokesmen of the laborers. Increasingly, the workers turned to the secret Workers' Commissions, and many factory owners found it expedient to come to terms with the commissions as the latter's strength and influence grew among the laboring masses. For all practical purposes the official bargaining bodies began to be bypassed. Gradually, however, the legally established *jurados* were infiltrated and taken over by legally elected *vocales*, who themselves made up the Workers' Commissions and who were members of associations either totally illegal like the Communists or potentially illegal like the militant Catholic groups. The state, however, could not dismantle the *jurados*—the instrumentalities through which the commissions operated—nor could it delegalize collective bargaining without jeopardizing the neocapitalist economic order. The regime, therefore, attacked the commissions themselves by declaring them illegal in 1968, but the commissions had an amorphous shape, established ad hoc at the plant level without a centralized, national organization, and therefore, they were almost impossible to crush out. By the early 1970s, they had lost some strength not only because of the sanctions used by the regime but also because of friction within the commissions between Catholics and Communists. The strength of the Communists prevailed, however, and their achievement seemed crowned in the syndical elections at the factory level in June, 1975, when members of the Workers' Commissions—Communists primarily but other leftists as well—won almost 80 percent of the seats.

Political Opposition

All political organizations, parties and pressure groups, were dissolved by Franco when he created by fusion the F.E.T. y de las J.O.N.S. on April 19, 1937.[31] More specifically, Communism and Freemasonry were suppressed on March 1, 1940, in a decree that was broad enough to embrace almost all other organizations as well. Article 3 of the decree reads:

> All propaganda that exalts the principles and pretended benefits of masonry or communism, or that seeds ideas which weaken religion, the fatherland and its basic institutions, and [is] against social harmony, shall be punished by the suppression of the periodicals or entities that sponsor them and by the confiscation of their properties, and with the penalty of long prison sentence for the major guilty person or persons and of shorter sentence for those who co-operated.[32]

Under the blanket of these decrees, the regime could find grounds to declare any organization illegal and thus in opposition.[33] Yet from its very inception the Franco regime tolerated certain kinds of opposition. In fact, given its nonideological nature, the system unwittingly encouraged them. The regime had no official party line or rigid belief system that compelled orthodoxy and conformity. True enough, the political system was structured on organic, Catholic concepts, but these theories were infinitely varied and complex and impossible to synthesize into a popular, political catechism. As Juan Linz has written, there was no ideology, there were only mentalities.

> We will purposely use the term mentality rather than "ideology." The German sociologist Theodor Geiger has formulated a useful distinction between *ideologies*, which are systems of thought more or less intellectually elaborated and organized, often in written form, by intellectuals, pseudointellectuals, or with their assistance, and *mentalities*, which are ways of thinking and feeling, more emotional than rational, that provide noncodified ways of reacting to situations. Ideologies have a strong utopian element; mentalities are closer to the present or the past. Totalitarian systems have ideologies, a point emphasized by all students of such systems, while authoritarian regimes are based more on distinctive mentalities which are difficult to define.[34]

Within flexible boundaries the Franco regime was pragmatic. In operation this means that certain groups or individuals could be allowed to follow an old course of action while a new one was pursued. Until the lag could be made up, those left behind would be "in opposition."

Opposition also was inevitable because of the way Franco himself used power, forever balancing political forces. Some groups would find themselves not included in a particular equilibrium and thus be in opposition to the coalition from which they were, for the time being, excluded. They made up what Juan Linz calls the semiopposition, "those groups that are not dominant or represented in the governing group but are willing to participate in power without fundamentally challenging the regime."[35] At any particular time any of the groups making up the Franco coalition—the military, the oligarchy, the Church, the Falange, the monarchists, Acción Católica, and later the Opus Dei—could find itself in opposition. For example, the Falange was in opposition to the neocapitalism of the Opus Dei. The monarchists were in opposition until the plebiscite in 1947 that restored the monarchy. Until Franco decided to make Juan Carlos his heir, the Alfonsine and Carlist monarchists found themselves in opposition as each jockeyed for the successional rights of its pretender. And within the Alfonsine monarchists there were those who preferred to see Don Juan on the throne and those who supported his son, Juan Carlos.

Characterized in this way, semiopposition would seem to appear to have been little different from legal opposition in a pluralist democracy. The similarity is much less obvious than it might seem for two reasons. First, oppositional status was determined not by those in opposition but by those in power. Second, the semiopposition, like all opposition during Franco's lifetime, was unorganized. The very act of organization would have immediately made it illegal. As a corollary, semiopposition was unaccountable, unlike opposition in a democratic polity. Linz writes:

> The main difference between a semiopposition in an authoritarian regime and an opposition in a democracy is the lack of accountability (through some formal mechanism like free elections) to potential, organized or unorganized "constituencies." In fact, the free organization of potential constituents is seriously handicapped. Plural groups share power in authoritarian regimes as a result of decisions made by the leader or the inner group of the regime and their willingness to co-opt them (often in response to changing situations and/or public opinion at home and abroad). Authoritarian regimes are likely to be somewhat responsive (largely through the rule of anticipated reactions) but not accountable.[36]

Beyond the semiopposition lay the alegal opposition made up of those who would peacefully alter the system if they were able. They were too estranged from the regime to be brought into the ruling elite (even though they often maintained personal friendships within it). They would not have been asked to join the elite nor would they have accepted had they been asked. Moreover they were too alienated to have been co-opted. Their position was precarious because with little difficulty they could either have moved into or have been pushed into the illegal opposition. Like the semiopposition they were not organized, and, again like the semiopposition, they had no official constituency. The alegal opposition often took amorphous shape around a personality: the Catholic Manuel Giménez Fernández, who in 1956 formed the Unión Demócrata Cristiano (Christian Democratic Union); the Catholic monarchist José María Gil Robles, who in 1957 formed the Democracia Social Cristiana (Social Christian Democracy); the socialist professor Enrique Tierno Galván; the social democrat Dionisio Ridruejo, an ex-Falangist; leftist Catholics like Ignacio Fernández de Castro and Julio Cerón, associated with the Frente Popular de Liberación (Popular Liberation Front). Like most alegal groupings whose existence is so tenuous, most of these associations were very short-lived. Often alegal opposition operated through a publication like the still existent and influential magazine of Christian Democratic persuasion, *Cuadernos Para El Diálogo*, established by Joaquín Ruiz Giménez, a former minister of education who went into opposition; the magazine *Diálogo y Convivencia* whose initials could cryptically stand for *Democracia Cristiana* (Christian Democracy); and the newspaper *Madrid*, which went beyond the tolerance of the regime and was forced to close down, its publisher Rafael Calvo Serer going into voluntary exile at the end of 1971.

Students

Student protest is difficult to assess because it oscillated between the alegal and the illegal. When violence broke out and the regime responded repressively, the opposition became clearly illegal. This was the case in 1956 and in 1965. But until that extreme was reached, student protest was considered by the regime to be primarily alegal if for no other reason than the fact that Spanish university students are overwhelmingly middle to upper-middle and upper class. The students in the last two categories are the children of the pillars of the Franco regime. To attack the students too brutally would have been to attack their parents as well, and the state grudgingly was forced to demonstrate caution. Middle-class students were in large part the children of that class, the new urban middle class, which the Franco regime courted so assiduously and whose parents often traded political apathy for economic prosperity. Again, as it was with the upper-middle and upper-class students, to have attacked the students would have been to attack their parents.

Opposition came only from a small percentage of the university student body, and Spain has yet to witness opposition from students in secondary schools like that which occurred in France in 1968. The majority of Spanish university students has not been radicalized. In 1966 Enrique Tierno Galván estimated that only about 10 percent of the approximately 27,000 university students in Madrid were activists, but as many as 75 percent could be mobilized for different sorts of protest. In Barcelona, because of the Catalan issue, Tierno Galván estimated the activists to number almost 20 percent.[37]

Student protest was of two types, each of which often spilled over into the other, making them difficult for the regime to evaluate.

> If we examine the protest movement as a whole, we can detect two levels of protest, both among staff and students. The first reflects the attitude of those who show concern for the social and political problems of the country above all. At the second level the protest is based more generally and somewhat vaguely on the concepts of democracy and liberty. This second group is more influenced perhaps by the observation, through reading, travel, films, and plays, that the principles of life in other countries and cultures are different from those which the present regime defends as universally valid. There are thus generic, unspecific protests and more specific identifiable protests.[38]

It was perhaps protest of the first variety that erupted in February, 1956, when students in Madrid for the first time demonstrated against the Franco regime and particularly against their compulsory membership in the official falangist syndicate for university students, the Sindicato Español Universitario. Among the students taking part in the riots were the sons of many distinguished families, including the son of a former cabinet minister. Violence broke out between the police and the students, and one student was seriously hurt. The regime suspended Articles 14, 15, and 18 of the Charter of the Spanish People for the first time since its promulgation in 1945. As a result of the confrontation, the minister of education, Joaquín Ruiz Giménez, upon whose liberalizing policies much of the blame was heaped, was relieved of his post as were Antonio Tovar, the rector of the University of Salamanca, and Pedro Laín Entralgo, the rector of the University of Madrid.

Conflict between university students and the regime continued from

1956 onward until February, 1965, when it erupted seriously again in Madrid in a protest containing elements of both types of opposition described by Tierno Galván. Part of the protest was concerned with purely academic or professional matters. It is ironic that the regime in embracing neocapitalism unwittingly contributed to the unrest of students who came to realize that the curricula and facilities in Spanish universities were antiquated and inadequate for the needs of a modern, industrialized, urbanized, and secularized society. These students were among the new breed of technicians whose services were indispensable if Spain was to progress economically. Thus the regime could not do without the new breed but did not know what to do with it.

The demonstrations in 1965 also had characteristics of the other type of student opposition, i.e., overt political protest. The students demanded amnesty for fellow students, freedom of expression within the university, freedom to form associations, and release from obligatory membership in the official student syndicate. Within days the protests spread to other Spanish universities, among them Barcelona, Bilbao, Valencia, Oviedo. The students were joined by many of their more progressive professors, among them the nationally known Enrique Tierno Galván, José Luis Aranguren, Santiago Montero Díaz, Augustín García Calvo, and Mariano Aguilar Navarro. The regime retaliated by removing Aranguren, García Calvo, and Tierno Galván from their academic chairs for life; Montero Díaz and Aguilar Navarro were suspended from their faculties for two years. In 1968, violence once more broke out on university campuses, beginning at the University of Madrid in January and spreading in the following months to other universities. On March 28 the University of Madrid was closed for an indefinite period of time. Student demands in 1968 were similar to those made in earlier years, particularly the demand for the right to reject compulsory membership in the state-controlled student syndicate and the right to form independent, autonomous student associations. After months of unrest the regime relented, and on September 28, 1968, Franco issued the decree on student associations allowing university-level students to form their own representative groups. The groups had to have specific, nonpolitical goals, however, and in the event they stepped beyond their limited spheres of activity, they could be suspended for three months by governing authorities of the universities and for longer periods of time by order of the courts. The groups had to meet the following rather vague criteria:

> To be a student association a group must be inspired by and oriented toward the specifically academic goals of growth and development, of

cultural benefits, of responsible personal and professional formation with respect for the fundamental legal order which makes possible the mutual well-being, harmony, and development of all the sectors of the nation of which it forms one part.[39]

But the regime did not heed the deeper discontent that came out of the demonstrations in 1968. Echoing slogans from the student rebellion that broke out in France in March of the same year, some of the Spanish students manifested more than professional, academic, or narrowly political disenchantment. For the first time there were protests about the quality and purpose of modern life, particularly the excesses of the consumer society most Spaniards were fast beginning to enjoy. It is paradoxical—profoundly paradoxical—that the students speaking primarily from the Left were making much the same criticisms against modern, urbanized, industrialized, technological life that Franco had made from the Right in the days before he embraced neocapitalism. The spiritual life he had extolled and identified with Catholicism during the first twenty years of his regime had much the same ring as the ethical life some present-day students identified with leftist thinkers like Camus, Sartre, Che Guevara, Camilo Torres, and Marcuse. The regime, having made its new commitment to materialism, ignored the students, but their cries were echoed by elements within the Spanish Church that spoke not of the old spiritualism identified solely with the Right and oriented toward the hereafter but instead of the new spiritualism that sought reconciliation with the Left and looked not just to the hereafter but also to the here and now.

The Catholic Church

Without doubt the most profoundly disturbing opposition to the Franco regime came from within the Catholic Church in Spain, and not only from distinguished laymen but also more significantly from some of the clergy. Ignacio Camuñas Solís wrote in 1973:

> With all sincerity I believe that the regime, for the first time since its inception, is facing its first great historic test. The earlier crises were political and economic. The present one affects its spirit and its substance. It concerns the placement of the regime within the present historic period and the incorporation once and for all of those generations which were not present at its birth.[40]

Student protest, though shocking when it first erupted in 1956, could (or should) have been foreseen. Such protest has been a part of European society since the founding of the great universities in the Middle Ages. The student riots that broke out in 1965 and again in 1968, while primarily of domestic origins, were at the same time a part of the student violence shaking the entire world in the 1960s. Given the antiproletarian bias of the Franco regime from the very beginning (made even more untenable by the decision in the 1950s to embrace neocapitalism), opposition from the laboring class also could (or should) have been foreseen. Opposition within the Church was not foreseeable, however, nor could the regime resist it even with those weapons used against the students much less with those used against the workers. Moreover, opposition from the Church (or more precisely from certain elements within the Church) could not be classified as either semiopposition, alegal, or illegal opposition. It is true that from time to time certain clergymen were disciplined by the regime when their behavior spilled over into blatant illegality, but the developing opposition was spiritual not physical and therefore essentially intangible. It was opposition to the very concepts upon which the Franco regime had been founded.

The Franco system had always been vulnerable to this disaffection, but the political elites had not expected its occurrence. Since the middle of the nineteenth century, the Catholic hierarchy in Spain had been a friend of the Right. In the second half of the 1800s, the Church made its peace with the state that had confiscated its property and sold it to the emerging bourgeoisie and to the established oligarchy. At first the Church had fiercely resisted this treatment but eventually accepted reality and became the friend and apologist of the state and its elites. By embracing the new bourgeoisie, the Church abandoned the lower classes and in exchange for protection and subvention accepted and defended the socioeconomic creed of the privileged classes.[41] This alliance continued through the Restoration, the dictatorship of Primo de Rivera, the Second Republic, and into the Franco era. As already emphasized, the Church became one of the pillars of the Franco regime, and its teachings sustained the Spanish organic polity. The superstructure of the Franco system was on the firm foundation of Catholic thought. But the regime could not control that thought as it developed within the universal Church headquartered in Rome. What the Vatican accepted in the way of new teachings or of new interpretations of old teachings became canons to be accepted by all the faithful everywhere. This would be especially true for Spain with its history of militant orthodoxy and for the Franco regime in particular, which boasted the kind of reverence for and devotion to Catholicism of which martyrs are made. Parenthetically it may be said on the behalf of the regime that the very fact that its philosophy was the expression of a creed beyond its control offers evidence that the Franco regime was not totalitarian. No totalitarian system ever in existence has been posited on a belief system that was not created and manipulated by its own "theologians."

The watershed in the change in contemporary Catholic thinking was the Second Vatican Council opened by Pope John XXIII on December 7, 1965. Essentially the council forced the Church's recognition of the reality of urbanized, secularized, and industrialized modern life. The political and economic rights of the individual—his claims for a share of the good things of *this* world and his demands for political freedoms— became the rallying cry of the progressives within the council whose voices shook the assembly and shaped its decrees. It is far beyond the scope of this study even to attempt to summarize the profound impact the council had upon both the Catholic and non-Catholic worlds. Suffice it to say that whatever impact it may have had elsewhere, the force exerted in Spain was even more explosive. Of all the countries in the Catholic world, Spain had most resolutely resisted the great transformative phenomena of modern Western civilization—the Reformation, the Renaissance, and the Industrial Revolution. For all practical purposes, she kept them out. Thus Spain did not learn, as did her sister Catholic nations, how to live with and adapt to threatening forces of change. Rather she fought and destroyed those forces in the name of religious purity. In fact, her battle goes back to the Reconquest, the seven-centuries-long crusade against the infidel that is the centerpiece of her entire history. But as a contemporary Catholic nation Spain could not resist the great transformative phenomenon of the Second Vatican Council *because that phenomenon emerged from within the Church itself.* Spain could not keep out the new doctrines and directives and still proclaim her loyalty to the Church. Moreover, the Franco system was constitutionally confessional. The Catholic belief system was written into the Spanish Fundamental Laws, but beginning with the Vatican Council the Catholic belief system underwent profound reappraisal. This reappraisal offered the progressive elements within the Spanish Church—with the laity as well as within the clergy— the opportunity to challenge the Franco regime by doing no more than accepting the tenets of the Vatican Council. The regime in turn was confronted with a dilemma from which there was no escape.

The Spanish reformists would no longer tolerate the dichotomy between religion and politics that had characterized the relationship between the Church and state since the mid-1800s. At that time the Spanish Church had withdrawn into its spiritual home, there offering to the faithful resignation to their fate in this world with the joys of eternity held out as the reward for their forebearance. The Spanish Church would not venture outside the house of God unless escorted by the state, which was always honored within its holy doors, nor would the Church address itself to the plight of the faithful compelled to live within the state. The things that were Caesar's and the things that were God's were clearly delineated. The post–Vatican Council reformists in Spain would no longer accept this relationship.

> The polemic . . . simply swirls about this proposition: is salvation which forms an essential part of the evangelical message reduced solely to the individual spiritual realm projecting exclusively to the hereafter or does it include, in equally essential form, the liberation understood as the overcoming of all that which here and now alienates man or which impedes the full realization of his potential as a person and as a member of a totally fraternal society?[42]

For the new Catholic militants it would no longer be religion *or* politics but religion *and* politics, a union having the paradoxical result of turning into anticlericals the traditional forces within Spanish society, elements both in the laity and in the clergy that accepted the classical relationship between Church and state. The postconciliar reformists believed that the Church should no longer remain silent before what it considered to be abuse. The Church should no longer decamp from the grounds of sociopolitical criticism and allow that territory to continue to be occupied by the unbelieving or agnostic Left. Their voices were strong enough to influence the hierarchy of the Spanish Church. An official pronouncement of the Plenary Assembly of the Spanish Episcopal Conference held in 1972 reads:

> No Christian can under the pretext of pluralism make his faith compatible with a sociopolitical system which opposes liberty or the growing socioeconomic equality among citizens or the participation of everyone in the political decisions which affect the common good. The term liberation includes the demands of Christian duty in the transformation of the social, political, and economic structures which may be the causes of oppression and exploitation. The gospel rejects all slavery as ultimately originating in sin.[43]

During the same Assembly the Spanish bishops declared:

> We refer to the duty, consciously accepted, to fight for justice. It is not the duty of a particular party or faction; it is a pastoral duty; the Church, as the city of God, is duty-bound to the process of the liberation of humanity. This process is dedicated firstly and most importantly to the liberation from sin and death and to the reconciliation of all men through Jesus

Christ; but it also includes the liberation from all slavery, be it economic, political, social, or cultural.[44]

The progressive postconciliar Spanish clergy sought the complete divorcement of Church and state in Spain. It called for: (1) the removal of all clergymen from official statist positions, e.g., membership in the Cortes, on the Council of State, in the syndicates, and in the chaplaincies of the armed services; (2) the reinstitution of the validity of both civil and religious marriage ceremonies with the former obligatory and binding and the latter optional; (3) the rescision of compulsory religious instruction in all Spanish schools and universities; and (4) either the renegotiation of the concordat signed between Spain and the Holy See in 1953 or preferably its permanent abrogation.

In regard to concordats which, like the Spanish, granted special rights to political authorities in their relationship with the spiritual authorities, the Vatican Council had issued the following pronouncement:

> In order to defend the liberty of the Church as it should be and to promote better and more expeditiously the good of the faithful, the Sacred Council wishes that in the future neither rights nor privileges of election, nomination, presentation or designation to the episcopal ministry be accorded to the civil authorities, and with all delicacy the Council asks the civil authorities, whose goodwill and obedience the Church recognizes and the Council appreciates, to renounce voluntarily and with the approval of the Holy See the rights and privileges which are now enjoyed either by custom or convention.[45]

Speaking of the privileges that would no longer exist if the concordat were revoked, the Jesuit magazine *Razón y Fe* editorialized that the Catholic Church should be treated no differently from any other Spanish association. The statement is of particular importance because it was issued by what is considered to be the most establishmentarian religious order in Spain, but of equal importance because no order in the Church is more sensitive to and adaptable to the changes in prevailing political winds.

> The Church . . . has no reason sociologically to enjoy a special position of power. Moreover, it ought not to. . . . But like any group formed by men—even if its reason be religious faith—it has the right to legal identity and freedom within the political community. What do we mean when we affirm the right of the Church to have its legal identity? Simply that the Church—a Christian community—should be recognized as such in the same way as all other groups in society and history which seek to find and wish to honor God.[46]

Antonio Palenzuela, the Bishop of Segovia, wrote in 1972:

> The Spanish Church finds herself at a crossroads. Facing completely
> new situations in Spanish society she has to decide if these situations call
> anew for her missionary action. But in this sense the necessary decisions
> cannot be taken if, in the coming years, she does not define and clarify her
> position before the new conscience of the Church in relation to the world
> opened by the last Council. She will have to abandon all nostalgia for
> some ideal "Christianity" and for any kind of identification with the
> established powers. . . . Without the liberation of the Church as an
> institution or [the liberation] of those groups formed within her that are
> associated with the economic and political powers that be, a healthy
> pluralism . . . compatible with a communion of faith will be impossible.[47]

Enrique Miret Magdalena, among the most articulate Catholic laymen
in Spain, wrote in 1970:

> In my opinion we should go one step further if we are profoundly aware
> of these convictions of the twentieth century: the suppression of all
> Condordats, adjusting the Church to a position like that of any other
> citizen or social group.[48]

The division between reformists and conformists within the Spanish
Church lay primarily along generational lines. The Jesuit magazine
Vida Nueva conducted a poll—the first of its kind ever carried out in
Spain—whose results were published in the issue dated March 21, 1970.
The poll revealed not only the depth of the disquiet within the Spanish
clergy but also its pervasiveness within the younger clergy. Question-
naires were answered by approximately 7,000 clergymen in twenty-two
dioceses. The data revealed that:

1. An immense majority believes that the Council was very
   necessary;
2. Sociopolitically there is a clear tendency toward more socially
   open and advanced forms and a decline in traditional and
   conservative postures;
3. A large majority shows its disagreement with the political and
   social line followed by the Spanish Church;
4. [Extreme] radicalism and conservatism in things pastoral appear
   reduced to very small groups vis-à-vis the majority situated on a
   line of clearly innovative equilibrium;
5. It cannot be said that the clergymen's posture is antihierarchical

even though the majority strongly questions the way in which that authority has been exercised until now.[49]

The data break down into the following detail; all numbers are percentages. To the question asking if the Vatican Council was necessary, the answers were:

No, not at all	3.0
Very little	0.8
Little	2.4
Somewhat	13.8
Very	26.0
Very, very much	51.2

By ages, the answers to this question were:

	Over 64	*Under 30*
No, not at all	9.8	0.4
Very little	2.5	0.1
Little	5.5	0.5
Somewhat	23.6	6.7
Very	23.2	20.4
Very, very much	26.7	71.2

To the question asking if the respondent was in agreement with the Spanish Church's position on social and political matters, the answers were:

No, not at all	29.8
Very little	14.6
Little	18.4
Somewhat	26.2
Very	6.5
Very, very much	5.0

By ages, the answers to this question were:

	Over 64	*Under 30*
No, not at all	11.3	50.5
Very little	4.3	23.1
Little	13.0	16.0
Somewhat	31.2	6.9
Very	15.8	0.4
Completely	12.6	0.6

To the question asking to what form of political ideology the respondent was most sympathetic, the answers were:

No response	16
Modern Socialism	26
Monarchy	19
Workers' Movements	12
Regional Autonomy	6
Republic	4
Existing Spanish Political System	11
Falange	2
Communism and Anarchism	Negligible

It is interesting to note that the responses to the last question total 96 percent. What made up the additional 4 percent if not Communism and Anarchism? If it were Communism and Anarchism and each received 2 percent, that percentage would have been as high as that received by the Falange. If, on the other hand, one of the others had received 1 or less than 1 percent or between 1 and 2 percent, the others would have received either 3 percent or between 2 and 4 percent, percentages larger than that received by the Falange. On this particular question, the editors approached the data gingerly as if they were concerned about possible confiscation of the issue. They reported that no choice exceeded 26 percent, but if one adds those choices that could be interpreted to be on the Left (including Regional Autonomy), the total is 48 percent, a figure indicating a high degree of politicization and alienation on the part of the clergy.

There are those, in fact, who speculate with concern that the "new Left" within the Spanish Church may now be doing what the "old Right" once did, i.e., identifying too closely with a particular political ideology and failing thereby to maintain the distance necessary for objectivity and a critical posture. The forward-looking Bishop of Segovia quoted earlier warns:

> The positive involvement of Christian faith in our world may run the risk of immediately "identifying" . . . the faith with the content and objectives of a particular historical process. There are within us [the Spanish Church] groups which, without sufficient thought, link their faith with the ideological and practical support of the capitalist society and economy. Others identify their faith with participation in the revolutionary movements of liberation of mankind. Here one runs the risk

of emptying the faith of its meaning, of reducing it to the sphere of private religiosity. The faith should be concerned about all human realities but should not identify with any of them; it must be involved in all efforts for the authentic liberation of man in every situation but at the same time it should maintain an attitude of detachment and criticism with its sights on the gospel and its objectives in the gospel's hopes. But Christians cannot achieve this if they do not share the fate of the oppressed and the marginal of all the classes in this world without falling into the temptations of power and dominance.[50]

Robert Moss, writing in 1973, makes a similar observation:

> The problem here could be that the Church may be making the very same mistake it made during the Civil War—of letting itself be sucked into a position of political commitment when it might do better to stay outside politics altogether. . . . On the other hand it is still hard to see how the Church leaders could go all the way and adopt a revolutionary position, because sooner or later they are bound to remind themselves that 11 bishops and 4,500 priests died in the Civil War mainly at the hands of Republican supporters. The radical posture of the Church in Spain cannot, of course, be fully understood unless it is related to the broader changes taking place within the Catholic Church in other countries.[51]

One can perhaps already see evidence of the kind of situation against which both Moss and the Bishop of Segovia warn. The following quotation concerns the circumstances surrounding the assassination of the Spanish Prime Minister Admiral Luis Carrero Blanco on December 20, 1973. There are those in the Spanish Church who blame the reformists in the Church for Carrero's death because it is said they wanted radical change and, by extension, encouraged and sanctioned violence.

> The bomb on Claudio Coello was going to be a test of fire for the Spanish Church. Those who tended to see the Spanish hierarchy and clergy as radical enemies of the regime because of the "crime" of seeking evangelical independence were going to find in the Church the sacrificial lamb for their fury. During the days which followed the assassination of Prime Minister Carrero bishops received more insults than the very groups which had organized the crime. When, during the funeral services of the admiral, we heard one bishop called "assassin" by the same people who applauded another bishop we understood that we had reached the summit of misunderstandings.[52]

Notes

1. J. M. Maravall, "Modernization, Authoritarianism, and the Growth of Working-Class Dissent: The Case of Spain," *Government and Opposition* 8 (Autumn 1973): 438.

2. Tamames, *La República, la Era de Franco*, p. 418.

3. Ibid., p. 420.

4. Ibid., p. 419.

5. Fundación Foessa, *Informe Sociológico sobre la Situación Social en España* (Madrid: Editorial Euramérica, 1966), p. 72.

6. Ibid.

7. Ibid.

8. Fundación Foessa, *Síntesis del Informe Sociológico sobre la Situación Social en España, 1970* (Madrid: Editorial Euramérica, 1972), p. 91.

9. Ibid., p. 92. By comparison, in France in 1966, 61 percent of homes had a refrigerator, 47 percent a television set, 49 percent a washing machine and 42 percent an automobile.

10. Fundación Foessa, *Informe Sociológico sobre la Situación Social en España*, p. 75.

11. For an interesting development of these ideas, see Guy Hermet, "Les Espagnols devant leur Régime," *Revue Française de Science Politique* (February 1970): 5-36; and Enrique Tierno Galván, "Students' Opposition in Spain," *Government and Opposition* 1 (August 1966):467-86.

12. See pp. 143-144 in this study and Appendix B.

13. Years later the term "stagflation" was coined in the United States to describe just this sort of economic situation.

14. See Amando de Miguel and Juan Linz, *Los empresarios ante el poder público* (Madrid: Instituto de Estudios Políticos, 1966).

15. For a detailed study of the *jurado de empresa*, see Jon Amsden, *Collective Bargaining and Class Conflict in Spain* (London: Weidenfeld and Nicholson, 1972).

16. The first strikes occurred in 1947 but were limited to Vizcaya. The strikes in 1951 were the first to spread and to have popular support and participation, e.g., the boycott of public transportation in Madrid.

17. Ibid., pp. 108-9.

18. For a detailed study of collective bargaining, see Amsden, *Collective Bargaining and Class Conflict in Spain*.

19. Maravall, "Modernization, Authoritarianism, and the Growth of Working-Class Dissent," p. 441.

20. Tamames, *La República, la Era de Franco*, p. 597.

21. See Manuel Fernández Areal, *La Libertad de Prensa en España (1938-1971)* (Madrid: Cuadernos Para El Diálogo, 1968) and Guy Hermet, "La Presse Espagnole depuis la Suppression de la Censure," *Revue Française de Science Politique* 18 (February 1968): 44-67.

22. *Libertad de Prensa e Imprenta* (Madrid: Servicio Informativo Español, 1966), p. 2.

23. See p. 70 in this study.

24. See p. 103 in this study.

25. Don Juan had gone into exile with his parents in 1931. When the Civil War broke out, he offered to fight for the Nationalists, but Franco not only refused his offer but also refused to allow him to return to Spain.

26. Opposition in the name of the monarchy continued into the third period of opposition. In 1959 the Unión Española (Spanish Union) was formed. It was short-lived, and it appears to have been repudiated by Don Juan, who found its views too far to the Left.

27. See pp. 96-97 in this study.

28. While these three organizations were formed in the 1940s, their strongly oppositional behavior dates to the 1950s and 1960s.

29. *Collective Bargaining and Class Conflict in Spain*, p. 90.

30. See pp. 214-216 in this study.

31. See p. 102 in this study.

32. María Carmen García-Nieto and Javier María Donézar, *La España de Franco, 1939-1973* (Madrid: Guardiana de Publicaciones, S.A., 1975), p. 112.

33. Through the years dozens of associations have been declared illegal and their members prosecuted (and persecuted). The best known and most dangerous are probably the Frente Revolucionario Anti-fascista y Patriótico (Antifascist and Patriotic Revolutionary Front, F.R.A.P.), a Maoist wing of the Communist party, and the Marxist-regionalist organization known by its Basque name as Euzkadi Ta Azkatasuna (E.T.A.), translated into Spanish as Patria Vasca y Libertad and into English as Basque Fatherland and Liberty. This organization was created in 1952 as the propaganda organ for the illegal regionalist Partido Nacionalista Vasco—P.N.V. (Basque Nationalist Party). The P.N.V. was founded in 1894 seeking autonomy for the Basque provinces. Because of republican support of regional autonomy, the Basques fought with the Loyalists during the Civil War. After the war Basque regionalism was anathema for two reasons. First, all regionalist sentiment was declared subversive by the Franco regime; second, Basque regionalism was particularly hated by the regime because of Basque loyalties during the war. The P.N.V. went underground still pursuing its cause: regional autonomy. Because of its separatist program it was considered to be leftist (as opposed to rightist) centralism, but religiously and socioeconomically it would have to be considered rightist. In 1952 the E.T.A. was created as an organ of the P.N.V., but the new group grew increasingly militant and moved farther and farther to the Left. In 1958 the E.T.A. broke away from the P.N.V. and became an avowedly Marxist, terrorist, regionalist association among whose victims was Prime Minister Luis Carrerro Blanco, assassinated on December 20, 1973, on the streets of Madrid. The E.T.A. is considered to be responsible for the crime.

Since the 1960s, there have been spectacular trials for members of these and other groups, like the Communists, accused of killing policemen, soldiers, and Civil Guardsmen. The trials, all of them before military tribunals and without the possibility of appeal, have drawn intense and passionate response not only from Spaniards but from leaders all over the world. The first trials took place in 1963, and three men were executed. The next trials, and probably the ones that received the most publicity, occurred in 1970. Franco commuted the sentences of the convicted terrorists probably because of world opinion. But world opinion did not deter Franco in March, 1974, when he allowed a young convicted member of another terrorist group, the Iberian Liberation Movement, to be executed by the garrote, the ancient and still used method of execution for certain kinds of violent blood crimes.

In August, 1975, a new antiterrorist law was passed commanding the death penalty for those who carried out terrorist acts that caused the death of a member of the police, or security, or armed forces, and for the death or mutilation of a kidnap victim. In addition, the law stipulated that all political groups of Communist, anarchist, or separatist tendencies and any other group that recommended or used violence as an instrument of social and political action would be subject to maximum penalties. Moreover, it was made a crime to condone or defend acts of terrorism and to criticize a sentence passed on a convicted terrorist, or to call for solidarity with a convicted terrorist. Punishment for such actions could include imprisonment for up to two years or a fine of 50,000 to 500,000 pesetas, or both.

In late August, 1975, four trials took place under the new law which resulted in the conviction of eleven men and women. Five were executed (all men) and six were reprieved by Franco. Once again international response was angry. Most European nations withdrew their ambassadors when Franco refused to heed their pleas for clemency. Even the pope took the regime to task but to no avail. (World opinion being what it is, however, all the ambassadors soon returned.)

34. Juan Linz, "An Authoritarian Regime: Spain," in Eric Allardt and Stein Rokkan, eds., *Mass Politics: Studies in Political Sociology* (New York: Free Press, 1970), pp. 257-58.

35. Juan Linz, "Opposition to and under an Authoritarian Regime: The Case of Spain," in Robert A. Dahl, ed., *Regimes and Oppositions* (New Haven, Conn.: Yale University Press, 1973), p. 191.

36. Ibid., p. 193.

37. "Students' Opposition in Spain," *Government and Opposition* 1 (August 1966): 478.

38. Ibid., p. 479.

39. García-Nieto and Donézar, *La España de Franco*, p. 591.

40. Igancio Camuñas Solís, "Introdución," in *España Perspectiva, 1973* (Madrid: Guardiana de Publicaciones, 1973), p. 18.

41. See pp. 22-24 in this study.

42. José María González Ruiz, "Panorama Religioso," in *España Perspectiva, 1973*, p. 156.

43. Ibid., p. 159.

44. Ibid., p. 159.

45. Enrique Miret Magdalena, "La Revisión del Concordato," *Triumfo*, April 4, 1970, p. 38.

46. *Razón y Fe*, December 1970, p. 429.

47. Monseñor Antonio Palenzuela, "Meditación Urgente sobre la Iglesia en España," in *España Perspectiva, 1972*, pp. 148-49.

48. Enrique Miret Magdalena, "Un Año Confuso de la Iglesia," in *España Perspectiva, 1970*, pp. 146-47.

49. *Vida Nueva*, March 21, 1972.

50. "Meditación Urgente sobre la Iglesia," p. 149.

51. Robert Moss, "Spain After Franco," *The World Today* 29 (August 1973): 333.

52. J. L. Martín Descalzo, "Panorama Religioso," in *España Perspectiva* (Madrid: Guardiana de Publicaciones), p. 201. Claudio Coello is the street on which Carrero Blanco was assassinated.

PART 4
AFTER FRANCO

Con la España que acaba y la que empieza canto y auguro,
profetizo y creo.

With the Spain that is ending and the Spain that is beginning,
I sing and foretell, prophesy and believe.

—*Rubén Dario*

11
The Reign of Juan Carlos

The Transition

Juan Carlos came to power at an inauspicious time. Perhaps there would never have been a propitious time for a king whose claim to the throne was challenged even by some monarchists in a country where ideologically committed monarchists are only a small minority of the vast majority of politically inexperienced subjects.[1] But there could have been at least a time less inopportune. Juan Carlos had been standing in the wings waiting to go on for over a year. He had been made acting head of state on July 19, 1974, when Franco suffered the first of the attacks that would lead eventually to his death. At that time the prince had been advised by some not to accept power if he could not keep it, for to do so would weaken his authority and undermine his tenuous prestige. But he rejected this counsel, and when Franco rallied and took back his power, Juan Carlos once more was a gentleman-in-waiting. He became acting head of state again on October 1, 1975, at the beginning of the last phase of Franco's illness and became king when Franco died six weeks later on November 20. But the long wait and the short substitute appearances demonstrated what was already clear, that the prince was, first of all, the understudy for a role that in time would be his but whose occupancy by him was already compromised. In the minds of many Spaniards his role was irremediably dishonored from the beginning because of its origin in Franco; in the minds of others it became compromised by the subservient behavior forced upon Juan Carlos in the months preceding Franco's death.

Moreover, Juan Carlos came to the throne at a time when Franco had once again demonstrated to an already unfriendly world what was considered to be the cruelty and repression of the Spanish political system. It will be remembered that in August, 1975, a severe new antiterrorist law had been passed that seriously restricted personal freedom in the name of national security.[2] On September 27, 1975, five terrorists were executed following trials which many called unjust. The outcry from Western Europe, including the voice of Pope Paul VI, was deafening, but Franco ignored the pleas for clemency and gave orders for their execution after having commuted the sentence of six others.[3] Thus in one of his last official acts, Franco seemed to be telling the world what both his domestic and foreign enemies had been claiming all along—that the regime remained unchanged from what it had been at the beginning of the Franco era. And in his last public message, read posthumously to the Spanish people by the prime minster, Franco added strength to that evaluation when he spoke in language that rang with the sounds of 1936:

> Now that the time is near for me to stand in judgment before God Almighty, I ask that He look kindly upon me since I have striven to live and to die a good Catholic.
>
> It has always been my desire to be a faithful son of the church in whose bosom I shall die. I ask forgiveness from all, as I give my most heartfelt forgiveness to those who declared themselves my enemies.
>
> *I believe and hope that I had no enemies other than those who were enemies of Spain*—Spain, which I will love until the last moment and to which I promised to serve until my death, which is near.
>
> I want to give my thanks to all those who have worked enthusiastically, devotedly and unselfishly in the huge task of making a united, free and great Spain. Out of the love that I feel for our country, I beg you to continue in peace and unity and to extend the same affection, loyalty and continued show of strength and support that you have given me to the future King of Spain, Don Juan Carlos de Borbón.
>
> *Do not forget that the enemies of Spain and of Christian civilization are watching*, and you should lay aside all personal gain in favor of the goals and interests of our homeland and of the Spanish people. Continue striving to obtain social justice and education for all Spaniards and make use of the rich multiplicity of its regions as a fountain of strength for a continued united Spain.
>
> I would like in these, my last moments, to join the names of God and Spain, and for us all to embrace one another and to shout for the last time on the threshold of my death: Up with Spain! Long live Spain![4]

Although Juan Carlos did not inherit the tranquil country envisaged by Franco in his valedictory, Spain was not ripe for revolt, its citizens awaiting the chance to overthrow a detested regime. To many, possibly to most, the political system may have lacked legitimacy, but violence as a way of seeking its reform was not a popular, viable alternative. The Civil War is still too recent an event for its memories to have died away. Most of those who fought the war may now be dead, but their children are alive, and their recollections form part of the patrimony of the present generation, the grandchildren of those who fought the war. Yet the calm that characterized Spain following the assassination of Carrero Blanco in December, 1973, and which many had hoped and believed would characterize the transition from Franco to Juan Carlos, proved to be deceptive. Franco's twelfth and last government, which he created to succeed that headed by Carrero, was under the prime ministership of Carlos Arias Navarro, the tough former mayor of Madrid, and was dominated by men associated with the forces of order, the National Movement and the army, appointed in reaction to the violence that had caused Carrero's death. Arias' program promised liberalization as a counterbalance to the obvious strongman character of the cabinet, but most of the projected reforms became dead letters as internal strife swept through Spain.[5]

There were two categories of antisystemic opposition during this period, both of which were illegal, but one of which was more immediately dangerous than the other. This latter type was openly violent and bloody, but its activists spoke for only a small minority of Spaniards. At the beginning, this opposition was identified primarily with the Euzkadi Ta Azkatasuna (E.T.A.) and the Frente Revolucionario Anti-fascista y Patriótico (F.R.A.P.) The E.T.A. (Basque Fatherland and Liberty) is a revolutionary group seeking not only regional separatism but profound socioeconomic change as well. It has been repudiated by the vast majority of Basque autonomists who resolutely seek home rule but who by and large are moderately conservative, socially, economically, and religiously. The Basques have the highest standard of living in Spain, and most of them do not wish to jeopardize their good life by radical action. The F.R.A.P. is a Maoist, revolutionary, terrorist group repudiated by the Spanish Communist party, which eschews violence. The second category of opposition is identified with a growing number of groups among which are the long-existent regionalist associations seeking autonomy (for the Basques, the Catalans, and the Galicians primarily), the Workers' Commission, the clergy, the students, and some newer groups made up of individuals hitherto politically passive—professional men and women, lawyers and journalists, clerks and government employees, housewives and consumers.

In the months between Franco's first illness in 1974 and his death in 1975, terrorism—bombings, killings, kidnappings—dominated the national scene and prompted a reaction from the regime, the anti-terrorist law of August, 1975, which many Spaniards foresaw as portending renewed repression that would not only delay for the immediate future the continuation of any sort of liberalization but would also destroy whatever progress had been made to date. There are those who believe that the campaign of violence was designed to provoke just such a reaction from the regime and thus create a self-fulfilling prophesy from the Left that would make a revolutionary response attractive to the masses in the post-Franco period. Immediately preceding and following Franco's death, terrorism abated, perhaps awaiting events, but it resumed in the early part of 1976 after it became obvious that the new regime planned no fundamental changes.

In the meantime, however, antisystemic reaction increased from the second category of oppositional groups. In early November, 1975, the Madrid Press Association, in a highly unusual move, loudly denounced the government's harassment of the media. In December there was a strike by the taxi drivers of Madrid followed by one of bank employees, the latter a normally acquiescent group. In early January, 1976, the subway workers of Madrid went on strike, and in sympathy with them went workers in banking, metals, construction, electronics, auto-mobiles, and aviation. In mid-January railway employees struck, and the government retaliated by drafting more than 70,000 of them. They joined the 55,000 postal strikers already under military rule and subject to court martial. In Barcelona electrical workers went on strike. On January 18, the government arrested 22 lawyers and 33 other professional men with their wives at a private party, which the police said was an unauthorized political gathering. Later in the day 150 lawyers went in protest to police headquarters where they were dispersed and where some were badly beaten. In February 5,000 students protested in Madrid, and in the same city housewives, from both middle-class and proletarian neighborhoods, took to the streets to protest inflation and the high cost of living. In an unprecedented action, 500 civil servants asked for governmental reform. In March statistics were released indicating that in the first two months of 1976 36 million man-hours had been lost in strikes, a figure double that for all of 1975.

On February 9 violence broke out again. The E.T.A. burst back into the news when a band of its members shot to death the mayor of the Basque town of Galdacano, outside Bilbao. In early March the police in the Basque city of Vitoria killed in a skirmish four workers who were taking part in a massive labor demonstration demanding the right to organize independent unions. In addition to those killed, over 100 participants were injured, many seriously. The reaction among the Basques was immediate and bitter, and within the following days a general strike in protest against the killings took place involving hundreds of thousands of people throughout the Basque provinces.

While these demonstrations were taking place, the Civil Guard killed an eighteen-year-old man near Bilbao on March 8. On March 19 the E.T.A. kidnapped a Basque industrialist who was found murdered on April 8. On July 18, the anniversary of the outbreak of the Civil War, bombs were exploded in Madrid, Barcelona, Bilbao, Seville, Segovia, Baracaldo, and El Ferrol (the birthplace of Franco). Their detonations were too synchronized to have been coincidental, and they were attributed to the E.T.A. and the F.R.A.P. In those attacks no one was killed and only seven persons were injured, but by August, 1976, 27 people had died violently as a result of terrorism or of skirmishes with the police since the death of Franco nine months earlier.

During that same nine-month period, the government began its moves toward liberalization. For the progressive political activists, the moves were too slow. For those who wanted the Franco regime to continue as it was at the caudillo's death, they were too fast, and for many the fact that there was any movement at all was ominous. It appears that those who sought an immediate and radical break with the past were naive. Irrespective of how desirable that break may have been, the political elite of the old regime was too entrenched to relinquish its power suddenly and willingly. On the other hand, a failure to respond to legitimate demands for liberalization could force the opposition into more radical postures and play into the hands of the extremists who have always contended that only violence could bring democracy to Spain.

Juan Carlos began his reign tentatively. He could not have done otherwise. Not only was he totally unpracticed in the art of politics, but he also was Franco's designated heir and could not have failed to pledge his allegiance to the system from which he had emerged. Moreover, his constitutional oath required it.[6] Juan Carlos kept Arias Navarro as his prime minister because of conservative pressure the untried king was unable to resist, but in the first royal cabinet, which took office on December 13, 1975, Arias introduced men with liberal leanings. It must be kept in mind, however, that a liberal leaning among those "politically available" (i.e., those who would be acceptable for high office at this stage of Spain's political evolution) is a relative position. By standards applied in a democratic polity, the two outstanding liberals in Juan Carlos' first government would, without doubt, be considered to be conservatives. José María Areilza, Count of Montrico, the minister of foreign affairs, is a monarchist who describes himself as a member of the "civilized right." Manuel Fraga Iribarne, the deputy prime minister for political affairs,[7] is a product of the old Falange. His political ideas have evolved far beyond their narrow origins, but his political style is considered to be abrasive and authoritarian and, it is said, he ill tolerates contradiction and opposition to his opinions. Thus it would be difficult to characterize ideologically Juan Carlos' first cabinet, and if the observer is left in something of a quandary in his attempt at evaluation, the confusion is exacerbated when one considers Torcuato Fernández Miranda, the extreme right-wing opponent to Western-style democracy, whom Juan Carlos appointed on December 2 to be president of the Cortes, a position that automatically made him simultaneously chairman of the politically powerful Council of the Realm.[8]

Irrespective of the undeniably right-of-center cabinet, on January 29, 1976, Arias announced a program of political reform. The opposition was too restive for him to have delayed its presentation, but its reception was cool. The forces seeking change found it inadequate and couched in ambiguous language; the forces seeking to maintain the status quo found it precipitant. Arias called for: (1) the creation of a two-house parliament with the lower house popularly elected; (2) a revision of the electoral laws to allow the formation of certain political groups, excluding "subversive and totalitarian" associations, like the Communist party, for example; (3) a change in the laws to allow freedom of assembly; (4) a modification of the laws on royal succession to permit a woman to inherit the throne and to lower from thirty to twenty-one the age at which a monarch could accede. Arias had already announced on January 15 that elections to the Cortes would be delayed at least a year. This decision was considered to have been a victory for the progressives because an election held when due in 1976 would have renewed the Cortes for four years under the existing representational laws.

On February 6 the reform program began to be actualized. The cabinet sent to the Cortes a bill under whose terms prior official authorization would no longer be necessary for public *indoor* meetings "provided they were held for legal ends." Of course, it would still be within the authority of the government, the police, and the courts to determine what would be considered legal ends. Public *outdoor* meetings would still require prior authorization, however. The cabinet also submitted a bill that modified the antiterrorist law of August, 1975, and made it discretionary not mandatory for the courts to hand down the death penalty for terrorist crimes. Moreover, in the future it would be ordinary not military courts that would try terrorist offenses except for those carried out by armed groups organized along military or paramilitary lines or those that attacked the country's institutions. On March 6, the government approved a bill providing for freedom of political association and on May 7 approved a two-house parliament. On June 9, following furious resistance from archconservative *procuradores*, the Cortes, by a vote of 338 to 91, passed into law the bill of March 6. Twenty-four *procuradores* abstained, and slightly over 100 absented themselves. Under the terms of the law, the government had the right to determine which groups may or may not be legally organized, and the government made it immediately clear that the Communist party would remain outlawed. What was not clarified or even broached, however, was the role the National Movement, hitherto the only legal political association, would play. If the law meant that the National Movement would determine the legitimacy of political organization under the terms of the Organic Law of the Movement and of its National Council and under the terms of the Organic Statute of the Movement, then as presented in Chapter 8 of this study, the coexistence of other political parties along with the National Movement could be rationalized.[9] If they could not coexist, however, then constitutional revision would eventually have to be forthcoming, for the existence of the National Movement is integral to the Francoist system.

Disassociation and Political Reform

On July 1, 1976, Juan Carlos accepted Arias Navarro's resignation. The prime minister's dismissal came as a surprise even to some of his fellow ministers, but his resignation had been in the king's hands for several months because of friction within the cabinet and between the cabinet and the king (primarily over the pace of change), and between the government and the Spanish people. The deputy prime minister for economic affairs, Juan Miguel Villar Mir, had particularly incensed the laboring masses when he blamed the inflationist spiral in 1974-75 on their demands for increased wages. The workers countered with an attack on the government and said that Villar continued to sound like the businessman he was rather than like the minister he had become. Before his appointment to the cabinet, he had been the head of the largest steel plant in Spain.

The cabinet change was inevitable, however, irrespective of the political maladroitness of men like Villar. Juan Carlos, eight months into his reign, was more comfortable and secure in his job than he had been at the start and could begin his external and public disassociation from the Franco regime. Moreover, the king's prestige had grown enormously during the difficult months of succession, and the Spanish people were beginning to accept him as the symbol of national unity and as a progressive force urging political change while maintaining continuity and stability. Juan Carlos was performing a delicate balancing act with unexpectedly subtle skills that surprised most of his subjects, particularly those detractors who had said that he would go down in history as John the Brief. Arias was a tangible reminder both to the king and to the Spanish people of the hovering spirit of the caudillo. Furthermore, Arias himself, irrespective of the liberalization initiated under his leadership, was not a man deeply committed to political reform, and change associated with him would always be suspect. Thus, in the name of progress, Arias was replaced by Adolfo Suárez González.

Here one encounters a paradox that gives evidence of the depth of confusion and unrest within the post-Franco regime and of the profound (but understandable) ignorance of the game of democratic (or incipiently democratic) politics among the Spanish governing elite. When the appointment of Suárez was made public, Areilza and Fraga, the two so-called liberals in the outgoing cabinet, announced to both the king and to the new prime minister that they could not serve in the new government because to do so, they claimed, would compromise their political beliefs. It seems that they could serve under the conservative Arias but could not do so under the more moderate Suárez, yet both Areilza and Fraga, each of whom had had eyes on the prime ministership, have a great deal in common with Suárez. Like Areilza, Suárez is, by Spanish standards, a moderate conservative (a "civilized rightist?"). Like Fraga, Suárez had long been identified with the National Movement. Suárez had risen to become its secretary-general (and automatically a cabinet minister) but broke his relations with it in order to form a new political association. In mid-1975 Suárez had left governmental service to help promote the Union of the Spanish People, a conservative, middle-class organization made up of individuals (much like Fraga and Areilza) who had supported Franco but who saw the need for change. Fraga, about the same time, founded a centrist association called Democratic Reform, different in degree but not in kind from the Suárez group.

At forty-three years of age, Suárez is one of the new breed, those who came to maturity with no direct knowledge of the Civil War. He is the youngest Spanish head of government in this century and irrespective of his conservatism, he has said, "I feel myself and I believe I am a democrat." Early evidence of Suárez's democratic commitment can be seen in the amnesty declared less than a month after he took office. In the days immediately following Franco's death, the cries for amnesty for political prisoners had been the strongest sounds in Spain. For countless Spaniards clemency symbolized the new Spain being born with the death of the old leader. But amnesty was freighted not only with deep emotion but also with highly volatile political reality. As a consequence a general pardon would be more than a humanitarian gesture performed by a young king generously celebrating his accession. It would also be a gesture that could be interpreted as a repudiation of Franco.

Of necessity Juan Carlos' first proclamation of amnesty was less than sweeping. On November 25, 1975, two days following Franco's burial, the government announced clemency for what would eventually number approximately 6,370 prisoners of whom 528 were declared to be political offenders. The decree, in addition to freeing many, reduced the sentence of others and barred the death penalty for those awaiting trial on charges of having committed terrorist acts before the declaration. But the decree denied freedom or reduction of sentence to all those found guilty of or charged with crimes of terrorism, propagandizing for terrorism, or being a member of a group such as the Communist party, the E.T.A., or the F.R.A.P. condemned by antiterrorist legislation. Thus the pardon primarily affected common criminals and left most of the political prisoners—those around whom the controversy swirled—still in jail. Moreover, the critics of the limited amnesty claimed that under the language of their indictments many persons imprisoned for terrorism or for terrorist-related crimes were in reality guilty of nothing more than being members of an illegal political association or of a labor group, like the various socialist parties or the Workers' Commission, none of which was terroristic. Once again, as with other aspects of liberalization, it was jejune on the part of the critics to have expected other than limited clemency. Political reality in the immediate aftermath of Franco's death would have allowed nothing more, yet both the diehards who shouted "no amnesty" and the radical reformers who cried "total amnesty" took violent issue with the proclamation.

By mid-1976 Juan Carlos felt sufficiently secure with his new cabinet to grant further pardons, and on July 30, the government announced that between 400 and 500 of some 650 political prisoners would be freed. Thus membership in certain organizations or participation in propagandistic activities were removed as impediments to clemency, but the decree did not apply to those prisoners who had taken part in acts that had endangered or taken human life. The following week on August 7, in an additional gesture of conciliation, the government reinstated the three prominent professors who had been removed from their academic chairs by Franco in 1965—Enrique Tierno Galván, José Luis Aranguren, and Augustín García Calvo.[10]

On September 10, 1976, Suárez announced the timetable for the following nine months. He promised that by June, 1977, there would be elections for a new parliament that would be empowered to change the constitution. He made clear, however, that the procedures for altering the system would not bypass the provisions of the existing Fundamental Laws that make it obligatory for the National Council of the

Movement to give its opinion on constitutional reform. Suárez insisted that until the constitution was changed, he intended to abide by the letter of the law. Moreover, the prime minister said that any basic changes in the laws concerning the syndicates, regional autonomy, and fiscal reform would be left to the new parliament.

Between September, 1976, and June, 1977, Suárez and Juan Carlos gradually but relentlessly pursued political change in the face of stiff resistance from the establishment of the old regime. In particular the army and the police grew restive as violence and internal disorder countered the political liberalization. The government moved to prevent potential military reaction and began the task of depoliticizing the armed forces. On September 23, 1976, Juan Carlos replaced his vice premier in charge of defense. The progressive Lt. Gen. Manuel Gutiérrez Mellado took over from the conservative Lt. Gen. Santiago Díaz y Mendivil, who opposed any systemic change, particularly regional reform, that would weaken national unity. On December 23 the hardline commander of the Civil Guard, Gen. Angel Campano López, was replaced by an officer known to be sympathetic to the king's reforms, Lt. Gen. Antonio Ibañez Freire. In February, 1977, and again in the following April, the king issued decrees forbidding the military to participate in politics or to show public preference for the political options being presented to the nation.

The first limited steps toward regional reform were taken in December, 1976, when, for the first time in forty-one years (it appeared that everything in Spain was taking place "for the first time in forty-one years"), the Catalan language was legalized for use in the regional bureaucracy in the four Catalan provinces. Even though nothing fundamental was altered in the relationship between Catalonia and Madrid (a change Suárez had said would occur only after the elections), the government's action had symbolic meaning particularly considering the obsessive repression of native languages other than Spanish and dialects other than Castilian during Franco's regime. The new law gave notice to all Spaniards that regional demands would eventually be heeded in some form or another.

Partial judicial reform accompanied the progressive action dealing with the military and with Catalonia. On December 30, 1976, the Suárez government abolished the Court of Public Order. The decree then went on to place all future judicial action involving terrorism before the regular court system. The military tribunals were stripped of their authority to adjudicate terrorist offensives, even those carried out against the country's institutions by armed groups organized along military or paramilitary lines. This reform did more than affect the judicial process, however; it also continued to relegate the military to strictly professional duty.

In the field of labor relations the Suárez cabinet began to loosen the state's stranglehold on the worker. On March 9, 1977, the government legalized nonpolitical strikes. Under Franco these kinds of strikes had come to be tolerated by the regime, but they had remained illegal nonetheless. On April 3, 1977, the worker was given the right to form unions industry by industry. No nationwide organizations were yet allowed, but even this partial step, by comparison to the past, was a giant step toward the dismantling of the corporative syndicalist structure.

All these reforms, while essential to the gradual liberalization of the political system, would have been almost meaningless had the Suárez government failed to confront the most pressing of all demands made by the Spanish people: the right to associate freely and to create political parties totally independent of the National Movement. In Chapter 8 the manner by which Spaniards could possibly have come to enjoy full political participation under the umbrella of the Movement was analyzed. But the mood of post-Franco Spain would tolerate no such evolution of the old regime. As a consequence, the king and the prime minister faced a dangerous dilemma over freedom of association. Without political liberty Spain could not hope to take her place among her democratic European neighbors, particularly in the Common Market, a place that the nation needed both politically and economically. Political freedom could not, therefore, be disallowed to any group in Spanish society, including, of course, the Communists. Yet the military elite, whose attachment to the evolving political system could not be taken for granted irrespective of the decrees of Suárez and Juan Carlos, anathematized the Communist party. The Communists remained, for most of the older officers, the great enemy, the very reason for having fought the Civil War.

If the inevitable legalization of the Communist party was to be successful, the steps toward it had to be meticulously choreographed by both Suárez and Juan Carlos, particularly in regard to the military. The role of each man was absolutely essential, and they worked in tandem in the manner of a constitutional monarchy. Under the Fundamental Laws still in force, the king had power almost commensurate with that of Franco—the prime minister was in reality his servant—but this was not the relationship maintained by Suárez and Juan Carlos during these precarious nine months. They were in effect coequal partners. The prime minister took the political initiative while the king maintained through his person the loyalty of his subjects, especially the military elite, which like Juan Carlos and Suárez also faced a dilemma. Unless the armed forces were prepared to revolt against political liberalization and set up a military dictatorship, they were almost compelled by circumstances to remain faithful to their sovereign and thus to the system. They had taken an oath of loyalty that passed from Franco to the king according to ritual and formula devised by Franco himself. To repudiate the oath would not only deny fidelity to Franco (in the name of whose regime a revolt would be led) but also to his chosen successor. Unlike the revolt in 1936, a rebellion in 1976-77 would not be against a hated republic but against a monarchy, the form of government considered to be most legitimate by the military. It would be a form of regicide even if the king were spared. Thus Juan Carlos and Suárez enjoyed an advantage that would redound to the benefit of a democratically evolving Spain.

Yet that advantage could not be flouted, and the armed forces would have to be conciliated gradually, allowing the military establishment time to adjust to each forward step. In September, 1976, the government allowed a group of leftist leaders—whose organizations were still illegal—to meet under no specific auspices in order to discuss a coordinated drive for political change. In late November of the same year two hundred delegates from thirteen parties and from four labor unions were permitted to meet. They demanded, among other things, the immediate dismantling of the National Movement and the liberty to form political parties and trade unions. Finally in December, 1976, after its first request for permission had been denied in October, the Socialist Workers' Party, Spain's largest socialist party, held its first congress in over forty-one years. Socialist leaders from around the world came to celebrate the occasion with their Spanish brethren: from Italy came the venerable Pietro Nenni; from France, François Mitterand; from Germany, Willy Brandt; from Sweden, Olaf Palme; from Great Britain, Michael Foot, the deputy leader of the British Labor Party. Spain survived the socialist "invasion," and the army remained quiet.

Two weeks later Santiago Carrillo, the exiled leader of the Spanish Communist party, openly appeared in Madrid and was arrested. Since Franco's death Carillo had been coming clandestinely into Spain from his home in Paris, but on this occasion he in effect dared the authorities to arrest him. He gave interviews to two European television crews while driving around midtown Madrid, and on December 10 he held a full-dress press conference. He was arrested on December 22, and on December 26 he and seven other Communists were indicted for illegal association. Yet four days later, on December 30, to the shock or delight of many Spaniards, Carrillo was released from jail and allowed to remain in Spain.

Obviously the way was being paved for the legalization of the Communist party, but Suárez, ever mindful of the precariousness of his maneuvers in regard to the Communists, particular vis-à-vis the military, sought to free himself from the hazardous decision to approve the party's legality. Under existing law it lay within the power of the cabinet to grant or to deny legality to a political party. On February 8, 1977, the Suárez government had the law changed. From that day forward any political association seeking legality would have only to deposit its statutes with the government, which had ten days in which to inscribe them in a register—and thus by inscription legalize them. If the ten days passed and no action were taken by the cabinet, the statutes would be turned over to the Supreme Court for a ruling. One provision of the old law remained in force, however. No political party that was subject to international discipline or that sought to establish a totalitarian system could be legalized. Irrespective of this legal holdover, the Communists activated the provisions of the new law, and Suárez tossed the political explosive to the judiciary. In the meantime the government gave permission to the Communists to meet in Madrid. No other event could have more significantly symbolized the emergence of a new Spanish political age than the delirious celebration which began in Madrid on March 2, 1977. All the Western European Communist chiefs came to Madrid, including Georges Marchais from France and Enrico Berlinguer from Italy. The leaders affirmed that their parties should be considered Eurocommunist, and it is from this meeting that the term moved into popular, universal usage. Essentially the word meant that each country had its own brand of communism and that no national leader took orders from any other national leader. Moreover, Eurocommunism, according to its founding fathers, accepted the rules of the democratic game and eschewed violence and revolution.

Already in July, 1976, Carrillo had spoken in what would later be labeled Eurocommunist terminology, separating himself from Moscow's domination:

> Yes . . . we had our pope, our Vatican and we thought we were predestined to triumph. But as we mature and become less of a church, we must become more rational, closer to reality. We must see that each individual has his private life, his individual sense of things. I told the last party executive meeting that a person's preference of friends, of music and literature, whether to be religious or atheist, has nothing to do with the party. The party can only be concerned with problems of politics and social struggle. . . .
> And why not make a comparision with Luther. . . . Nowadays, he wouldn't be burned by the Inquisition. Heretics usually turn out to be all

right. They are ahead of their time, but after all they are right. We want
Communists to be heretics. When we are conservatives, we are no longer
right.[11]

Speaking of democracy, Carrillo said in the same interview with a
reporter from the *New York Times:*

> We want a type of socialism with universal suffrage, alternation of
> government, not control of power for the Communists, but an alliance of
> forces that in no way would allow a Communist monopoly. . . . We mean
> the Communist Party could be in one coalition government, and if it lost
> out in the next elections, it would be outside.[12]

At the historic meeting in Madrid, Carrillo reiterated his position but
went further than either Marchais or Berlinguer in affirming national
independence from Moscow and in criticizing communism as practiced
in the Soviet Union. Carrillo said that his stand and that of his French
and Italian confreres were characterized by "the rejection of any
directing center that tries to intervene in the internal affairs of other
parties and other peoples" and by the respect for "the richness of
individual and collective liberties."[13]

If Carrillo could be taken at his word, then the Communist party in
Spain was no longer either the puppet of a foreign force or an advocate of
totalitarianism and was therefore a proper candidate for legalization.
The courts, where the issue of legalization now lay, refused to make a
judgment and in behavior never before witnessed in Spain tossed the
issue back to Suárez. The death of one justice and the illness of another
had conveniently reduced the court to eight members deadlocked four to
four. Suárez could no longer temporize, and on April 9, 1977, the
Communist party was legalized. At almost the same moment the
National Movement ceased to exist as a political entity. Spain was now
ready for elections with no party deprived of the right to participate.
There was grumbling among the military elite, particularly within the
deeply conservative navy. There were some dramatic resignations from
military posts in protest. But the armed forces remained loyal to the
king, and on April 13, 1977, the seventeen members of the Supreme
Council of the Army, composed of the nation's top officers and regional
commanders, issued the following statement:

> The Supreme Council of the Army believes that the Government should
> be informed that the army is indissolubly united in its defense of the
> fatherland, the national flag, the permanence of the Crown, and the good
> name and discipline of the army.[14]

By this action, the army was in effect giving its approval to what had already taken place in Spain and what would take place in the future as a result of the upcoming elections.

The Elections

The Spanish people had already given its overwhelming approval for the Suárez reforms and for the legislative elections the prime minister had promised would take place before the end of June, 1977. Following the procedures set forth in the still operative Fundamental Laws, a nationwide referendum was held on December 15, 1976. The Fundamental Laws also required that the electoral proposal be set before the Cortes for its approval or disapproval. A month earlier, on November 18, 1976, the parliament approved the elections for a new legislature by a vote of 425 to 59 with 13 abstentions. By this ballot the *procuradores* effectively voted the Cortes out of existence forever. In the December referendum, 94.2 percent of the electorate (about 16.5 million people) gave its endorsement for the following changes in the political system. All qualified men and women over twenty-one would elect a new parliament made up of two houses whose first incumbents would sit as a constituent assembly. The lower house would have 350 deputies elected by proportional representation. The upper house would have 4 senators from each of Spain's fifty provinces. Seven additional senators would be distributed among the Canary Islands, the Balearic Islands, and Ceuta and Melilla, the Spanish enclaves in Morocco. Up to 40 more senators would be appointed by the king to sit for each four-year legislative term.

On March 16, 1977, Suárez set June 15, 1977, as the date for the elections and announced the procedures that would govern them. No cabinet minister (with the exception of the prime minister), no high-ranking governmental official (political or bureaucratic), and no military officer could run for office without first resigning his post. For the lower house, the government prescribed a modified system of proportional representation that would guarantee at least three seats to each province irrespective of how thinly populated. Voting would be for closed and blocked lists, i.e., the voter would cast his ballot for the party and not for an individual, accepting the order of priority assigned to the candidate by the party. A party would have to obtain at least 3 percent of the total vote within a province to have its candidates eligible for election. For the upper house, the voter would cast three ballots to elect the senators to fill the four seats allocated to each province. Victory would go to the four candidates receiving the highest number of votes.

Over one hundred parties were legalized by the time of the elections, but, as one wry Spanish observer commented, most of them could have fit all their members in two taxi cabs. Before the elections only six parties were of major importance; after the elections only two of those remained electorally significant. Aside from the Basque and Catalan regionalist parties, the four major parties in the campaign were the Communist party, the Socialist Workers' party, the Democratic Center Union, and the Popular Alliance.

The Democratic Center Union had been hastily assembled at the last moment to capitalize on Suárez's enormous popularity and to make a platform for his candidacy, which he announced on May 2, 1977. The party was to the left of Suárez's original political organization, the Union of the Spanish People. Many critics contended that the party's candidates, other than the prime minister, were second-rate and colorless men hand-picked by Suárez to do his bidding. Suárez's partisans countered that his party was put together to weaken the appeal of the Popular Alliance, the right-of-center party under the leadership of Manuel Fraga Iribarne.

The Popular Alliance was to the right of Fraga's original political organization, Democratic Reform, and reflected Fraga's significant shift to the right in the months since Suárez was made prime minister. Fraga formed the party with those elements from the respectable right that feared that the excessive liberalization, identified with Suárez, would undermine Spain's economic development and sense of law and order. Fraga considered these to be Franco's most important legacies and built a party around their defense. His alliance was composed of orthodox Falangists and conservative Roman Catholics from the Opus Dei (given recent past history, these made exotic bedfellows), and various elements from the industrial, commercial, and banking elite. Fraga and his followers accused Suárez of effectively pulling off a coup d'etat by legalizing the Communist party and claimed that the prime minister had betrayed his understanding with the Cortes, made in the previous September, not to allow the Communists to take part in the electoral process. Yet at the same time, Fraga observed that little separated him from Suárez philosophically and compared what was taking place in Spain between himself and Suárez to what was taking place in France between Giscard d'Estaing and Chirac, i.e., the division of the natural majority of the country.

Of the two Spanish leaders, however, Suárez emerged overwhelmingly the most popular man in Spain while Fraga was the most unpopular. Irrespective of how basically Fraga and Suárez resembled each other, Suárez, by speaking in a different political cadence, appeared to be forward looking, belonging to a younger generation, while Fraga reminded the people of the past. Thus Suárez could receive the progressive but non-Marxist vote to the left of center while at the same time attracting the moderately conservative vote to the right of center.

Felipe González, however, the leader of Spain's largest socialist party, the Socialist Workers' party, considered both Suárez and Fraga to be shams. He labeled Suárez's program renovated Francoism and branded Fraga's platform unalloyed continuism devoid of even cosmetic retouching. He claimed that the Socialist Workers' party offered the Spaniards the only true democratic alternative to include fundamental socioeconomic reform that would correct the imbalance between the haves and the have nots, a disequilibrium among the most severe in the Western world even after Spain's economic miracle in the 1960s. In addition to attacking Fraga and Suárez, González claimed that popular sentiment in Spain was republican and accused the Communist party of opportunism in failing to condemn the monarchy as an institution.

Indeed, Marcelino Camacho, the second-ranking Communist in Spain and the leader of the powerful Workers' Commissions, had indirectly said that the Party was prepared to accept the reality of a monarchy if the system were reformist: "We Spaniards must not be obliged, when we speak of freedom, to think of the republic."[15] The same grudging concession was made by the Party's leader, Santiago Carrillo. While he called the present system a relic, he also said that it was up to the Spanish people to decide if it wanted a monarchy or a republic, implying that the Communists would accept either decision. Of the four major nonregionalist parties, the Communists were considered to have the weakest preelectoral appeal. It was classified as a major party because of its organization and its control of the powerful Workers' Commissions, and because of its historic reputation as the bitterest enemy of Franco and his regime. But numerically the Party was small, and it was not expected to do well in the elections.

As the result of the elections, the 350 seats in the new lower house were distributed as follows: the Democratic Center Union received 166; the Socialist Workers' party, 118; the Communists, 19; the Popular Alliance, 16; the Catalan Democratic party, 11; the Basque Nationalist party, 8; and minor parties, 12.

The Campaign of Violence

Violence plagued the Suárez reforms and the electoral campaign almost until the day of the elections. During the last years of the Franco regime, violence had already begun to mount, culminating in the assassination of Prime Minister Carrero Blanco in December, 1973.

Franco struck back brutally at the extremists, and at the time of his death
Spain appeared to be more openly repressive than it had been in many
years. In the immediate aftermath of the caudillo's death, however,
violence abated, only to resume when Juan Carlos decided to keep Arias
Navarro, Carrero's successor, as his first premier. Perhaps Arias'
conservatism and his intimate links with the old regime led the
extremists to believe that no real change would be forthcoming in post-
Franco Spain. Yet when the king dismissed Arias and appointed Suárez
in his place, the extremists were not assuaged. On the contrary, it
appeared that violence increased in almost direct relation to the efforts
by the king and the prime minister to liberalize the political system.

Until more is known about the terrorists' operations during this
period of Spanish history and until contrary evidence is revealed to
prove otherwise, it would seem that the violence from both the Right
and the Left was aimed at the destruction of the reformist program and at
the disruption of the timetable leading to the parliamentary elections. It
should be clearly understood that the leftist and rightist opposition
discussed here was not what might be called loyal opposition willing to
take part in the political process according to the democratic rules of the
game (as, for example, the Communists and the various socialist parties
that had openly disavowed violence in any form) but was the opposition
whose only political instrument was violence. It appeared that leftist
opposition rejected the reforms because deliverance from oppression
could no longer be offered to the Spanish people as the rationale for
bloodshed and brute force. Leftist terrorists would be rebels without a
cause in a free and open society. Rightist opposition was perhaps more
straightforward in its animus toward Suárez and his program. It simply
wanted to crush out the emerging freedom and return Spain to what it
had been during the Franco regime, in fact, to what it had been in the
opening years of that era.

Perhaps the E.T.A., the most notorious of the left-wing extremist
groups, wanted to free itself from just that sort of dilemma in which are
trapped most leftist extremists who speak in the name of freedom in a
nondemocratic regime. For that reason it announced, during the last
week of September, 1976, that it was renouncing violence and would
seek to become a legitimate organization and eventually a legal political
party. It cannot be known with certainty if the E.T.A. lived up to its
word, but if, in reality, it did forswear bloodshed, the techniques of
violence were adopted by a new group speaking for Basque regional
freedom, the E.T.A.-V under the leadership of Migel Angel Apalategui
Ayerbe. This organization claimed responsibility for the killing on
October 4, 1976, of Juan María de Araluce, a liberal-leaning Basque who

was a member of the Council of the Realm. In this instance Basques were killing Basques, but Araluce was a particularly symbolic victim, a Basque in the governmental elite. In the minds of the terrorists he was a traitor in the service of Madrid.

Other terrorist groups appeared after September, 1976. On December 11, 1976, Antonio María de Oriol Urquijo, president of the Council of State, was kidnapped by members of the First of October Anti-Fascist Resistance Group (G.R.A.P.O.). The group appeared to come from the radical left, but certain informed sources in Madrid believed that in reality the members of G.R.A.P.O. were right-wing commandos masquerading as leftists out to destroy Suárez's reforms. A few weeks later on January 23, 1977, G.R.A.P.O. claimed responsibility for kidnapping Lt. Gen. Emilio Villaescusa Quiles. (Until the summer of 1976 Villaescusa had been army chief of staff and at the time of his abduction was head of the military tribunal that, until recently, had had jurisdiction over terrorist offensives.) Later on the same January 23, five Communists, two of whom were lawyers, were murdered in a labor office in Madrid. A heretofore unknown terrorist band from the right proudly claimed responsibility—the Anti-Communist Apostolic Alliance. On that same day, between the time of the kidnapping of Villaescusa and the killing of the five Communists, a female student was accidentally killed in Madrid during a street battle between students and the police. The demonstrators were protesting the killing of a male student the day before during another demonstration demanding amnesty for political prisoners. The young man had been shot by two unidentified assailants thought to be members of an ultrarightist organization. Three days later unidentified gunmen shot and killed three policemen in Madrid. In one horrific week in Janurary, 1977, ten persons died violently in Madrid, bringing to a total of forty-eight the number of political deaths since the passing of Franco fourteen months earlier.

In order to prove that the streets were not slipping from his control, Suárez suspended two constitutional guarantees for a month beginning January 28: the legal protection against search and seizure and the right to be charged within seventy-two hours of arrest. Between the end of the emergency period in late February and the elections in mid-June, violence never again reached either the proportions or the virulence it had during January. But violence still persisted, particularly in the Basque territory. In a gesture designed to ease tension in that region, Juan Carlos announced in March that the fourth major amnesty since his accession would soon be decreed. It would extend to all political prisoners except those who had committed violent acts against persons, and even those who had been directly involved in such crimes would have their sentences reduced by twelve years. Yet before the pardons were granted on March 18, gunmen in the Basque provinces killed one trooper of the Civil Guard and wounded two more.

Thirty Basque political prisoners still remained in jail following the amnesty, and their continued detention rankled the Basque people, whose dark mood was used by the extremists to set off another wave of violence, the last, as it turned out, before the elections. In mid-May four people were killed and over fifty wounded as a result of clashes with the Civil Guard and the police. Not even the return of Dolores Ibarruri ("La Pasionaria") from her thirty-eight-year exile in the Soviet Union quieted the Basques. On the contrary the presence on native soil of this famed octogenarian Basque Communist increased the rhetoric of the extremists. From its headquarters in France, the E.T.A., which had renounced violence the previous September, threatened to resume the armed struggle. In the final effort at appeasement, Suárez announced that twenty-three Basque prisoners accused of blood crimes would be released from prison but would be immediately sent out of the country. On May 22 five of them were flown to Belgium. On the day of the election all were said to be out of Spain.

In the end, the violence was self-defeating. The reform program was carried out as planned by Suárez and Juan Carlos. Moreover, far from being undermined by his inability to handle crises, Suárez's position and prestige were incalculably strengthened by his steadfastness, his coolness under pressure, and his courage in the face of opposition. He was intimidated neither by those opponents willing to play the democratic game nor by those enemies who took to the streets with bombs and bullets. Toward the end of 1976, a cartoon in a Spanish publication showed Suárez dressed up as Superman and renamed the prime minster "Suárezman." This image was enormously enhanced in the following six months. Not only was he considered to be the most trusted man in Spain by the leaders of the loyal opposition, from Communists to Christian Democrats, but polls also showed him to be the most popular person in all Spain on the eve of the election. Yet Juan Carlos deserves equal credit. He had had the foresight to choose the relatively unknown Suárez, a former activist in the Franco regime. For whatever reasons—politic or altruistic, selfish or self-serving—Juan Carlos and Suárez saw that Spain's future lay in democracy, and they pursued that goal in concert.

Interestingly, Juan Carlos and Suárez received invaluable support from the most unlikely of all sources—the leader of the Communist party, Santiago Carrillo. For whatever reasons—politic or altruistic, selfish or self-serving—Carrillo played the game of democratic politics.

During the months in which the king and his prime minister were setting the goals and the pace of reform, Carrillo held the Communists in check, refusing to be goaded into reaction even when violence was done to his followers. The slaying of the five Communists in January, 1977, was a very special test to his forbearance. He realized that had he ordered his comrades to take to the streets the army would probably have taken after them, and the entire program of reforms and the elections in which they were to culminate would have been laid to waste. One of Carrillo's spokesmen reiterated the Communist position when he declared at the wake of his five companions that the Communists would never fall into the trap of provocation. Throughout the entire post-Franco period they kept their word, and Carrillo's discipline aided Juan Carlos and Suárez to prepare Spain for democracy. Almost nothing could be more symbolic of the end of the Franco era than the three men who were creating a new life for Spain: an ex-Falangist, a revisionist Communist, and the caudillo's hand-picked successor.

Résumé and Speculation

It is not possible to know what Spain would have been like if muscular and militant fascism had been triumphant in the 1940s. Nor is it possible to know if Franco ever was a totalitarian, given the immobilism of the early years of his regime—the very antithesis of the relentless dynamism of totalitarianism. Once the Spanish Civil War was over, however, and the European war had moved in favor of the Allies, Franco used his power to force Spain back into a traditional mold. His policy was designed to prevent change in Spanish society through isolation and economic self-sufficiency.

He built his supports on a socioeconomic base made up of the oligarchy, the agricultural and industrial elite which profited from politics and society as it existed and resisted all social experimentation; the military, which supplied the force to maintain the inertia; and the Church, which furnished the philosophical rationale. The price for maintaining the static polity was paid primarily by three groups: the urban proletariat, the rural subproletariat, and the small middle to lower-middle classes that had begun to grow during the Second Republic. The urban and rural workers suffered the most grievously because, in a frozen economy built on cheap labor and protected industry, forced to pay artificially higher prices for products out of often less than subsistence wages, they lived on the border of destitution. Moreover, they were prevented by the regime from participating either economically or politically in the decision-making process. They could not vote, organize into unions, or strike. The middle and lower-middle classes suffered materially in much the same manner as did the urban and rural working classes, but in addition they also suffered psychologically. They were not pariahs in the society as were the working masses. But they were allowed no participation in the system, and their aspirations for upward mobility could seldom be fulfilled in the arrested development of the early Franco regime, which offered little room for careers open to talent.

In the early 1950s events occurred which upset the inertial smugness of the conservative Spanish elite. Economically the system was no longer viable. It could not continue to sustain itself in self-sufficient isolation from the rest of the world. It had ceased to be a question of maintaining a frozen polity advantageous to only a few. It had become the reality that the economic disintegration of the system was beginning to impair the security of even the few. Nothing less than massive repression would have been sufficient to crush all those elements of society beginning to grow restive because of continued deprivation. Moreover, events from outside Spain intruded: the cold war between the democracies and the Soviet Union made Spain's strategic geography attractive to the West, and the Vatican Council generated a fundamental change in Catholic thinking. The Roman Church began to retreat from its active involvement with political regimes around the world, particularly nondemocratic, right-wing regimes whose benefactor it has so often been in the past. The Church whose philosophy undergirded the Francoist regime was beginning to liberalize itself. How, then, could a regime like the Spanish, linked intimately to Catholic concepts, fail to change when the Church itself changed?

In the mid-1950s Franco made the momentous decision to alter the system economically by throwing the country open to those who had come courting Franco's favor with money for development, in particular the United States, which came looking for defensive alliances. But Franco, who had lived in such hermetic isolation for so long, failed to realize that by opening his society along one dimension he was setting in motion a process of modernization that could not be reversed— except, again, by total repression—and that would reverberate throughout the country transforming all those systems by which men organize their society: the political, economic, intellectual, religious, psychological, moral, and ethical. Spain, as a result of Franco's decision, ceased to be a traditional, or closed, society and became a transitional society. Manfred Halpern uses the word "transitional" in the following way:

> The term "transitional" applies to any political system in which the

structural changes and demands set loose by the uncontrolled forces of transformation exceed the will or capacity of political authority to cope with them.[16]

Yet, Franco was unwilling or unable to allow the system to move forward and become a modern political system. Halpern considers a modern system to be one that maintains its stability through its ability to absorb *continuing* transformation:

> The revolution of modernization closes, as fully adequate responses for the successful survival of societies, all three roads which constituted the premodern alternatives for confronting stability and change: (a) changes *in* certain structures and functions within some systems of a society without altering the core pattern of the systems . . . ; (b) changes *of* some of the systems of a society and the patterns relating them to each other, but not involving a change of all systems or all patterns of relationship . . . ; or (c) resistance to change through isolation. By contrast, the revolution of modernization for the first time raises the opportunity and need (which represent at the same time the minimum and maximum modern chance for wedding stability and change) to create systems which derive their stability from their intrinsic capacity to generate and absorb continuing transformation.[17]

Beginning in the late 1950s, Franco attempted to reconcile change and stability by using his old techniques, but he was unable to hold these opposing forces together because he would not or could not allow change to gather its full momentum. In the long run his authoritarian, technocratic regime could not reconcile economic development and mobility with tight social control. Franco was successful for a short period of time, but he was eventually undermined by the very stratum of society he sought to incorporate into his authoritarian technocratic regime—the emerging middle and professional classes. His plan was to close the system once again to the advantage of a few, but a few significantly increased by the addition of this new stratum. This class was initially attracted to Francoism by the economic prosperity that resulted from Spain's reopening to the world, by the relaxation of the restrictions on civil rights (particularly freedom of expression, conscience, and religion), and by limited political participation through the family representatives in the Cortes. Franco sought to bend material well-being to his advantage just as he had once bent fascism and orthodox Catholicism. These two forces were now either moribund or no longer available for use by the regime. Fascism had been abandoned years earlier, and Catholicism was no longer a trustworthy agglutinant. Not only was the Church moving away from the orthodoxy that had given Franco's early regime its rationale, but the Spaniards themselves were increasingly less faithful to Catholicism in any form, orthodox or reformed.

But the middle classes—whose successful amalgamation into his regime was the key to Franco's strategy—would not stay bought. Furthermore, Spanish prosperity was not sufficiently deep or wide to compensate for the restrictions still placed upon society. The increase in economic well-being was just enough to make the middle classes want even more, to make them want the remaining rights and privileges enjoyed by members of those classes in all the other Western countries, above all freedom of assembly and the right to organize into political parties and to form pressure groups. The working classes were even more resentful and alienated than the bourgeoisie. They had been offered little during the early years of the Franco regime, and in the period beginning in the late 1950s they were rewarded with scarcely more. True enough, they benefited from the relaxation of the restrictions on civil rights that had been forthcoming in order to attract the new middle class, but such relaxation—particularly on rights like freedom of expression and worship—was in reality an extravagance when basic political privileges, such as the workers' right to organize and to strike, were still forbidden. Moreover, the new prosperity, though benefiting the whole nation, had not spread evenly enough to fill the demands of the middle classes, much less to satisfy the needs of the working class, which still included the necessities of life not the luxuries.

Thus the Spanish regime during the last years of Franco was a transitional sociopolitical system temporarily derailed, and the forces of change that had unwittingly been released in the decade of the late 1950s to the late 1960s were temporarily stopped in the late 1960s and early 1970s when the regime returned once again to repression. But it was the repression of a regime in its death throes, a regime thrashing out at forces it could not contain but would not tolerate. After Franco died, the forces of change were released, and the momentum begun in the late 1950s accelerated once again. The early moments of the succession, during which Juan Carlos and Suárez began to execute their program of liberalization, witnessed the first tentative steps moving Spain out of the transitional state initiated by Franco into the stage of modernity.

Spain's future depends upon how skillfully modernity is embraced and actualized. The task before the constituent assembly elected in June, 1977, will be to establish a constitutional framework that will allow Spain to change itself as necessity demands without that change threatening the stability of the entire political system. The political system created must not be one that could lead to stalemate in the manner of the Third and Fourth Republics in France, for example. Nor must a system be created that could lead to possible confrontation in the manner of France's Fifth Republic, where the president and the prime minister could be antagonists. Yet it is the model of the Fifth Republic that seems best suited to Spain. A parliamentary system like the British—with its two dominant political parties loyal to the system but disciplined by their leadership—seems totally out of the question even for the relatively distant future. And a parliamentary system like the Italian (reminiscent of that of the Third and Fourth Republics in France) would give Spain no more stability than it has given Italy. A presidential model like the American—with a single, independently elected chief executive representative of a national consensus—is alien to Spanish experience and impossible in the highly fractionalized Spanish polity. The position of the king will be pivotal in the emerging polity, and a way must be found to allow him sufficient power to provide stability yet have that power contained within limits tolerable in a constitutional monarchy.

The signs are relatively good so far. "Relatively" is the operative word. Even when stability amid change becomes a reality, Spain will tend to resemble her Catholic sister nations, like Italy and France, far more than she will resemble the Anglo-Saxon democracies. In other words conflict will be endemic in Spanish politics for even the distant future. But at least those forces that have resisted change in Spain's past appear to be willing to allow the momentum toward modernization to take place: the Church (if one has faith in postconciliar Catholicism); the military (if one can believe the statements of its hierarchy made after the legalization of the Communist party); the oligarchy, apart perhaps from the diehards huddled together in the bunker (if one is willing to believe that, from the point of view of simple economic reality, the present day economic elite sees itself more prosperous and more stable as a part of the Western European community, a place unattainable except through the continued democratization of Spanish society). And even the old revolutionaries on the Left have become tractable (if one can believe Carrillo and his philosophy of Euro-communism).

The working classes are more unpredictable. They are at the moment suffering seriously from Spain's rampant inflation, and their continued forebearance cannot be taken for granted. They have not yet even begun to approximate the standard of living obtained by their fellow workers in the rest of Western Europe. As a consequence, should economic conditions worsen, their long-range cooperation with the system (in the manner of the pact made between the government and the laborers in

Great Britain, for example) cannot be anticipated. The workers represent emergent Spain's second most serious threat to stability. Only the centrifugal separatist forces appear more ominous, but the present regime has already moved gingerly toward granting autonomy. Yet national unity remains the single most passionate obsession of the military. To dare even conjecture what could happen if separatist forces began to speak as do their counterparts in Scotland and Quebec, for example, would be impossible.

Notes

1. In this context the word "subject" carries more than its traditional, monarchical meaning. It also carries the modern meaning given to it by Gabriel Almond and Sidney Verba in their classification of political cultures. Spain, at the moment of Juan Carlos' accession, was still what these authors would call a "subject political culture."

> Here [in a subject culture] there is a high frequency of orientations toward a differentiated political system and toward the output aspects of the system, but orientations toward specifically input objects, and toward the self as an active participant, approach zero. The subject is aware of specialized governmental authority; he is affectively oriented to it, perhaps taking pride in it, perhaps disliking it; and he evaluates it either as legitimate or as not. But the relationship is toward the system on the general level, and toward the output, administrative, or "downward flow" side of the political system; it is essentially a passive relationship. (Gabriel A. Almond and Sidney Verba, *The Civic Culture* [Boston: Little, Brown and Co.], pp. 17-18.)

2. See note 33, pp. 239-240 in this study.
3. In defense of Spain and in rebuttal against foreign interference in Spain's domestic affairs, Prime Minister Arias cited the European Security Pact, which had been signed only the month before on August 1 in Helsinki. Under terms of the pact the signatories agreed not to interfere in each other's internal affairs or to help either directly or indirectly terrorist or subversive activity. But evidently, according to Arias, such guarantees were not meant to apply to Spain.
4. *New York Times*, November 21, 1975. Emphasis added.
5. The reform program included an elective system for mayors, greater separation of the legislative and executive functions, more freedom of association for labor, and freedom of political association.
6. The oath answered affirmatively by Juan Carlos read: "Sir, do you swear by God Almighty and the Gospels to carry out and to have carried out the Fundamental Laws of the Kingdom and to maintain loyalty to the principles that govern the National Movement?"
7. Under the governmental reorganization which came into operation

in Franco's last cabinet (appointed on January 3, 1975), three deputy prime ministers were created: one for economic affairs, which incorporated the Ministry of Finance; one for labor affairs, which incorporated the Ministry of Labor; and one for political affairs, which incorporated the Ministry of the Interior, which controlled national security.

8. For a description of the political functions of the Council of the Realm, see Chapter 7.

9. See pp. 188-189 in this study.

10. See p. 228 in this study.

11. *New York Times*, July 7, 1976.

12. Ibid.

13. *New York Times*, March 4, 1977.

14. *New York Times*, April 14, 1977.

15. *New York Times*, July 15, 1976.

16. "The Revolution of Modernization in National and International Society," pp. 185-86, in *Revolution*, Carl J. Friedrich, ed. (New York: Atherton Press, 1966).

17. Ibid., pp. 182-83.

Appendixes

Appendix A:
The Syndicates

The syndicates are the associations that link employer and employee and carry out in the area of work the organic societal doctrine similarly manifested in the family and in the community. In theory the syndicates serve two purposes. First, they provide the employer and employee with the mechanism through which to meet and solve problems. In the organic concept, employers and employees within the same occupation share similar outlooks and goals. Furnished with the means to resolve conflict their communality will produce a harmony unattainable either in coercive communist systems like the Soviet or in aggressive capitalist systems like the American. As shown in Chapter 9, however, theory broke down in practice after 1945. Second, the syndicates offer the employer and the employee political representation in the Cortes through *procuradores* who emerge from the Syndical Organization. Some of the syndicalist *procuradores* are indirectly elected by the members of the twenty-nine individual syndicates, which together make up the national Syndical Organization. Other syndicalist *procuradores* occupy their legislative seats ex officio because of their positions within the national Syndical Organization. The remaining *procuradores* are chosen by the Permanent Committee of the Syndical Congress.

The syndicates were provided for in Article 8 of the Labor Charter promulgated on March 9, 1938,[1] but did not come into being until the Ley de Unidad Sindical (Law of Syndical Unity) was decreed on January 26, 1940. On February 17, 1971, the Cortes approved the Ley Sindical (Syndical Law), which modified but did not basically alter the syndicalist structure set up thirty years earlier. Every employer and employee in Spain must, under the law, be a member of a syndicate created around a particular economic activity. The only exceptions are the professions (which have their own organizations), civil servants, and domestics. Over 90 percent of the working force is organized into these syndicates: (1) Diverse Activities; (2) Health Care; (3) Water, Gas, and

Electricity; (4) Food Suppliers; (5) Sugar; (6) Banking, Savings Associations, and Stock Exchange; (7) Grains; (8) Combustible Fuels; (9) Construction; (10) Teaching; (11) Entertainment; (12) Fruits and Vegetables; (13) Livestock; (14) Hotels and Tourism; (15) Chemicals; (16) Wood and Cork; (17) Merchant Marine; (18) Metals; (19) Olives and Olive Oil; (20) Paper and Graphic Arts; (21) Fishing; (22) Hides and Skins; (23) Press, Radio, Television, and Advertising; (24) Insurance; (25) Textiles; (26) Transportation and Communication; (27) Wine, Beer, and Beverages; (28) Glass and Ceramics; and (29) Farm Workers and Herders.

Each of the twenty-nine syndicates is organized from the local to the national level in the following manner. Let us take sugar for our example.[2] Everyone in the sugar-growing business in a particular area within each separate province belongs to the local sugar syndicate, which is divided into two sections, the association for employers *(empresarios)* and the association for employees. The latter represents workers *(trabajadores)* and specially trained workers called technicians *(técnicos)* who might also be in lower-level managerial or overseeing positions. All of those who work in the sugar-growing business within a province belong to the provincial syndicate also divided into associations of employers and employees. The provincial syndicate is headed by a chief appointed by the president of the national sugar syndicate. All those in the sugar-growing business at the provincial level make up the national sugar syndicate, which like the local and provincial organizations beneath it, is divided into associations of employers and employees. The national syndicate is headed by a president chosen by the national representatives of employers and employees. By a three-quarters majority vote they select the individual who will be president and forward that nomination to the minister of syndicalist relations, who makes the appointment. In the event no one receives a three-quarters majority, the minister makes the appointment from among five nominees chosen by the executive committee of the syndicate.

The employers and employees who make up the two sections of each syndicate at each level are chosen in the following manner. At each place of employment, the workers and technicians choose a representative to the local syndicate. The employer does the same thing, choosing either himself if it is a small firm, or someone from management to represent him. It is only within the individual firms that direct elections take place. Every other elective post within the syndicalist organization is filled indirectly. The representatives of the employers and employees who sit in the local syndicates choose delegates from among themselves to represent their respective sections of employers and employees at the provincial level. Those delegates at the provincial level choose from among themselves the delegates who will represent each section at the national level. Among other functions the national delegates choose the *procuradores* who will represent each individual syndicate in the Cortes.

Paralleling the vertical organization of each of the twenty-nine syndicates is a horizontal organization bringing together all of the sections of employers and all of the sections of employees, cutting across the separate syndicates at the local, provincial, and national levels. Thus there is a Local Council of Employers that brings together all the representatives of employers from each separate syndicate found at the local level. There is also a Local Council of Employees that brings together all the representatives of employees from each separate syndicate found at the local level. In other words, the representatives of employers and employees act in two capacities—one role within each separate syndicate, and one within the Local Council. The same organizational structure is found at the provincial and at the national level. The presidents and secretaries of the National Council of Employers and of the National Council of Employees sit ex officio as *procuradores* in the Cortes.[3]

At least once every two years all those delegates who represent their syndicates at the national level, i.e., all those representatives of employers and employees who have been chosen in the manner described above, meet in the Syndical Congress, where each syndicate, irrespective of size, has the same voting strength. The congress is the highest representative body of the national Syndical Organization, but its function is primarily advisory. Authoritative decision making is carried out neither in the congress nor in the national organization of each individual syndicate but in the national Syndical Organization, which controls all twenty-nine syndicates. In other words, syndicalist representation, which is primarily advisory, is elected indirectly from the bottom up, but authoritative decision making not only moves from the top down but also is carried out by appointed officials not responsible to the representatives. Before 1969 the secretary-general of the Movement, a cabinet minister, controlled the Syndical Organization, which was run on a day-to-day basis by his appointee, the *delegado nacional* (national delegate). As described in Chapter 9, the power of the movement was seriously eroded in the 1960s, and a major manifestation of its weakening was the loss of control over the Syndical Organization it had had since the 1940s. Since 1969 the Syndical Organization has been headed by a separate cabinet minister who acts as liaison between the government and the Syndical Organization, which is run on a day-to-day basis not by the minister but by his appointees, the secretary-general and the deputy secretary-general, both of whom sit ex officio as *procuradores* in the Cortes.[4] Subordinate to the national Syndical Organization are the fifty provincial Syndical Organizations headed by chiefs appointed by the minister or by his appointees. The structures of the provincial organizations are duplicates of the national Syndical Organization.

Notes

1. *Fundamental Laws of the State: The Spanish Constitution*, Labor Charter.

2. Even though all syndicates are organized nationally, not every syndicate can be found in each province. There are no fishermen in Madrid, for example.

3. Because employees far outnumber employers, the latter are heavily over-represented in the Cortes since both National Councils have the same representative strength in the legislature.

4. Nothing could better symbolize the separation of the syndicates from the party than the appointment of Enrique García-Ramal Cerralbo as the first minister of syndical organization in 1969 (renamed minister of syndical relations after 1971). García-Ramal was identified with the Opus Dei, the most powerful antagonist of the Falange, which had controlled the syndicates through the party from 1940 to 1969.

Appendix B:
The Opus Dei

The Societas Sacerdotalis Sanctae Crucis (Priestly Society of the Holy Cross), known as the Opus Dei (God's Work), is a secular institute of the Catholic Church. The Opus is headquartered in Rome and is worldwide in membership. But it was founded by a Spaniard, José María Escrivá de Balaguer y Albás, and its membership is far larger and its strength far greater in Spain than in any other country. Escrivá was born in Aragon in 1902 and became a lawyer and a priest, pursuing both studies simultaneously. Perhaps it was this combination of the sacred and the secular that inspired Escrivá to create an association primarily of laymen who would dedicate their lives and energies to the pursuit of "God's work" not by withdrawing from the world into convents and monasteries but by remaining in the world, pursuing a secular occupation while personally leading a dedicated Christian life and influencing others by word and deed.

The Opus Dei was founded in Madrid on October 2, 1928, around an original nucleus of thirteen male university students with Escrivá acting as spiritual advisor. A branch for women was founded on February 4, 1930, and in 1934 the society established its first residence for men. The Civil War interrupted the group's expansion; moreover republican Madrid was enemy territory for any religious association. Escrivá went into hiding and eventually escaped to France but returned to Nationalist Spain and regrouped his society in Burgos, the Rebel capital. After the Civil War was over, the religiosity of the Franco regime offered the perfect atmosphere for the growth of a spiritual society like the Opus. In 1941 it was recognized by the Bishop of Madrid-Alcalá as a "pious union" and later by the Holy See as a diocesan "Communitarian Institute." But Escrivá had visions that went beyond the diocesan, and he moved to Rome in 1946, seeking to universalize his society. In 1947 the Opus Dei received its *Decretum Laudis* (Decree of Praise) from the Pope, the Church's preliminary approval of a group's activity and goals.

On June 16, 1950, the Opus Dei became the first secular institute in the
history of the Church. By encyclical in 1947 the Pope had created secular
institutes perhaps to accommodate societies like the Opus.

> The Vatican describes Secular Institutes as associations of priests and
> laymen who pursue Christian perfection by exercising their apostolate in
> the world. . . . It is perhaps too often overlooked that the Opus Dei is first
> and foremost a religious organization whose primary aim is the
> sanctification of its members in the fulfillment of their ordinary secular
> professions. As its founder never tires of saying the basic principle of the
> society is "to sanctify work, to sanctify oneself in work, and to sanctify the
> rest through work."[1]

The Opus Dei is not a religious order; it requires no vows that are
canonically binding. Its members do not wear special dress, nor must
they live together in identifiable places of residence like convents,
monasteries, or rectories. Its membership is made up primarily of men,
but there are also sections for women. The two branches are totally
autonomous, so in that sense there is no mixing of the sexes. Priests may
also become members. Priests who are already ordained remain subject
to the discipline of their bishops, but priests who were members of the
Opus before ordination devote their time primarily to the society. Even
though priests make up only a small percentage of the membership—
estimated to be about 3 percent—they dominate the organizational
hierarchy. In command of the international Opus Dei is Escrivá, now a
monsignor, the president-general for life. He is aided in his governing
by a council made up of members from around the world. His orders go
to the director-general, a layman, in each country where the Opus Dei is
organized, but the orders are communicated through the member-priests
who form the actual Priestly Society of the Holy Cross.

There are four ranks of membership in the Opus Dei, admission to
each of which follows a probationary period during which the candidate
undergoes rigorous philosophical and theological training. The
classification of the postulant is made by the society. The first and
highest rank are the Numeraries, unmarried members who are
university educated, have no physical handicaps, and come from good
social background. They pursue their occupations in public life but give
their income to the society. They take noncanonical vows of poverty,
chastity, and obedience and most often live together in special but
anonymous residences. The second are the Oblates, unmarried
individuals of more humble origin who do not have the special
characteristics of background, physical attributes, and education
necessary to become Numeraries. Ordinarily they continue to live at

home and contribute only a small portion of their income to the society, but they devote their life fully to the Opus just as do the Numeraries. The third are the Supernumeraries. These are the married members, many of them of great professional prominence and social position, whose secular commitments prevent total dedication to the society but whose ardor for its goals is no less intense that that of the Numeraries and Oblates. The fourth are the Co-operators. "Their only obligation," as Vicente Pilapil writes, "is that they must do something for the society (pray or help in any way) every day."[2]

Very little is known of the inner workings of the Opus Dei. Silence, discretion, and obedience are the bywords of Escrivá. As a consequence his followers very seldom talk about the society, and when they do, they reveal almost nothing. No official publication concerning the Opus has ever appeared, nor is it likely that it ever will. Its wealth remains a mystery because it is held not *by* the society but *for* the society in the name of individual members or in dummy corporations. Even its residences are not its own; they are most often rented or leased, usually from members. Its membership can only be approximated. While the society does not forbid a member to make his relationship known publicly, he or she is strongly discouraged from doing so. It is estimated that in Spain there are 18,000 members and 32,000 Co-operators, but no outsider knows for sure. It appears that there is no rigid belief system, philosophy, or ideology that commands absolute obedience, but it also appears from the social, economic, and educational background of the leaders of the Opus that there is a shared world view—elitist, conservative, and disciplinarian. The Opus Dei would have to be classified as a semisecret organization. It is for this reason that the Opus Dei is looked upon with suspicion and fear and has been called by its detractors the "white Freemasonry" and the "holy Mafia."[3]

In Spain the Opus Dei has gone through an interesting transformation in its sociopolitical concepts. Its earlier spokesmen, writing in the late 1940s and early 1950s, were traditionalists who believed that Spain was set apart from the historic mainstream as the guardian of Western civilization against the perversions that had been unleashed by the French Revolution.

> This early Opus group's interpretation of the state of Western civilization was totally pessimistic. Western civilization was seen to be in a terrible crisis. Liberal democracy had failed twice since it had proved unable to resist communism. The fascist alternative had failed—they had lost the war. The communist menace was looming increasingly threatening over the whole precarious structure. Western civilization was basically incapable of facing communist dialectic materialism since it has

abandoned Christianity for the treacherous path of nationalism, pragmatism, and de-spiritualization of man.

Spain, as the only European country with the will to retain the Catholicity of its culture was, therefore, to lead the errant Western culture back to Christianity. . . .

Spain was also considered to be organized in political and economic terms as a model superior to that of the rest of Europe. Politically the Spanish model was seen as ideal organic democracy with the "natural" representative institutions: the family, the municipality, the "organic" syndicates, and the leadership of an "enlightened" minority. . . .

Spain was thus to act as the "third force" in the world, the alternative to the equally decadent Russian and Western civilizations.[4]

Yet irrespective of its early disdain for modernity, the Spanish Opus Deists in the 1950s came to accept the reality of technology. While they believed that Spain was ahead of the rest of the world in spiritual and political values, they realized that Spain had no modern technological know-how and as a consequence was being outdistanced by what they considered to be inferior nations (that is, every other nation except Spain). The Opus Deists made the decision to embrace technology and to adapt it to Christian values. Rafael Calvo Serer, a prolific Opus Deist intellectual, wrote: "Modern techniques originated in a Christian culture which explains why they contain positive values. This means that they are not and cannot be incompatible with the spirit of Christianity."[5] The confessional Spanish state would maintain political stability and uphold Christian values while the new technocrats from the Opus Dei would solve the problems of Spain. The emphasis would be on economic development—lifting the standard of living and improving the material quality of life. The governmental form would be of little consequence; only political stability that allowed development to take place peacefully would matter. For this reason the Opus Dei in Spain supported the Franco regime and championed the succession of Juan Carlos.

The idea that Spain was a country on the road to "development" carried a series of implications—most of which justified the existence of Franco's regime. Firstly in relation to democracy. Since it had been agreed that, in a situation of development, ideology was unnecessary and in fact irrational, it followed that dialogue was also redundant since the state legitimized itself by its efficiency in achieving a series of pragmatic goals. The concept of the politician was also revised. They now became the "rational" elite acting in the long-term interests of the people.

The theorists also argued that freedom was primarily a function of material wealth since the individual's range of choices varied directly with his degree of material well-being. His freedom was thus best guaranteed if the society he happened to have been born in developed as quickly as possible. One of the greatest threats to rapid development was social disorder. If a development-oriented government such as the Spanish one put down social disorder it was therefore operating in the real interests of the whole people.[6]

According to the sociopolitical theorists among the Spanish Opus Deists, political development would follow economic development, but the process would not disrupt the polity. By the time the country was ready for democracy (which would occur, according to one distinguished Opus Deist, Laureano López Rodó, when the average yearly per capita income reached the equivalent of one thousand dollars), most Spaniards would have a vested interest in the political system that had provided the good life and would wish to make no fundamental changes in it.

Raúl Morodo, an outspoken antagonist of the Opus Dei, makes a fascinating analogy between the Society of Jesus (the Jesuits) and the Opus Dei and compares their roles in Spanish politics:

> If the Society of Jesus was the clearest and most coherent response to the ideological formalization of the imperial system of the Hapsburgs, the Opus Dei is the intent to formalize, in this latest period, the present-day sociopolitical Spanish regime. The Jesuits intuitively knew where effective power resided and understood its rationalization and subsequent control. Without the Jesuits it would be generally impossible to understand the political and social history of the past centuries. . . . In the same way, the Opus Dei is the response to the political and socioeconomic situation in postwar Spain, above all after 1945. A Spanish economic and intellectual history of the present establishment cannot be understood without analyzing this religio-political institution. The Opus Dei has understood where the effective power lies and has directed its strategy to controlling it, applying in this task modern methods of control. The Opus Dei is, in this sense, a technological-integralist ideology applied to a semi-developed country.[7]

Notes

1. Vincente R. Pilapil, "The Opus Dei in Spain," *The World Today* 27 (May 1970): 214.
2. Ibid., p. 216.
3. Probably the most critically damning study of the Opus Dei is by Jesús

Ynfante, *La prodigiosa aventura del Opus Dei* (Paris: Ruedo Ibérico, 1970). A more balanced yet highly provocative study has been written by a former member of the Opus, an ex-nun, María Angustias Moreno, *El Opus: Anexo a una historia* (Barcelona: Editorial Planeta, 1976).

4. Leslie Mackensie, "The Political Ideas of the Opus Dei in Spain," *Government and Opposition* 8 (Winter 1973): 77-78.

5. Rafael Calvo Serer, "El fin de la época de las revoluciones," *Arbor*, no. 41, p. 187.

6. Mackensie, "The Political Ideas of the Opus Dei in Spain," pp. 87-88.

7. Raúl Morodo [Rogelio del Moral], "Opus Dei y la Vida Intelectual y Política Española," *Ibérica* (February 15, 1966), p. 7.

Index

Index